No one has explored the link between value pluralism and liberalism with more persistence and precision than George Crowder. *The Problem of Value Pluralism* is Crowder's best treatment of this issue, and it deserves a wide readership.

— William A. Galston, Senior Fellow, The Brookings Institution

George Crowder's well-established reputation as an expert on Isaiah Berlin's value pluralism and its implications will be further burnished by this new volume. Once more he displays the clarity, thoroughness, coherence, ingenuity and command of the literature that characterise all his work. After helpfully recapitulating his view of Berlin's own seminal contribution, he turns to a critical examination of the work of Berlin's contemporaries and successors, most of it inspired or provoked by Berlin. The result is the most complete treatment of this crucial seam of moral and political thought that has yet been given to us, and required reading for all serious students of pluralism.

— Henry Hardy, Fellow of Wolfson College, Oxford,
Isaiah Berlin's principal editor,
and author of *In Search of Isaiah Berlin: A Literary Adventure*

The Problem of Value Pluralism

Value pluralism is the idea, most prominently endorsed by Isaiah Berlin, that fundamental human values are universal, plural, conflicting, and incommensurable with one another. Incommensurability is the key component of pluralism, undermining familiar monist philosophies such as utilitarianism. But if values are incommensurable, how do we decide between them when they conflict?

George Crowder assesses a range of responses to this problem proposed by Berlin and developed by his successors. Three broad approaches are especially important: universalism, contextualism, and conceptualism. Crowder argues that the conceptual approach is the most fruitful, yielding norms of value diversity, personal autonomy, and inclusive democracy. Historical context must also be taken into account. Together these approaches indicate a liberal politics of redistribution, multiculturalism, and constitutionalism, and a public policy in which basic values are carefully balanced.

The Problem of Value Pluralism: Isaiah Berlin and Beyond is a uniquely comprehensive survey of the political theory of value pluralism and also an original contribution by a leading voice in the pluralist literature. Scholars and researchers interested in the work of Berlin, liberalism, value pluralism, and related ideas will find this a stimulating and valuable source.

George Crowder is Professor of Political Theory in the College of Business, Government and Law, Flinders University, Australia. His books include *Liberalism and Value Pluralism* (2002), *Isaiah Berlin: Liberty and Pluralism* (2004), *The One and the Many: Reading Isaiah Berlin* (co-edited with Henry Hardy, 2007), and *Theories of Multiculturalism* (2013).

Routledge Innovations in Political Theory

Compromise and Disagreement in Contemporary Political Theory
Edited by Christian F. Rostbøll and Theresa Scavenius

Democratic Political Tragedy in the Postcolony
The Tragedy of Postcoloniality in Michael Manley's Jamaica and Nelson Mandela's South Africa
Greg A. Graham

Epistemontology in Spinoza-Marx-Freud-Lacan
The (Bio)Power of Structure
A. Kiarina Kordela

Aesthetics and Political Culture in Modern Society
Henrik Kaare Nielsen

Post-Fukushima Activism
Politics and Knowledge in The Age of Precarity
Azumi Tamura

Reconstructing Nonviolence
A New Theory and Practice for a Post-Secular Society
Roberto Baldoli

Rethinking Positive and Negative Liberty
Maria Dimova-Cookson

The Problem of Value Pluralism
Isaiah Berlin and Beyond
George Crowder

For more information about this series, please visit: www.routledge.com/Routledge-Innovations-in-Political-Theory/book-series/IPT

The Problem of Value Pluralism
Isaiah Berlin and Beyond

George Crowder

NEW YORK AND LONDON

First published 2020
by Routledge
605 Third Avenue, New York, NY 10017

and by Routledge
2 Park Square, Milton Park, Abingdon, Oxon, OX14 4RN

First issued in paperback 2021

Routledge is an imprint of the Taylor & Francis Group, an informa business

© 2020 Taylor & Francis

The right of George Crowder to be identified as author of this work has been asserted by him in accordance with sections 77 and 78 of the Copyright, Designs and Patents Act 1988.

All rights reserved. No part of this book may be reprinted or reproduced or utilised in any form or by any electronic, mechanical, or other means, now known or hereafter invented, including photocopying and recording, or in any information storage or retrieval system, without permission in writing from the publishers.

Trademark notice: Product or corporate names may be trademarks or registered trademarks, and are used only for identification and explanation without intent to infringe.

Publisher's Note
The publisher has gone to great lengths to ensure the quality of this reprint but points out that some imperfections in the original copies may be apparent.

Library of Congress Cataloging-in-Publication Data
Name: Crowder, George, author.
Title: The problem of value pluralism : Isaiah Berlin and beyond/ George Crowder.
Description: New York, NY: Routledge, 2020. | Series: Routledge innovations in political theory; Volume 75 | Includes bibliographical references and index. |
Identifiers: LCCN 2019043543 (print) | LCCN 2019043544 (ebook) | ISBN 9781138724822 (hardback) | ISBN 9781315192208 (ebook) | ISBN 9781351754385 (adobe pdf) | ISBN 9781351754361 (mobi) | ISBN 9781351754378 (epub)
Subjects: LCSH: Berlin, Isaiah, 1909–1997-Political and social views. | Values. | Pluralism.
Classification: LCC B1618.B454 C76 2020 (print) | LCC B1618.B454 (ebook) | DDC 192–dc23
LC record available at https://lccn.loc.gov/2019043543
LC ebook record available at https://lccn.loc.gov/2019043544

ISBN 13: 978-1-03-208522-7 (pbk)
ISBN 13: 978-1-138-72482-2 (hbk)

Typeset in Times New Roman
by Scientific Publishing Services

Contents

Preface and Acknowledgments viii
List of Abbreviations x

   Introduction 1

1 Berlin and the Problem of Value Pluralism 11

2 The Great Goods 43

3 Agonism and Context 66

4 Realism and History 91

5 Diversity and Liberalism 116

6 Toleration and Autonomy 142

7 Democracy and Compromise 165

8 Constitutionalism and Public Policy 192

9 Conclusion 218

   Index 229

Preface and Acknowledgements

In this book I aim to identify the problem of value pluralism as presented by Isaiah Berlin, to map a number of different attempts, advanced by Berlin and his successors, to solve the problem, and to construct and defend my own response. I hope, of course, to persuade readers to accept my own view, but even if they do not they may still find the problem stimulating and the map useful.

The problem of value pluralism is the problem of how to choose among conflicting fundamental values if they are conceived as incommensurable with one another in the manner of Isaiah Berlin. Should liberty come first, or equality or justice or tradition? Berlin, I argue, formulates the problem but does not provide a convincing answer to it. He throws out numerous suggestions, but he does not develop any of these systematically or investigate their political implications thoroughly.

That task has been taken up by others, including myself, and our various attempts to solve the problem of value pluralism are the book's immediate focus. Those attempts can be reduced to three main approaches: one based on universal values, or in Berlin's phrase 'the great goods'; a second that emphasizes various dimensions of context (personal, cultural, political, and historical); and a third that seeks normative guidance in the concept of value pluralism itself.

I argue that, while each of these approaches is valuable to some degree, it is the last-mentioned 'conceptual' approach that is the most fruitful. However, this needs to be combined with insights from the other approaches, in particular historical context.

The argument builds on my previous work, in particular *Liberalism and Value Pluralism* (2002) and *Isaiah Berlin: Liberty and Pluralism* (2004). In the current book, I try to improve on those earlier arguments, respond to criticisms, and attend to areas of inquiry I have previously neglected or covered inadequately. These latter include the bearing of pluralism on historical context, political realism, democracy, compromise, constitutionalism, and public policy.

Some of these ideas have appeared in chapters and articles I have published over the past decade and a half. The book incorporates published work as follows:

Chapter 1: 'Pluralism, Relativism and Liberalism', in Joshua Cherniss and Steven Smith, eds, *Cambridge Companion to Isaiah Berlin* (Cambridge: Cambridge University Press, 2018).

Chapter 4: 'Value Pluralism vs Realism in the Political Thought of Bernard Williams', *Journal of Value Inquiry*, published online 12 April 2019, DOI https://doi.org/10.1007/s10790-018-9674-5, Online ISSN 1573-0492.

Chapter 5: 'Value Pluralism, Diversity and Liberalism', *Ethical Theory and Moral Practice*, vol. 18, no. 3 (2015): 549–564.

Chapter 6: 'Two Concepts of Liberal Pluralism', *Political Theory*, vol. 35, no. 2 (2007): 121–146.

Chapter 8: 'Value Pluralism, Constitutionalism and Democracy: Waldron and Berlin in Debate', *Review of Politics*, vol. 81, no. 1 (Winter 2019): 101–127.

I am grateful to the relevant publishers (Cambridge University Press, Springer, and Sage) for permission to reproduce material from these pieces.

No one can tackle philosophical questions with any hope of success without the advice of others. I have benefited from the thoughts of many people, including the editors and reviewers of the journals to which I have contributed the pieces listed above and audiences at various conferences and workshops where I have presented parts of the argument in this book. I would especially like to thank Karen Austin, Joshua Cherniss, Andrew Cole, Kim Economides, William Galston, Elizabeth Handsley, Henry Hardy, Rob Manwaring, Lionel Orchard, Sharyn Roach Anleu, Michael Spicer, and Miguel Vatter. At Routledge, Natalja Mortensen and Charlie Baker have been very helpful and supportive.

Some of the basic research for the book was undertaken at St Catherine's College, Oxford, where I was a Visiting Fellow in 2014. I acknowledge the hospitality of the Master and Fellows.

Most importantly of all, I could not have completed this book without the patience and support of my partner, Sue.

Abbreviations

The following abbreviations are used in the text. Abbreviations of Isaiah Berlin's books follow the model set by Berlin's editor, Henry Hardy.

Caps	Martha Nussbaum, *Creating Capabilities* (2011)
CIB	Ramin Jahanbegloo, *Conversations with Isaiah Berlin* (1992)
CTH	Isaiah Berlin, *The Crooked Timber of Humanity* (2013)
Deed	Bernard Williams, *In the Beginning Was the Deed* (2005)
ELP	Bernard Williams, *Ethics and the Limits of Philosophy* (1985)
FG	Martha Nussbaum, *The Fragility of Goodness*, 2nd edn (2001)
IE	Stuart Hampshire, *Innocence and Experience* (1989)
JC	Stuart Hampshire, *Justice Is Conflict* (2000)
L	Isaiah Berlin, *Liberty* (2002)
LAP	Richard Bellamy, *Liberalism and Pluralism* (1999)
LK	Martha Nussbaum, *Love's Knowledge* (1990)
LP	Williams Galston, *Liberal Pluralism* (2002)
LVP	George Crowder, *Liberalism and Value Pluralism* (2002)
Min	Jonathan Riley, 'Isaiah Berlin's "Minimum of Common Moral Ground"' (2013)
MP	John Kekes, *The Morality of Pluralism* (1993)
OC	Avishai Margalit, *On Compromise* (2010)
POI	Isaiah Berlin, *The Power of Ideas* (2013)
PLP	William Galston, *The Practice of Liberal Pluralism* (2005)
PPT	Jeremy Waldron, *Political Political Theory* (2016)
TR	David Thacher and Martin Rein, 'Managing Value Conflict in Public Policy' (2004)
UD	Isaiah Berlin and Beata Polanowska-Sygulska, *Unfinished Dialogue* (2006)
WHD	Martha Nussbaum, *Women and Human Development* (2000)

Source: Photo of Isaiah Berlin reproduced by courtesy of the Trustees of The Isaiah Berlin Literary Trust

Introduction

In both personal and political life, fundamental values are frequently in conflict.[1] People struggle to balance the goods of family life with those of professional success. Taxpayers want both the liberty to spend their income as they please and the public services that can only be funded by taxation. Reconciliation clashes with justice when one regime succeeds another. Value conflict is ubiquitous, and the fact that values conflict is uncontroversial.

What is more controversial is how we should understand and respond to that conflict. When important values collide, how should we rank them or trade them off against one another? Does family come before profession, liberty before equality, reconciliation before justice, or is it the other way round?

One theoretical answer is provided by the broad idea of ethical 'monism'. According to monists, we can resolve fundamental value conflicts by referring to a single formula for ranking or trading off that applies in every case. The clearest example is utilitarianism, which proposes that any value conflict can be resolved by choosing the option that maximizes 'utility', in whatever way this is defined – as happiness, pleasure, or the satisfaction of preferences. Liberty comes before equality in cases where that ranking will maximize utility; equality before liberty where utility demands the opposite. Another instance of monism is where a single value dominates and orders the best way of life – for example, the philosophical knowledge that overrides all other goods for Plato and Aristotle.

An alternative view is that there is no such single formula that applies in every case. This is the idea of 'value pluralism'.[2] At the heart of the pluralist idea is the thought that fundamental values – which may include goods like liberty, equality, justice, and so on – are 'incommensurable' with one another. Values are incommensurable when they share no common measure and are not subject to any superior value. Each is intrinsically valuable, speaking as it were in its own unique voice. So, if liberty and equality are incommensurable, each makes ethical claims that are wholly its own. Neither is ultimately more important than the other. And if that is so, they cannot be subjected to a single rule for ranking them that applies in all cases. There can be no universally applicable rule to the effect that liberty must always come before equality or equality before liberty.

This pluralist way of seeing matters is widely associated with the work of Isaiah Berlin, and that work is my starting point. For Berlin, pluralism has a very significant political implication: it is an antidote to utopian political theories that lead to authoritarian and even totalitarian outcomes. If monism were true, then the possibility of a single correct formula for resolving all moral conflict implies the possibility of a single uniquely perfect form of society. For the sake of such perfection, no price in human effort and suffering can be too great to pay. But if pluralism is true, then utopianism dissolves, and with it a central justification of authoritarianism.

The trouble is, if pluralism is true it seems to undermine not only the utopianism and authoritarianism that Berlin opposes but also the liberal politics he supports – indeed, it seems to undermine the justification of any political position. Without a general rule for ranking, why should we uphold the values characteristic of liberalism – individual liberty, equality of opportunity, toleration – rather than those emphasized by socialists (equality of outcome, solidarity) or conservatives (respect for tradition) or even fascists (uniformity, violence)?

This political issue is an instance of a broader question which I call 'the problem of value pluralism'. If values are incommensurable and there is no general rule for ranking them, how do we choose between them when they conflict? Standard monist responses to this question are ruled out because they rely on the kind of general rule for ranking that pluralism denies. Utilitarianism, for example, requires that value conflicts always be resolved by the maximization of utility. For pluralists, utility may well be an important value but it can be only one value among others and fundamentally no more important than they are. However, if we reject monist solutions, what should we do?

Berlin advances various answers to that question but only briefly and unsystematically. Sometimes, he suggests that in the face of conflicting incommensurables we can only 'plump' for one or the other, meaning choose non-rationally (Berlin 1975; Berlin 2015: 277). At another time, he supposes that pluralists tend to possess a certain psychological make-up that predisposes them to liberal solutions (*UD* 226). In several places he thinks that pluralist conflicts can be resolved in context by following a personal or cultural way of life (*L* 42, 47; *CTH* 19). Elsewhere, he speculates that we can get answers by drawing out the conceptual implications of the idea of value pluralism itself (*L* 214). He does not develop any of these ideas or investigate their political implications in detail.

The task of following through on these and other suggestions has been taken up by other writers, including many directly influenced by Berlin.[3] It is the work of these 'successors' of Berlin that will be my central concern. They include, in order of their principal appearance in the book, Jonathan Riley, Stuart Hampshire, Martha Nussbaum, John Kekes, Bernard Williams, John Gray, William Galston, Richard Bellamy, and Avishai Margalit. I also consider Ronald Dworkin and Jeremy Waldron as critics of Berlin, and I discuss Max Weber, Carl Schmitt, and Chantal Mouffe as writers not influenced by Berlin but whose 'agonist' approach to pluralism aligns with Berlin's plumping suggestion but contrasts with his more characteristic approaches and conclusions.

Although there is something to be learned from all these writers, I shall be especially interested in three broad approaches to the problem of value pluralism. There are traces of all these in Berlin himself, but again they are developed more fully by his successors. First, there is an appeal to 'the great goods' (Berlin's phrase) or those basic values that apply universally. Riley (*Min*), Hampshire (*JC*), and Nussbaum (*WHD*, *Caps*) all argue, in different ways, that conflicts among incommensurable values can to some extent be regulated or mitigated by respect for universal goods.

Second, there are those writers who, again in different ways, try to resolve conflicts among incommensurables by reference to the context in which the conflict occurs. Nussbaum (*LK*, *FG*), for example, explains how such choices may be guided by Aristotelian practical reason within the context of an individual life. Kekes (*MP*) extends this kind of thinking into the public realm by appealing to cultural tradition. The role of historical context is emphasized by Bernard Williams (*Deed*), who defends liberalism in the face of pluralist value conflict by connecting it with the notion of modernity. Several pluralists are drawn to the context of 'the political', although their interpretations of this vary. Weber, Schmitt, and Mouffe, for example, advance 'agonist' accounts stressing the centrality in politics of conflicts irresolvable by reason, while Williams argues for a link between pluralism and 'realism', involving an emphasis on the goods of social order and legitimacy.

Third, there is a conceptual approach in which norms are derived from reflection on the concept of value pluralism itself. This kind of argument is present in the work of Galston (*LP*, *PLP*), who links pluralism with democracy and with toleration of different ways of life, including non-liberal outlooks. Pluralism is also connected with democracy by Bellamy (*LAP*), who highlights the pluralist role of negotiation and compromise. In addition, these latter themes are developed by Gray (2000) and Margalit (*OC*).

However, when it comes to the conceptual approach I rely more on my own arguments. My thesis is that the idea of pluralism itself implies norms of value diversity (which I distinguish from cultural diversity, although the two are connected), personal autonomy, and inclusive democracy and that these norms lead in the direction of a certain conception of liberalism. I concede, however, that this conceptual argument has to be qualified by attention to context, in particular historical context. As explained by Williams (*Deed*), whose argument I supplement with the work of Christian Welzel (2013), it is only under conditions of modernity that the pluralist case for liberalism is persuasive. On the other hand, Williams's historical case for liberalism needs to be reinforced by a conceptual argument.

Plan of the Book

Each chapter focuses on one or more lines of thought about how to tackle the problem of value pluralism. Moreover, each of these discussions will enable me to take another step in constructing my own view.

Chapter 1 sets out the framework of the problem as this is found in Berlin. I begin by tracing the idea of value pluralism in his work before analyzing it into its component parts, opening up issues of interpretation that will recur in later chapters. This leads to a critical discussion focusing on the following issues: (1) Is pluralism true? (2) Is it a form of relativism? (3) How can we choose among plural values when they conflict? (4) What are pluralism's political implications? Question (3) is, of course, the central 'problem of value pluralism'. Berlin offers various suggestions in response to it, including psychological affinity, universalism, compromise, non-rational agonism, contextualism (in various dimensions), and a conceptual approach. He does not pursue any of these suggestions in detail, but they offer clues that have been taken up by later writers.

In Chapter 2, I consider arguments from Riley, Hampshire, and Nussbaum that appeal to the great goods, or universal values, as a way of dealing with the problem of value pluralism. I argue that these proposals have merit in two respects: first, in giving content to the goods that are said to be plural and conflicting; second, in establishing these goods as overriding less fundamental goods, hence narrowing down to some degree the range of reasonable choice when goods conflict. However, difficulties arise over how to identify the great goods, and how to choose when the conflict is among the great goods themselves.

At this point, some writers will say that there is simply no reasoned choice among fundamental values when they conflict; in such cases, we must simply choose in a way that is ultimately non-grounded. To use Berlin's term, we must simply 'plump' for one option or the other. In Chapter 3, I begin by looking at views along these lines, including those of Weber, Schmitt, and Mouffe – the 'agonistic' school of pluralism. The basic problem with this outlook, I argue, is that it fails to account for the fact that we do in reality manage to rank conflicting incommensurables, for decisive reason, in context. While it is true that there is no such reason to rank fundamental values in the abstract, in concrete situations we may have good reasons for ranking fundamental goods. Liberty does not override equality in every case, but it could be that there are good reasons to prioritize liberty over equality in a particular set of circumstances – say, where equality has been achieved but liberty is desired but lacking.

Consequently, Chapter 3 continues with an examination of the view, found in many pluralists, that a reasoned ranking of incommensurable values is possible if it is contextual. At the level of individual decision making, the model is that of Aristotle's situated ethics, which is employed in a pluralist setting by Nussbaum. Within a personal context, individuals can navigate among conflicting incommensurables by reference to their background conception of the good life. Further, such an approach is often reinforced by an appeal to cultural tradition, suggesting both a wider social or public-policy application and also a conservative political bent, a tendency defended explicitly by John Kekes. I argue that while there is good reason for pluralists to accept contextualism in general, there are problems with the narrowly traditionalist reading of context, since within a single modern society traditions tend to be multiple and conflicting and their merits disputed. These difficulties either send us back to universal standards or push us forward to a broader understanding of context.

Such broader contexts include those of politics and history. These are considered in Chapter 4, which examines pluralist issues in the work of Bernard Williams. The chapter opens with a consideration of Williams's 'realism', in which the value of social order is emphasized within the context of 'the political'. Here I use the pluralist perspective to question why such an emphasis should be maintained in preference to that of Rawls, which sees the paramount political value as justice. I argue that if Williams's realist claim is that order is normatively superior to justice, then even within the political context that claim is unconvincing. On the other hand, if the claim is only that order is a 'precondition' for justice, and so sequentially rather than normatively prior, then that position is compatible with pluralism but no longer distinctively realist. Realism, in short, is in tension with pluralism.

The second theme of Chapter 4 is Williams's approach to the problem of value pluralism through historical context. For Williams, any ethical and political system is hedged by historical circumstances; liberalism, for example, is defensible only within the bounds of 'modernity'. However, what exactly the link is between modernity and liberalism and how strongly that link holds are matters that Williams does not fully explain. I supplement Williams's argument by bringing in the work of Christian Welzel, who makes a nuanced developmental case for the 'emancipatory values' of liberalism. I argue, however, that even once Williams's case has been reinforced by that of Welzel, there is reason to believe that liberalism is not *uniquely* justified by modernity. Authoritarian political models, including most recently that of China, also flourish under modern conditions. A more complete justification of liberalism remains to be pursued (see Chapters 5, 6, and 8).

In Chapter 5, the discussion takes a crucial turn, shifting from a contextual to a conceptual approach. The basic idea is that when incommensurable values conflict we can look for guidance by reflecting on aspects of the concept of value pluralism itself. Berlin hints at this possibility in 'Two Concepts of Liberty', but I argue in Chapter 1 that his reasoning along these lines does not succeed. Nevertheless, similar links can be made more convincingly. My starting point is again the work of Bernard Williams, who sketches the idea of an intimate relationship between value pluralism and the promotion of a 'diversity' of values, and suggests that this diversity is best promoted by liberal institutions. Once again, his case is not complete but it can be supplemented and made more persuasive. Diversity should not be seen as a matter of multiplicity alone, since some values cannot be promoted together, but rather as a combination of multiplicity and coherence. The necessary balance between these principles connects with the political balance represented by liberalism.

Chapter 5 continues with an examination of a series of objections to the diversity argument. For example, the passage from pluralism to diversity faces the complaint that this violates 'Hume's law', which forbids attempts to derive values from facts. I reply that the starting point of the argument is in part a normative position, since most pluralists identify and are committed to the great goods they say are plural. Another objection points out that liberalism inevitably places limits on the range of goods and ways of life possible in a society. If that is the case, how can we be sure that liberalism maximizes diversity? I respond that in no form of politics will value diversity be unlimited. Liberalism is simply less limited than the alternatives.

Chapter 6 serves two purposes. First, I consider another conceptual link between pluralism and liberalism, this time through personal autonomy. Second, this link adds further detail to my account of what liberal pluralism will look like. Both purposes are pursued through an engagement with the work of William Galston, who cites Berlinian pluralism as part of the framework for his picture of liberalism. For Galston, the incommensurability of fundamental human goods must be acknowledged, but when this is taken together with an emphasis on the value of 'expressive liberty' the result is a 'Reformation' liberalism that is based on toleration, including toleration of non-liberal groups. I examine Galston's position, questioning whether it is really preferable, from a pluralist point of view, to the 'Enlightenment' liberalism, based on personal autonomy, that he rejects. I argue in favor of the Enlightenment version of liberalism, both from within the logic of Galston's own position and by means of an independent link between pluralism and autonomy.

Chapter 7 investigates conceptual connections between value pluralism and two further ideas, namely democracy and compromise. The starting point is the readily apparent link between pluralism and democracy that associates multiple political voices with multiple values. The addition of liberal rights in liberal democracy prevents minority voices from being ignored or suppressed. But might there be a pluralist case for insisting that democracy be not merely liberal but 'deliberative' – that is, encouraging the direct participation of citizens in reasoned and 'reciprocal' political debate? This is the view of Richard Bellamy. I argue that pluralists should be aware that this move carries its own value priorities. The best pluralist view sees deliberation as supplementing rather than replacing the more orthodox liberal model.

Democracy is commonly linked to practices of compromise and negotiation, and these are also themes of Chapter 7. I consider the nature of compromise in general from a pluralist perspective before going on to discuss the typology of compromise presented by Bellamy and the modus vivendi theory of John Gray. Critical of 'traditional' or universalist liberalism, Gray interprets Berlinian value pluralism as having more radical, anti-liberal political implications than Berlin supposed. For Gray, a pluralist outlook supports a political focus on modus vivendi, or compromise for the sake of peaceful coexistence. However, one may wonder whether Gray is not presenting a monist formula in which the overriding value is peace.

Further, the notions of modus vivendi and compromise more generally raise the question of limits. Which modi vivendi and which compromises are ethically acceptable and which are not? Gray appeals to the idea of a universal minimum morality, but this takes us back to the great goods and their limitations. Margalit asserts that there is a class of 'rotten compromises' that should never be entered into, but again it remains unclear how these should be defined. Compromise, in short, needs the framework provided by the conceptual norms identified earlier.

In Chapter 8, I look at two other conceptual lines of argument. The first of these is from pluralism to the institutions of liberal-democratic constitutionalism. The complaint is now widespread that contemporary political theory spends too much time on ethical justifications and neglects institutions. Berlin is taken to task on this count by Jeremy Waldron (*PPT*). In this chapter, I defend Berlin against Waldron's criticism and go on to show how Berlinian pluralism can form the basis of a case for constitutional institutions much like those commended by Waldron. To begin with, there are conceptual links between pluralism and constitutionalism in general: the latter provides the political preconditions necessary for the diversity commended by the former. Where the constitution in question is democratic, pluralists would support the standard liberal institutions of separation of powers and checks and balances. Thus far, they would agree with Waldron.

However, pluralists should disagree with Waldron's rejection of judicial review of legislation. Judicial review is commended by context where it is an established component of a society's political culture, and more especially where it can help to offset populist political sentiments that threaten individual and minority rights and liberties. There is also a conceptual link between pluralism and judicial review by way of value diversity, since the courts represent a different set of values from those embodied by legislatures. A pluralist approach would suggest that both judicial and legislative values be respected in balance with each other.

The other connection drawn by the chapter is between pluralism and certain standard devices of public policy formation and advice. Cycling, firewalls, and casuistry are identified by David Thacher and Martin Rein (*TR*) as different means of managing conflicts among incommensurable values at a policy level. I connect these practices with approaches discussed earlier in the book and assess their strengths and weaknesses from a pluralist point of view.

The Conclusion draws together the strands of the discussion, summarizes my own response to the problem of value pluralism, and offers some brief remarks about the place of the pluralist literature in contemporary political philosophy. As noted earlier, my response combines insights from all of the approaches studied, but emphasizes two in particular: the conceptual approach, qualified by historical contextualism. This leads to a qualified case for liberalism. Assuming modern conditions, liberal principles and institutions are superior to the alternatives because they are the likeliest vehicles for promoting value diversity, personal autonomy, and inclusive democracy. I close by noting two general points demonstrated by this study. First, Berlin has created more of a 'school' of successors than he is sometimes given credit for. Second, the concerns of value pluralists are more central to contemporary political theory than is commonly realized.

Notes

1 My main concern is with the political implications of value pluralism, but I sometimes discuss pluralism in a personal setting too: see, especially, Chapters 3 and 5.
2 'Value pluralism' sometimes appears in the literature as 'moral pluralism'. I use either 'value pluralism' or simply 'pluralism' interchangeably.
3 For a brief outline of the post-Berlinian literature, see Crowder 2016.

References

In-text abbreviations are noted in brackets.

Bellamy, Richard (1999), *Liberalism and Pluralism: Towards a Politics of Compromise* (London: Routledge). [*LAP*]
Berlin, Isaiah (1975), 'The End of the Ideal of a Perfect Society', transcribed in Henry Hardy, ed., *The Isaiah Berlin Virtual Library*, http://berlin.wolf.ox.ac.uk
Berlin, Isaiah (2002), *Liberty*, ed. Henry Hardy (Oxford: Oxford University Press). [*L*]
Berlin, Isaiah (2013), *The Crooked Timber of Humanity: Chapters in the History of Ideas*, ed. Henry Hardy, 2nd edn (Princeton: Princeton University Press). [*CTH*]
Berlin, Isaiah (2015), *Affirming: Letters 1975–1997*, ed. Henry Hardy and Mark Pottle (London: Chatto & Windus).
Berlin, Isaiah and Beata Polanowska-Sygulska (2006), *Unfinished Dialogue* (Amherst, NY: Prometheus Press). [*UD*]
Crowder, George (2016), 'After Berlin: The Literature Since 2002', in Henry Hardy, ed., *The Isaiah Berlin Virtual Library*, http://berlin.wolf.ox.ac.uk/lists/onib/after-berlin.pdf accessed 10 July 2019.
Galston, William (2002), *Liberal Pluralism: The Implications of Value Pluralism for Political Theory and Practice* (Cambridge: Cambridge University Press). [*LP*]
Galston, William (2005), *The Practice of Liberal Pluralism* (Cambridge: Cambridge University Press). [*PLP*]
Gray, John (2000), *Two Faces of Liberalism* (Cambridge: Polity).
Hampshire, Stuart (2000), *Justice Is Conflict* (Princeton: Princeton University Press). [*JC*]
Kekes, John (1993), *The Morality of Pluralism* (Princeton: Princeton University Press). [*MP*]
Margalit, Avishai (2010), *On Compromise: And Rotten Compromises* (Princeton: Princeton University Press). [*OC*]
Nussbaum, Martha (1990), *Love's Knowledge: Essays on Philosophy and Literature* (Oxford: Oxford University Press). [*LK*]
Nussbaum, Martha (2000), *Women and Human Development: The Capabilities Approach* (Cambridge: Cambridge University Press). [*WHD*]
Nussbaum, Martha (2001), *The Fragility of Goodness: Luck and Ethics in Greek Tragedy and Philosophy*, 2nd edn (Cambridge: Cambridge University Press). [*FG*]
Nussbaum, Martha (2011), *Creating Capabilities: The Human Development Approach* (Cambridge, MA: Belknap). [*Caps*]

Riley, Jonathan (2013), 'Isaiah Berlin's "Minimum of Common Moral Ground"', *Political Theory* 41: 61–89. [*Min*]

Thacher, David and Martin Rein (2004), 'Managing Value Conflict in Public Policy', *Governance* 17 (4): 457–86. [*TR*]

Waldron, Jeremy (2016), *Political Political Theory: Essays on Institutions* (Cambridge, MA: Harvard University Press). [*PPT*]

Welzel, Christian (2013), *Freedom Rising: Human Empowerment and the Quest for Emancipation* (Cambridge: Cambridge University Press).

Williams, Bernard (2005), *In the Beginning Was the Deed: Realism and Moralism in Political Argument* (Princeton: Princeton University Press). [*Deed*]

1 Berlin and the Problem of Value Pluralism

Isaiah Berlin's work traverses many fields, and it has been subjected to a variety of interpretations.[1] Nevertheless, it is tolerably safe to say that his master-question is that of the intellectual origins of twentieth-century totalitarianism, especially in its communist form. Ironically, he finds these origins most immediately in the eighteenth-century European Enlightenment that most liberals would have championed. Berlin accepts the values of the Enlightenment – liberty, equality, toleration, rational inquiry – but worries that the scientism of the Enlightenment, its characteristic faith in the authority of scientific method in all fields of inquiry, has led to a narrow understanding of reason and eventually to a dangerous utopianism in social and political theory.

Behind Enlightenment scientism Berlin sees a more ancient Western belief in moral 'monism', the idea that all ethical questions can be answered by a single uniquely correct formula applicable in every case. A single correct formula in ethics suggests the possibility of a single correct formula for every individual life and for social and political organization. By definition, the prospect of such perfection would justify any sacrifice. The tyranny of the Soviet Union is merely the latest, scientific form taken by this old idea.

To moral monism, Berlin opposes the idea of value pluralism: human values do not fit neatly within a single monist structure but are deeply plural and often in conflict with one another. Berlin does not claim to have invented the concept of value pluralism; he traces its basic insights to Machiavelli, Vico, and Herder in particular.[2] There are other modern pluralist sources of which he does not seem to have been aware, the most notable being Max Weber (1948a, b).[3]

It is Berlin, however, who is the most influential pluralist in contemporary political thought, certainly in the Anglo-American literature. Berlin is a popularizer able to link the idea of pluralism with both deep philosophical trends and current political issues, a writer capable of inspiring friends, students, and readers with his vision of the plurality of values. Although it is often said that Berlin is not a careful or precise philosopher, it is often added that he has the ability, not universal among philosophers, to bring his subject alive. Berlin does not give us all the answers, but he asks the questions in an especially stimulating way.

This opening chapter outlines the fundamentals of Berlin's concept of value pluralism and examines his various responses to the problem at its heart. I begin by indicating the main passages where pluralism appears in Berlin's texts. The next section analyzes the idea into its component parts, highlighting the crucial idea of incommensurability and bringing out questions of interpretation. I then examine two background issues, namely whether pluralism is true and whether it is a kind of relativism, before arriving at my central question: how can we choose among plural values when they conflict? I review Berlin's answers to that question, argue that none is wholly satisfactory as Berlin presents it, but suggest that three in particular – his appeal to universal values ('the great goods'), to contextualism, and to conceptualism – offer valuable clues for his successors. The chapter concludes with some comments on Berlin's treatment of the political implications of pluralism.

Berlin and Value Pluralism

Value pluralism permeates Berlin's work but in a scattered, diffuse way. There is no single, extended discussion that can be regarded as the definitive statement. The closest Berlin gets to such a statement are three texts: the classic 'Two Concepts of Liberty', especially the last section, and two retrospective pieces, 'The Pursuit of the Ideal' and 'My Intellectual Path' – first published in 1958, 1988, and 1998, respectively. I begin with 'Two Concepts', Berlin's best-known work.

Berlin's immediate purpose in 'Two Concepts' is to define and contrast two conceptions of liberty, negative and positive – respectively liberty as non-interference and liberty as self-mastery. The immediate political context is the Cold War, and negative liberty is presented by Berlin as the liberty of the liberal-democratic West in conflict with the positive liberty of the communist world. On the whole, Berlin defends the negative liberty of the liberals and is critical of the positive idea.

The negative conception of liberty is the idea that I am 'free to the degree to which no man or body of men interferes with my activity' (*L* 169). Berlin conceives of the negative idea in terms of 'the area within which a man can act unobstructed by others'. The classic obstacle to negative liberty is therefore coercion, 'the deliberate interference of other human beings within the area in which I could otherwise act'. This immediately brings in the thought that not every obstacle is an obstacle to liberty. If I lack the ability 'to jump more than ten feet in the air', that is a lack of capacity, not a lack of liberty. What about poverty: is that a lack of liberty or of capacity? The answer depends on whether you explain poverty as more like 'a kind of disease', for which no one is responsible, or like a condition caused by the deliberate actions of other people (*L* 170).

Why does this matter? Berlin is introducing a theme he will return to repeatedly in 'Two Concepts', a theme that foreshadows the idea of value pluralism that he will make explicit in the final section. In the modern world, the prestige of liberty is so great that there is a temptation to present every public goal as a form of liberation. But this is a mistake. 'Everything is what it is; liberty is liberty, not equality or fairness or justice or culture, or human happiness or a quiet conscience' (*L* 172). There are many fundamental human goods, and we should be clear which we are pursuing at any given time. If a given policy promotes not liberty but some other good, still more so if the policy promotes that good by reducing liberty, we should acknowledge that fact and not pretend that liberty is somehow advanced by everything we do.

This does not mean that we should never diminish liberty for the sake of any other good. Berlin is clear that there are many cases where the reduction of liberty is justified for the sake of some other value (*L* 172–3). But then it is that other value that is being promoted, not liberty. Berlin is inviting us to be honest about the costs, especially in terms of liberty, of our policies. He has in mind the claptrap not only of the Soviet Union but also of Western social democracy (which on the whole he supports) when the promotion of any public good whatever is supposed to be liberating.

For Berlin, consequently, negative liberty is the central goal of liberalism, but liberals should take a balanced view of its value. On the one hand, there must be 'a certain minimum area of personal freedom'; 'a frontier must be drawn between the area of private life and that of public authority' (*L* 171). What exactly the minimum should be or where precisely the frontier should be drawn is a matter of dispute, although the basic rule is that the degree of individual liberty in a society should reflect that society's understanding of the fundamental requirements of human dignity as these have been accepted over long periods of history. In this the maximal demands for liberty of the most advanced liberal thinkers, such as Mill and Constant, have been exceptional, and most human societies will settle for less (*L* 207).

On the other hand, 'liberty is not the only good of men', and there may be good reasons to qualify it in the name of other values (*L* 172). Berlin is sometimes taken to treat negative liberty as overriding in contradiction to his own notion of moral pluralism, but this is clearly not true. A liberal society will, of course, place a certain emphasis on negative liberty, but that will never be absolute.

The second of Berlin's two conceptions of liberty, the positive idea, is the notion of liberty as self-mastery. 'I wish my life and decisions to depend on myself, not on external forces of whatever kind' (*L* 178). Negative liberty places limits on authority, while positive liberty locates authority in the right place (*L* 212). I have positive liberty to the extent that I really have control over my life.

As Berlin observes, this positive idea may at first seem to be 'at no great logical distance' from its negative counterpart, but he proceeds to explain how the two ideas have come into conflict (*L* 178). They have 'historically developed in divergent directions, not always by logically reputable steps, until, in the end, they came into direct conflict with each other' (*L* 179). The sequence of development he describes is not one of logical necessity but rather partly historical and partly associational.

The starting point is the idea that self-mastery may be obstructed not only by coercion from an external source, as with negative liberty, but also by aspects of a person's own psychology: fears, beliefs, emotions, appetites. People can experience a sense of their own self as being divided, perhaps between a more rational and a more emotional part. These conflicting selves are then experienced as 'higher' and 'lower', or more and less authentic. Typically, my rational self is thought to be more authentically 'me' than my emotional self. The next step is the thought that others may know my genuinely rational interests better than I do. Perhaps, then, this superior knowledge may be possessed by experts, or by authorities such as the state or the Church or the Party. If so, it might be argued that these authorities may justifiably coerce my lower self in the interests of my higher self. Finally, in doing so, they may justly say that they are not only acting for my own good but liberating me because they are placing my true or authentic self back in control of my life.

For Berlin, this conclusion is a 'monstrous impersonation' (*L* 180). Liberty has, by these gradual steps, been redefined as its opposite, coercion. This is the pattern that lies behind the outrageous claims of the twentieth-century dictatorships to have 'liberated' their people. Positive liberty need not necessarily be twisted in this way, but the fact is that it has been subject to this kind of distortion historically (while negative liberty has not), and that fact points to a vulnerability at its heart. This begins with the notion of the divided personality. People's actual wishes can be set aside if these are identified with a lower self whose claims are inferior to those of a higher self. Negative liberty is not so susceptible because its underlying conception of the self is more resolutely empirical: the individual's actual wishes cannot be second-guessed in the same way.

Some readers of 'Two Concepts' have the impression that Berlin rejects positive liberty completely, but things are not so simple. It is true that for much of his discussion he seems to be saying that, in the political realm at least, negative liberty is the safer and perhaps the more coherent ideal. Sometimes, indeed, he hints at the thought that the negative idea is the 'fundamental' or 'normal' form of liberty or 'the essence of the notion of liberty' and that the positive variations are metaphorical extensions or departures from it (*L* 48, 169, 204). Nevertheless, Berlin never condemns the positive idea completely. Moreover, toward the end of the essay, he is inclined to see the two ideas as moral equals: 'the satisfaction that each of them seeks is an ultimate value which, both historically and morally, has an equal right to be classed among the deepest interests of mankind' (*L* 212).

This theme of the ultimate equality of the two liberties is deepened in the final section of the essay, 'The One and the Many', where Berlin sets it in the context of his underlying idea of value pluralism. He begins by defining the critical target. 'One belief, more than any other, has been responsible for the slaughter of individuals on the altars of the great historical ideals' (*L* 212).

This is the monist idea that 'there is a final solution', a single formula that will answer all moral – and by extension political – questions correctly. A range of thinkers 'from Plato to the last disciples of Hegel or Marx' have embraced this ideal 'of a final harmony in which all riddles are solved, all contradictions reconciled' (*L* 213). It is no accident that these are the great authoritarians, thinkers who have argued that there is, in essence, only one right way to live and that those who disagree must be brought into line by force if necessary.

Moreover, the moral monism on which authoritarianism has thrived must be rejected as not only dangerous but false: 'The world that we encounter in ordinary experience is one in which we are faced with choices between ends equally ultimate, and claims equally absolute, the realisation of some of which must inevitably involve the sacrifice of others' (*L* 213–4). Human values do not form a unity, they are multiple and conflicting. Value conflict is not merely an appearance that a more refined reason can show to be an illusion, but a deep reality from which we cannot escape. It is the ambition of monism that is delusional.

In this light, the negative and positive conceptions of liberty are now revealed to be irreducibly plural and incommensurable values on a level with other basic goods such as equality, justice, and security. Each speaks with its own voice and cannot be reduced to terms of the other. There is no common measure by which we can weigh one against the other. Consequently, we must make hard choices between the two liberties, and between liberty and other goods, when they conflict.

The choices we make between such conflicting values reflect our cultural and historical situation rather than an eternal law grounded in metaphysics. To seek greater certainty and permanence for our values is understandable and may be inevitable, but it is a wish that is bound to be disappointed, 'perhaps only a craving for the certainties of childhood or the absolute values of our primitive past' (*L* 217). Nevertheless, our choices are our choices. 'Principles are not less sacred because their duration cannot be guaranteed'.

Where did Berlin's pluralism come from? What are its sources? He goes some way toward answering that question in two short pieces he wrote late in life. In 'The Pursuit of the Ideal' and 'My Intellectual Path', he looks back on his intellectual development and sees it as centrally shaped by an emerging sense of the plurality of values in opposition to what he sees as the dominant monism of Western moral and political theory. The two essays tell much the same story, but there are some odd differences. I shall focus primarily on 'Pursuit', taking note of 'Path' mainly at the points where it diverges.

In 'Pursuit' Berlin paints himself as initially an idealist, indeed a monist.[4] The turbulence of the twentieth century shows us that ideas matter and that political ideas are extensions of moral values. The Russian novelists of the nineteenth century, such as Tolstoy, 'did much to shape my outlook', Berlin reports, and theirs was an 'essentially moral' approach (*CTH* 3). The world is an arena of contending goods and evils: truth, love, honesty, and so forth are confronted by injustice, oppression, falsity. The goal of moral and political action is to find a general solution to all these problems, although there is widespread disagreement over what the solution may be. Is it, for example, the simple life commended by Rousseau, or religion, or scientific progress, or liberal democracy, or nationalism?

Whatever the answer, this general approach to life makes certain assumptions: first, that every moral question has a single correct answer; second, that 'a dependable path' to that answer can be discovered; third, that all correct answers are compatible, fitting together like a 'cosmic jigsaw puzzle' (*CTH* 6). In principle the goal is a 'perfect life'. Together these assumptions constitute the 'Platonic ideal' – or moral monism. This may take various forms. Perhaps we shall never attain the ideal completely. Even if the shape of human history assures us that we shall reach the goal eventually, as Hegel and Marx believe, that progress may be fraught with conflict ('dialectical') rather than smoothly linear. But the underlying faith remains that history has a meaning, that progress is at least conceivable, and that all this is underpinned by the notion of the uniquely correct general solution to all problems. This is the dominant outlook of Western thought, confirmed for Berlin by his philosophical education, and in 'Pursuit' he presents it as the faith of his youth.

This early monist view is then challenged in Berlin's reading by three writers in particular. First, Machiavelli 'shook my earlier faith' (*CTH* 8).⁵ Here was a writer who did not seem to believe in a single ideal. In his advice to the prince on how to retain political power, Machiavelli notoriously rejects the conventional Christian morality of love, compassion, and honesty in favor of the values of pagan civilization (more precisely, pre-imperial Rome): strength, courage, ethical flexibility, ruthlessness. On the other hand, Machiavelli does not reject Christian values outside the context of politics, so he does not oppose them entirely. For Berlin, Machiavelli sees the two sets of values as those of two incompatible civilizations with incommensurably distinct merits. Each announces its own ethical standard, and there is no 'overarching criterion whereby we are enabled to decide the right life for men' (*CTH* 8). Hence, there is no uniquely right answer to the question of how to live after all.

Similarly, Berlin finds in Giambattista Vico and J. G. Herder an understanding of human cultures as 'incommensurable' with one another – they are so deeply distinct as to be incomparable. For Vico, this occurs when cultures are separated by history. There is 'no ladder of ascent from the ancients to the moderns', but rather 'a plurality of civilisations ... each with its own unique pattern' (*CTH* 9, 10). Instead of progress toward a single universal ideal, we should be aware of multiple ideals expressed by multiple civilizations. Although these are not different in every respect, since they share a common humanity, they differ 'in some profound, irreconcilable way, not combinable in any final synthesis' (*CTH* 10). In Herder, Berlin sees the same idea extended from civilizations to 'national cultures'. Each possesses its own 'centre of gravity', profoundly different from that of others.

The insights from Machiavelli, Vico, and Herder enable Berlin to elaborate his idea of value pluralism:

the conception that there are many different ends that men may seek and still be fully rational, fully men, capable of understanding each other and sympathising and deriving light from each other, as we derive it from reading Plato or the novels of medieval Japan – worlds, outlooks, very remote from our own.

(*CTH* 11)

People pursue a multitude of different goods, different combinations constituting a multitude of different ways of life. These ways of life must have something in common – a universally human element – or we would not understand each other at all. But there is no single correct ideal to which all should conform. If ways of life are diverse, that is not in itself a sign of some failure of rationality or conduct in some of them, but a natural variation that is only to be expected – indeed, valued.

Questions of Interpretation

The reality of human values, Berlin argues, is not unity but deep plurality and conflict: the realm of human morality is one of multiple, clashing values requiring difficult choices. This is a matter not merely of appearances but of the deep structure of our ethical experience. Beyond this broad picture Berlin provides few details, and he does not develop the idea of pluralism or its implications systematically.

Gathering together what he does say, we may think of the basic concept of value pluralism as having four main elements: there are at least some fundamental values that are objective and universal; there is a plurality of these fundamental values; such values are liable to come into conflict with one another; and such conflicts are often hard to resolve because fundamental human values are incommensurable. But each of these claims is to some degree ambiguous or unclear in Berlin's account, and each therefore raises questions of interpretation.

First, Berlin's treatment of values, including the most fundamental, is ambiguous between seeing them as subjective and local – values are whatever particular individuals or groups happen to value – and seeing them as objective and universal – values are truths about the world, independent of any particular human judgment or recognition. On the one hand, Berlin is attracted to the idea that values in general are 'not found, but made', an idea he attributes to the German romantics; on the other, he regards certain 'human' values as having an 'objective' status independent 'of men's subjective fancies' (*POI* 11, 14).

To some extent, the subjective-objective ambiguity in Berlin can be accounted for by a distinction between values that are more basic or fundamental (objective and universal) and those that are less so (subjective and local).[6] However, even within the ostensibly objective and universal category of 'human' values, Berlin's account is less than completely univocal. Sometimes he seems to identify the human values with 'the essence of humanity'

(*POI* 14). In 'Two Concepts', he refers to values that are 'bound up with our conception of man, and of the basic demands of his nature' (*L* 215). By contrast there are passages in which Berlin insists on his credentials as an empiricist, relying solely on the evidence of experience and avoiding any kind of metaphysical speculation, which would include, apparently, speculation on the essential nature of man (e.g., *POI* 13).

Different again, and perhaps most characteristic, are those passages where Berlin strikes a compromise, describing the fundamental human values as 'quasi-empirical', or ends 'that dominate life and thought over a very large portion (even if not the whole) of recorded history' (*L* 45).[7] Neither unchangingly essential nor the mere inventions of individuals or even single societies, the basic human goods answer to fundamental human needs but in historically contingent ways.

What is the content of these basic values? Again, Berlin is more suggestive than definitive. In various places he gives the following examples: 'truth, love, honesty, justice, security, personal relations based on the possibility of human dignity, decency, independence, freedom, spiritual fulfilment' (*CTH* 3); liberty and equality, justice and mercy (*CTH* 12); 'justice, or happiness, or culture, or security, or varying degrees of equality' (*L* 171); courage (*CIB* 37). These remain suggestions, without any attempt to systematize them. All Berlin will say of their overall shape is that 'the number of human values, of values which I can pursue while maintaining my human semblance, my human character, is finite – let us say 74, or perhaps 122, or 26, but finite, whatever it may be' (*POI* 14). This cannot be literally true, since there is no theoretical limit to the subdivision of value.[8] Presumably, Berlin means only that there is some limit to the range of values recognizable as human. I take up this theme later in relation to Berlin's idea of the 'human horizon'.

The second element of Berlin's pluralism is, of course, plurality: the world of value is fragmented rather than unitary. But what exactly is it that is plural? Berlin gives two broadly different answers.[9] Sometimes, as we have seen, he refers to the plurality of individual values or goods such as liberty, equality, justice, and so on – as in his observation that 'liberty is not the only goal of men' (*L* 172). Call this the 'analytical' interpretation of value pluralism. At other times, he sees whole systems or packages of values as incommensurable: pagan versus Christian civilizations in Machiavelli's *Prince*, historical civilizations in the work of Vico, national cultures in Herder. Call this the 'holistic' interpretation. I shall return to this analytical-holistic distinction when I discuss the boundary between pluralism and relativism.

Third, Berlin emphasizes the potential for conflict among the plural values. A standard theme in his work is that to choose one value is often to forego another, or at least to call for a compromise where one value is partially traded off so that another can be partially realized. The general insight is that no single individual life, social order, or conception of the good can accommodate, or at any rate maximize, all genuine values. But there are different kinds of value conflict, and Berlin is not careful to distinguish these.

A useful typology is presented by Thomas Nagel. To begin with, value conflict may be merely contingent, the result of subjective or historical views that could be otherwise, or of other practical circumstances such as lack of time or resources. Alternatively, it may be 'noncontingent', arising 'essentially', or from the nature of the values themselves (Nagel 2001: 105–6). For example, the values involved in living a city life exclude those intrinsic to living in the country.

Further, noncontingent conflict may itself take weaker and stronger forms. In its weaker sense, it may be a matter of 'incompatibility', meaning 'the impossibility in principle of realizing one value while realizing the other, or without frustrating the other' – as in the city vs country example: both kinds of life may be valuable but their respective natures prevent them from being lived simultaneously (Nagel 2001: 106). In its stronger form, noncontingent conflict becomes 'opposition', where 'each value actually condemns the other, rather than merely interfering with it' (Nagel 2001: 106–7). An example is Machiavelli's opposition 'between the virtues of Christian humility and the pagan virtues of assertion and power'.

Although Berlin sometimes speaks in more contingent terms, Nagel argues that it is noncontingent conflict that is his more distinctive concern, since it is this that points more decisively toward the kind of pluralism that interests him, namely a deep plurality in the structure of value. Pluralism in Berlin's sense involves a meta-ethical thesis about the nature of value, and it is not just the uncontroversial empirical observation that opinions about value differ. If value conflict were merely a matter of different opinions, or of contingent circumstances such as time constraints, that would be consistent with monism: there could still be a 'final solution' or overriding formula, it is just that time or ignorance get in the way of its realization. Stronger forms of conflict are a stronger indication of value pluralism.

The noncontingent view of value conflict connects with the final element of Berlin's pluralism, its most distinctive and controversial component, namely the idea that fundamental human values are 'incommensurable' with one another. If we ask why it is that basic values can conflict with one another at these more profound levels, Berlin's answer is that each basic value stakes a completely distinct claim. No matter how deeply we look into the nature of these fundamental goods, we will find that there is no basis on which they can be commensurated – either cashed out according to a single measure (e.g., utility) or ranked within a single hierarchy subject to a super-good (e.g., Plato's philosophical contemplation). Basic human values are fundamentally too different to be brought within a single formula that solves all conflicts in the same way.

Here again there are divergent interpretations: most importantly, a distinction can be drawn between strong and moderate accounts of incommensurability.[10] The strong interpretation insists that there can be no reasoned ranking of incommensurable values *in any circumstances*. On this view liberty and equality, say, are such distinct considerations that we never, in any case, have any decisive reason to rank either ahead of the other. Of course, each generates its own reason for action, namely the intrinsic good of liberty or equality. But each of those reasons speaks with such a unique voice that there can under no conditions be any overarching or independent rationale for preferring either option. When we have to choose among such values in cases of conflict, our choice is always ultimately non-rational.[11]

By contrast, the moderate interpretation holds that although ranking for decisive reason may be impossible in the abstract, or in accordance with a final solution or single formula that applies in every case, that is compatible with there being a decisive reason for ranking incommensurable values *in a particular case*.

This view is advanced by Berlin in an article co-written with Bernard Williams, where they give the example of a conflict between justice and loyalty.

> What justice favours should in a wide variety of cases be pursued at the expense of loyalty, but it is not always so; in other circumstances it may be reasonable to see loyalty as more important than the considerations of justice that come into the matter.
>
> (Berlin and Williams 2013: 326)

While impartial justice should come first for the trial judge or public official, impartiality will legitimately come second to personal loyalty for the parent at her child's soccer game. Such rankings are not merely subjective expressions of feeling or taste but objectively appropriate in the circumstances, the product of, or in accord with, 'practical reason' (Berlin and Williams 2013: 327–8).

The moderate interpretation of incommensurability should be preferred to the strong interpretation for two reasons. First, it accords more closely with ethical experience. It captures the widely held sense that even when fundamental values are conceived as incommensurable, and therefore unrankable in the abstract, people are nevertheless capable of choosing between them for good reason in concrete circumstances. William Galston recounts his experience as a White House official faced with the 'irreducibly heterogeneous' views of the various government departments arguing their case before his interagency task force:

> I found it remarkable how often we could reach deliberative closure in the face of this heterogeneity. Many practitioners (and not a few philosophers) shy away from value pluralism out of fear that it leads to deliberative anarchy. Experience suggests that this is not necessarily so. There can be right answers, widely recognised as such, even in the absence of general rules for ordering or aggregating diverse goods.
>
> (*LP* 7)

Second, the moderate view is well developed philosophically, with a pedigree stretching back to Aristotle. But this is acknowledged less by Berlin than by his successors, so I shall postpone its discussion to Chapter 3.

Is Value Pluralism Dangerous and Untrue?

If the moderate account of incommensurability is accepted, that has important implications for the question of how to resolve the problem of value pluralism. I show this in greater detail later in the chapter when I review Berlin's responses to the problem. But the point is immediately relevant if we consider the view of Ronald Dworkin, who sees Berlinian pluralism as an unsatisfactory ethical basis for liberalism. In 'Do Liberal Values Conflict?' Dworkin (2001) neatly reverses Berlin's case against ethical monism. Where Berlin had argued that monism is dangerous and untrue, Dworkin says the same of value pluralism.

Value pluralism is dangerous, according to Dworkin, because it endorses a counsel of despair or indifference. Dworkin takes Berlin to be saying that 'important political values necessarily conflict, that no choice among these can be defended as the only right choice, and that sacrifices in some of the things we care about are therefore inevitable' (Dworkin 2001: 75). If there is no uniquely right choice, that gives us an excuse for doing nothing, indeed undermines any justification for action. So, for example, taxation to help the unjustly disadvantaged can be knocked back as an invasion of individual liberty. Similarly, if there is no right answer as between the rival claims of liberal societies and illiberal cultures like that of the Taliban, there is nothing decisive the former can say to the latter.

This part of Dworkin's argument rests on some basic misunderstandings about Berlin's pluralism. If we accept the moderate reading of incommensurability, then to say flatly that there can be no uniquely right choice among plural values is mistaken. It is true on the pluralist view that no such choice is possible in the abstract or that no single rule for ranking applies in every case. But that is compatible with there being a best course of action in a given context. As for the complaint that there can be no right answer where whole cultures are in conflict, this assumes the holistic interpretation of pluralism and equates pluralism with cultural relativism. This too is a mistake, as I explain in the next section.

What about Dworkin's contention that value pluralism is false or at least that there is no good reason to accept it? Berlin does not take much trouble to establish the truth of pluralism, simply appealing to the evidence of 'ordinary experience' to demonstrate that values are fundamentally plural in the sense he describes (*L* 213). By itself that is inadequate, since value pluralism is in part a meta-ethical thesis about the deep structure of human values, not simply a report of our experience of values. It might be the case that values are plural in this sense even if no one realized it. Indeed, that is Berlin's implicit claim when he says that values are plural even though the dominant view in Western thought has been monist.

But Dworkin argues that Berlin's notion of pluralism is too extreme and speculative to be accepted. According to Dworkin, Berlin is saying that under pluralism, at least in cases where the values in play are important, whatever choices we make will be made *against* some important good, and therefore, we will be acting wrongly: 'whatever we do, we do something wrong' (Dworkin 2001: 81). Moreover, because somebody will inevitably be attached to the values that lose out in the decision, we will be mistreating that person and violating his or her rights. Consequently, 'we must think a political community violates its responsibilities no matter what it does' (Dworkin 2001: 80). This view is not only dangerous but also ungrounded, Dworkin argues. It assumes that basic values are like 'independent and competing sovereigns' such that conflict among them is inevitable (Dworkin 2001: 83). But that assumption pre-judges what ought to be the outcome of a much longer investigation: 'it purports to see to the bottom of a dilemma and see that there is no escape. Are we ever entitled to so ambitious a claim?' (Dworkin 2001: 81).

Dworkin thinks we are not. If we look long and hard enough, we will find that our values are not independent but 'interdependent' (Dworkin 2001: 84). They possess what value they have only in relation to one another, so each is qualified or contoured by the values surrounding it. For example, individual liberty is valuable not in isolation as the bare absence of interference, as Berlin had said, since that would be compatible with valuing the liberty to murder. Rather, liberty is valuable only subject to the rights of others. Once we understand the value of liberty sufficiently, we see how it fits with, or is dependent on, other values. To insist on the reality of value conflict is a sign that we have not properly understood the values in play. We need to redefine them until we understand their interdependence.

An obvious initial reply to Dworkin is that if the pluralist position is speculative then so too is his monist position. Why should monists like Dworkin have any greater expectation of their view being borne out by further investigation than pluralists have of theirs being vindicated? Philosophers have sought after the monist answer for millennia without arriving at any generally accepted formula.

Dworkin does have a response to this. He proposes a 'test' to see if a given value is independent or interdependent, asking in each case whether the 'violation' of a supposedly independent value is 'really bad or wrong' (Dworkin 2001: 88). If the answer is no, that shows that the putative value is not a genuine value; our conception of it is defective and needs redefinition in the direction of interdependence. This is the case with Berlin's negative liberty, for example.

The trouble with Dworkin's test, and with his whole position, is that it is underpinned by a highly questionable assumption, namely that if one important value is diminished in the name of another, that must amount to wrongdoing and to the mistreatment of individuals and violation of their rights. If that were true, then we would have to say, with Dworkin, that in such cases we do wrong whatever we do. If that were what Berlinian pluralism amounted to, then it would indeed be problematic in the way Dworkin describes, and there would be substance to his plea for monism: that to avoid such outcomes we need to redefine the values involved until they harmonize.

However, Dworkin's account of Berlin's pluralism is quite misleading. First, we should recall the point already made that Berlinian pluralism does not insist that when important values conflict there can never be any right course of action. What Berlin's pluralism says is that is possible to do the right thing overall in a particular case, but that 'the right thing' cannot be determined by a single formula that applies in every case. Further, the right thing has costs. The best decision all things considered will typically involve the balancing of multiple considerations, among which there will be losses, sacrifices, trade-offs.

Berlin makes this clear in 'Two Concepts'. Social welfare, state education, national recognition, collective self-government – all these are policy goals that are justified given the appropriate economic, cultural, and historical circumstances, but they may all have a cost in terms of negative liberty or other values (*L* 172–3). Social-democratic programs require funding by taxes that diminish the liberty of individual taxpayers, and democratic decisions may reduce personal freedoms. This is not at all to say that such policies are not justified – Berlin is broadly in favor of them (Crowder 2013a: 53–7). But we should not pretend that there is no cost, still less that the policy somehow enhances liberty if only we redefine that term in some suitably convenient way.

The notion of losses or sacrifices or trade-offs or costs is not the same as the notion of wrongdoing, or the culpable mistreatment of other people, or the violation of their rights. On the Berlinian view, it is possible for a decision to be correct in the circumstances – that is, a decision may do the best job, in the situation, of ranking or balancing the relevant considerations. All such decisions will have costs, in terms of values forgone or diminished, since 'we cannot have everything' (*L* 215).[12]

As Bernard Williams points out, Dworkin's argument seems to rest on the model of American constitutional law (Williams 2001: 100–1). This is strongly apparent in Dworkin's recourse to the language of rights, absolute entitlements to a certain standard of treatment. If important values must always be expressed in terms of rights, then it is easy to see how conflicts of important values must be conflicts of absolutes. But that is not Berlin's pluralist view, which acknowledges the centrality of certain values in particular contexts without making them absolute. Thus, in 'Two Concepts', he emphasizes the value of negative liberty for liberal democracies, and especially within the political or public sphere, but without making this overriding: 'liberty is not the only goal of men' (*L* 172). Justice, equality, and so on are also valid concerns, and they must be balanced against liberty in any correct public decision.

In the end, it is Dworkin's monist picture that is the more extreme and speculative. In *Justice for Hedgehogs* (2011), he writes:

> My claim is not just that we can bring our discrete moral judgements into some kind of reflective equilibrium – we could do that even if we concede that our values conflict, by adopting some priorities for values or some set of principles for adjudicating conflicts in particular cases. I want to defend the more ambitious claim that there are no genuine conflicts in the values that need such adjudication.
>
> (Dworkin 2011: 119)

He gives the example of having to choose between being honest with a colleague about his poor manuscript and being kind to him. In such a case, Dworkin says, we should consider what the concepts of honesty and kindness 'really' mean in relation to one another: 'we reinterpret our concepts to resolve our dilemma: the direction of our thought is toward unity, not fragmentation'.

But surely the pluralist picture, where we acknowledge value conflict at a conceptual level and try to manage it in particular practical cases, is more realistic. When honesty and kindness appear to collide in the case of the colleague's manuscript, most people's central concern will be to resolve the issue in that case rather than to conduct an inquiry at the level of the concepts themselves. The usual inclination would be to acknowledge a conflict and try to work through it in the particular circumstances, balancing an understanding of the values involved with possible ways of respecting those values in the situation. In the circumstances, most of us will say, honesty weighs more heavily than kindness, or vice versa, or perhaps (more doubtfully) we can compromise: it will depend on a closer look at the situation. This is essentially the 'reflective equilibrium' or priority-setting response that Dworkin acknowledges and rejects. But few people will attempt to find, or even be interested in, the level of resolution that he proposes, in which the basic concepts themselves are contoured in such a way that the sense of conflict that set the process in motion must eventually be seen as an illusion.

Finding the 'right answer' in a particular case is one thing: that, to repeat, is compatible with Berlinian pluralism. Finding a 'final solution', as Berlin puts it, a unitary formula at the level of fundamental values themselves, is quite another. Dworkin wants a final solution but gives us no convincing reason to believe that this is either necessary or possible. Berlin wants us to accept the reality of value conflict at a fundamental level. Although he does not demonstrate that this must be so, his view remains, to say the least, highly plausible.

Is Value Pluralism a Kind of Relativism?

Another major area of controversy raised by Berlin's idea of value pluralism concerns its relation with ethical relativism. At its broadest, relativism in ethics is the idea that moral claims have no universal or objective validity but express some particular point of view, which may be that of a personal or cultural or some other perspective (Wong 1993). The practical implication is that relativists deny the universal application of any ethical norms, and so deny that beliefs and values can be validly criticized on the basis of any perspective except their own. All ethical claims are made from within some local or personal perspective, and none has any purchase on beliefs or practices endorsed from some other perspective. Cultural relativists, for example, tend to see the standard list of 'human rights' – including freedom of speech and religion – not as truly universal or objective but as reflecting a characteristically Western cultural outlook.[13]

Some critics see Berlin's pluralism as a species of relativism.¹⁴ The implication is that, given his pluralism, Berlin cannot justify his liberal political preferences, such as his emphasis on negative liberty, in the apparently universalist terms he asserts.¹⁵ A wedge is driven between his ethics and his politics, between his pluralism and his liberalism.

It is easy to see why the critics think as they do. As noted earlier, Berlin's work contains both analytical and holistic understandings of pluralism, the former stressing the incommensurability of individual values or goods, the latter the incommensurability of whole systems of value, such as those of civilizations or historical periods or national cultures. It is hard to see how the holistic version in particular can be separated from relativism. For example, if the value systems of national cultures are incommensurable, then they have nothing in common and there is no overarching measure or standard according to which one can be ranked above another. Therefore, there is no basis from which any national culture can be criticized on terms other than its own. The result is a world of deeply separate and indefeasible ethical perspectives – the world, essentially, of cultural relativism.

Berlin sometimes seems to endorse this picture, especially when he is discussing Machiavelli, Vico, and Herder. In his account of the last of these, for example, he refers with apparent approval to Herder's view that 'all these forms of life are intelligible each in its own terms (the only terms there are)' (Berlin 2013d: 290). Again, every national culture has its own 'ideal of indefeasible validity', from which it follows that 'we are forbidden to make judgements of comparative value, for that is measuring the incommensurable' (Berlin 2013d: 289). This is Berlin speaking in his holistic voice, which is indistinguishable from the voice of cultural relativism.¹⁶

When this was pointed out, however, Berlin sought immediately to argue that pluralism and relativism are distinct.¹⁷ In 'Alleged Relativism in Eighteenth Century European Thought' (in *CTH*), he tries to make this case in relation to the work of Vico and Herder in particular. Relativism he defines as 'a theory of ideology according to which the ideas and attitudes of individuals or groups are inescapably determined by varying conditioning factors, say, their place in the evolving social structures of their societies' (*CTH* 80). According to relativism, 'the judgement of a man or a group ... is the expression of a taste, or emotional attitude or outlook ... with no objective correlative which determines its truth or falsehood' (*CTH* 83). In short, all values under relativism are subjective and locally determined. Because they cannot be shown to be either true or false, they are immune to objective criticism.

Are Vico and Herder relativists in these terms? Berlin admits that he has, in the past, given the impression that they are, but that was a mistake (*CTH* 79–80). Rather, they are pluralists who urge us 'to look upon life as affording a plurality of values, equally genuine, equally ultimate, above all equally objective; incapable, therefore, of being ordered in a timeless hierarchy, or judged in terms of a single absolute standard' (*CTH* 82).

There are two key points here, both indicating important distinctions between pluralism and relativism. The first is that in this passage Berlin abandons the holistic interpretation of pluralism and shifts to the analytical reading, referring to a plurality of values rather than of systems of value or whole cultures. This is a move he must make. If pluralism is to escape from relativism it must make room for the possibility of critical judgments that transcend personal or local perspectives and that cannot happen if those perspectives are incommensurable. Pluralism is the view that incommensurability is a feature of fundamental values, not of whole systems of value such as cultures.

Still, Berlin finds it hard to let go of the holistic interpretation, since elsewhere in 'Alleged Relativism' he attributes incommensurability not only to values but also to 'social wholes', 'stages of development', 'visions of life', and so forth (*CTH* 87). Although the holistic-analytical distinction is implicit in what he says, he does not see it sharply enough or appreciate its significance. To the extent that he retains the holistic view, he does not altogether succeed in distinguishing pluralism from relativism.

Perhaps what Berlin really wants when he clings to the holistic view is the idea of the uniqueness of cultures, the notion that each culture has its own peculiar 'centre of gravity'. This is a plausible and attractive idea, but it does not depend on the notion of incommensurability. Cultures can be unique without being incommensurable. They overlap because they share the generic values of humanity, as I explain in greater detail in a moment, so they are to that extent commensurable and critically comparable. But they interpret and develop those generic values in distinctive ways, so they are to that extent unique. Germany and Japan have both distinct national cultures and shared human values. Their uniqueness implies neither incommensurability nor, consequently, relativism.

The second distinction between pluralism and relativism arising from the quoted passage is that pluralists acknowledge a framework of objective and universal human values while relativists deny this. Berlin refers in this connection to the notion of a 'human horizon'. 'Forms of life differ. Ends, moral principles, are many. But not infinitely many: they must be within the human horizon' (*CTH* 12). There is a (wide) limit to the range of values that are recognizable as human. It is this human limit that makes cross-cultural and trans-historical understanding possible, since human beings, even those distantly separated by space or time, share the same fundamental purposes.

This idea connects with a central theme that Berlin finds in both Vico and Herder: the human ability to 'feel oneself into', or exercise imaginative empathy with, other apparently quite alien ways of life (Berlin 2013d: 261). Hence, there must be something in even the most alien human culture that we can empathize with – namely, the generic ends pursued by all human beings. These are interpreted and applied in different ways in different cultural settings, but there must be a bedrock of common value that makes understanding possible. Although 'the world of the Greeks is not that of the Jews nor of the eighteenth-century Germans or Italians', nevertheless the 'values and ultimate ends' that constitute those different worlds are all 'open to human pursuit' (*CTH* 88). All human ends are comprehensible because 'all respond to the real needs and aspirations of normal human beings', so that 'members of one culture can understand and enter the minds of, and sympathise with, those of another' (*CTH* 87). Relativism, by contrast, turns cultures and civilizations into 'windowless boxes', making it hard to account for mutual understanding or any solid sense of humanity (*CTH* 88).

So, Berlin's view is that the 'many worlds' he speaks of 'overlap': all are worlds in which the ends pursued include interpretations of ends common to humanity (*CTH* 88). In principle, such universal ends could provide standards against which the performance of particular cultures, societies, institutions, and persons can be evaluated. This is not to say that human societies can be easily ranged in a single, fixed hierarchy of worth, since strengths in one value are likely to be mirrored by weaknesses in another – more freedom, for example, may result in less equality or solidarity. But it will not be true on the pluralist view, as it is for a relativist, that cultures or societies are immune to external criticism. On the contrary, the pluralist outlook demands that we take seriously the full range of fundamental human goods present in the human horizon, acknowledging the extent to which they are present or absent in particular social and cultural systems.

Unfortunately, while the idea of the human horizon shows that Berlin's value pluralism is not just the same thing as relativism, the problem of relativism persists in practice. The human horizon is so wide that it excludes hardly anything. By definition it includes all recognizably human purposes, so every human norm or practice or institution falls within it. It includes even the values of Nazi Germany, since Berlin is explicit that these, although grossly misguided and repulsive to most people, are not inhuman or insane (*CIB* 38). They are distorted expressions of recognizably human goals such as the quest for national or cultural recognition.

Consequently, the human horizon offers only the weakest basis for critical judgment. Someone might appeal to the horizon to make the point, for example, that society A is rich in individual liberty while society B is weak in liberty but, say, stronger in equality. But the human horizon itself tells us nothing about what priorities or balances should be struck between competing values, like liberty and equality, in particular circumstances. That question remains open, and so on the face of it the problem of how to defend specifically liberal values and institutions (or any other specific political position) remains.

If the horizon is not much help in this respect, what about Berlin's different idea of the 'core' human values?[18] While the human horizon primarily identifies those actions and institutions that are recognizably human and therefore comprehensible to others, the core is the narrower notion of those values that are not only universally comprehensible but actually endorsed by all or most human societies. So, for example, while the practice of human sacrifice falls (like almost all practices) within the human horizon, it is arguably outside the human core and potentially open to objection on that ground.

What, however, is the content of the core? We saw earlier that this is a question that Berlin answers only in an ad hoc way. Further, whatever the precise content of the core, it is likely to be highly generic if it is to be genuinely universal in Berlin's sense – that is, actually accepted by all or most human societies. The core, by being more specific than the horizon, may get us further away from relativism, but it is unlikely to be a sufficient basis for liberalism or indeed to indicate any particular form of politics.

Even Berlin's notion of the core human values, then, lacks critical teeth. Could a more substantial account be developed that balanced universality with greater critical potential than Berlin offers? I pursue this question in Chapter 2.

What Is to Be Done?

With a more detailed grasp of the nuances of value pluralism, I am now in a better position to look directly at the way, or ways, in which Berlin responds to the central question pluralism raises. 'If we allow that Great Goods can collide', he writes, 'how do we choose between possibilities? What and how much do we sacrifice to what?' (*CTH* 17, 18). This is the problem of value pluralism, as I term it.

Berlin's immediate response is that 'there is, it seems to me, no clear reply' (*CTH* 18), but scattered through his work are a number of suggestions.[19] Although none is developed in sufficient detail to be persuasive, it is essential to note what Berlin does say because these are the starting points for his successors.

The first suggestion is psychological. The basic claim is that acceptance of value pluralism aligns with a certain kind of temperament which in turn points in a particular ethical and political direction – more specifically, that of liberalism. Berlin mentions this idea only briefly in a very late interview (*UD* 226), but it has been taken up by others. Michael Walzer, for example, writes that 'I don't know anyone who believes in value pluralism who isn't a liberal' (Walzer 1995: 31).[20]

This approach suffers from the obvious problem that pluralist psychologies seem in fact to point in various different political directions, and therefore to be compatible with a range of different value rankings (Crowder 2013b). Not all pluralists are, in fact, psychologically disposed to be liberals. Berlin's own pluralist sources, Machiavelli, Vico, and Herder, are certainly not liberals. In our own time, the roll call of distinguished non-liberal pluralists includes John Gray, John Kekes, and Bhikhu Parekh.[21] Are these the exception or the rule? If the former, why have they deviated from the norm?

More important than the question of what we can say *about* these embarrassing non-liberal pluralists is the question of what liberal pluralists like Berlin can say *to* them. On the psychological view, there seems very little to say: some pluralists are psychologically disposed to be liberals, others are not – end of conversation. But surely there is more to be said. Even if every single pluralist were disposed to be liberal, it could still be reasonably asked whether that made sense. *Why* should pluralists be liberals? To answer that question, it is not enough to point to a (putative) psychological profile; we need an argument.

Might such an argument be provided by attending to the universality of the 'Great Goods' that Berlin recognizes? This is a second possible approach to the problem of value pluralism. If choices among incommensurables were completely open and unqualified, then anything would be justified – or perhaps nothing (as Dworkin argues), since no choice would be *uniquely* correct. But perhaps things are not so open-ended because choices under pluralism are constrained by the universal values that Berlin acknowledges. Thus, he writes, 'There is a great deal of broad agreement among people in different societies over long stretches of time about what is right and wrong, good and evil' (*CTH* 19).

Again, however, this would seem to be a limited solution. What are the values and principles that are supposed to be universal in this sense? As noted earlier, Berlin is cagey about their content. In 'Pursuit of the Ideal', he writes that 'there are, if not universal values, at any rate a minimum without which societies could scarcely survive' (*CTH* 19). But societies have survived over long periods while maintaining all manner of objectionable norms and practices: slavery, racism, xenophobia, imperialism, sexism, and so on. A minimum morality grounded in social survival is compatible with almost anything.

Moreover, even if Berlin presented a substantial and plausible account of a minimum human morality, this could not resolve conflicts among incommensurables because its component values would be multiple, conflicting, and incommensurable themselves. On Berlin's account, basic human values are subject to the problem of pluralism rather than standing above it. Take utility, for example. At one point Berlin rather desperately proposes utilitarianism as a method for deciding pluralist conflicts, since although 'utilitarian solutions are often wrong', they are 'more often beneficent' (*CTH* 18). This forgets that utilitarianism is one of the standard forms of monism that pluralism opposes, since it involves the reduction of all values to a common denominator, 'utility'. On Berlin's own view, utility can at best be one consideration among others.

Still, the identification of the great goods is an important part of a pluralist political theory for two reasons: it clarifies what the values are that are said to be plural and incommensurable, and it narrows down the range of legitimate choice among conflicting values by distinguishing between those 'primary' goods that contribute to any good life and those 'secondary' values that are no more than locally valid. The former override the latter. I pursue this matter in Chapter 2.

The question remains of how to rank the great goods when they come into conflict. One answer might be to avoid conflict altogether. So, for example, we might try to avoid having to choose between the values of career and family by reforming work life to be more accommodating of family obligations and pleasures (*Caps* 37–9). For Berlin, though, this is a very limited response because conflicts among fundamental values are inevitable. 'The human condition is such that men cannot always avoid choices' (*L* 43).

What we can do, however, is to mitigate our losses through compromise. This is Berlin's third suggestion. To the question, 'What and how much must we sacrifice to what?' there may be no clear reply,

> but the collisions, even if they cannot be avoided, can be softened. Claims can be balanced, compromises can be reached: in concrete situations not every claim is of equal force – so much liberty and so much equality; so much for sharp moral condemnation, and so much for understanding a given human situation; so much for the full force of the law, and so much for the prerogative of mercy; for feeding the hungry, clothing the naked, healing the sick, sheltering the homeless. Priorities, never final and absolute, must be established ... we must engage in what are called trade-offs – rules, values, principles must yield to each other in varying degrees in specific situations.
>
> (*CTH* 18)

Whenever we contemplate a conflict of fundamental values, we may be able to reach a compromise between them.

This seems eminently reasonable but the obvious question is, which compromises should we accept and which should we reject? Not all compromises are equally desirable. Even assuming that we are not dealing with cases where compromise is extorted, may there not be situations where someone freely but wrongly concedes too much of one value in return for too little of another? The idea of compromise seems empty without some kind of reasoned principle or norm to guide it.

It might be responded – Berlin's fourth approach – that there simply is no such reasoned principle or norm when we are dealing with a conflict of incommensurable values. Call this the 'agonistic' account of pluralist choice. As Berlin puts it in a lecture,

> you cannot say love is inferior to honour, and you do not want to say that honour is inferior to love. Both these are ultimate values, and there is no way of settling the issue: you must just plump in some sort of way.
>
> (Berlin 1975)[22]

When he writes about Machiavelli as straddling the distinct worldviews of Christianity and classical paganism, he observes that 'entire systems of value may come into collision without possibility of rational arbitration' (Berlin 2013a: 94). If I am faced with a choice between being just and being merciful, in the end I can decide between these options only by personal preference or sheer ungrounded commitment or some random decision procedure like tossing a coin. My choice is not wholly irrational, since each of the values at stake gives me a reason to act. Nevertheless, there is no overarching reason to judge one option as more compelling than the other.[23]

The trouble with the agonistic view is that it rests on the 'strong' interpretation of value incommensurability, according to which there is never a decisive reason to rank one incommensurable value above another in any circumstances. That interpretation was rejected earlier. It is true that at an abstract level there is no reason why one fundamental value is more important than another, but things are different at the level of concrete situations where these values have specific application. There is no hierarchy between justice and loyalty as such, but there may be good reason to place one before the other in a concrete situation.

However, this shortcoming of the agonistic account suggests a fifth, more promising possibility: a 'contextual' approach. This fits with the moderate interpretation of incommensurability recommended earlier. Even though there may be no decisive reason to choose between incommensurable values in the abstract, there may be reason to decide between them in particular cases. As Berlin writes, 'the concrete situation is almost everything' (*CTH* 19).

There are, of course, different kinds of context in which incommensurable values can conflict – personal, political, cultural, and historical, for example (although these interconnect). The first of these, the context of an individual life – its dominant or constitutive goods and overall shape – is not much discussed by Berlin, although it has been examined by other pluralists, such as Nussbaum.[24] Usually, Berlin is concerned with political judgment, whether that of individual leaders or of whole societies faced by conflicts among fundamental values. In the former case, he refers to the 'sense of reality' that enables the successful statesman to 'grasp the unique combination of characteristics that constitute this particular situation – this and no other' (Berlin 1996: 45).[25] When it comes to the judgment of whole societies, he appeals rather more narrowly to the authority of culture. Responding to pluralist conflict among public goods is 'not a matter of purely subjective judgement: it is dictated by the forms of life of the society to which one belongs' (*CTH* 19). 'To decide rationally in such situations is to decide in the light of general ideals, the overall pattern of life pursued by a man or a group or a society' (*L* 42).[26] By implication a similar role is accorded to historical context, the 'centre of gravity' of a period or age, when Berlin is discussing Vico and Herder in particular.

This is not to say that context always points to a clear answer. In many cases, the best decision will be hard to identify because there will be more than one relevant context and these will conflict – as, for example, in the conflict between private and public identities (family and city) dramatized in Sophocles' *Antigone*. Even wholly within the context of public culture, there may be conflict between rival cultural traditions.[27] There may sometimes be genuine dilemmas in which no option is preferable to any other.

Nor are our circumstances likely to throw up wholly painless solutions to conflict. The ubiquity of loss, even where a decision has been made that is the best possible overall, has already been mentioned (see also Williams 2001). Further, there is the possibility of tragedy – a frequent theme in Berlin – where losses are both unavoidable and severe. In such cases, the best we can hope for is the mitigation of losses through compromise.

So, Berlin's contextualist pluralism is not a view that expects neat and tidy formulas in ethics and politics; on the contrary, it is explicitly anti-formulaic. It recognizes uncertainty, dilemma, loss, tragedy, the need for compromise. On the other hand, the contextualist view denies that pluralism implies blankly non-rational choice in all instances. It is consistent with more routine cases in which basic values are ranked or traded off for good reason generated by given circumstances.

All this seems robustly realistic, but Berlin's contextual approach still has problems. What is the relevant context in any particular case? Should we give priority to the personal or the political, the cultural or the historical? Contexts may come into conflict, as where a given question would be answered differently by two rival cultures that both claim authority in the case. Further, even if we settle on, say, a culture as the relevant court of appeal, its ruling may still be open to interpretation or dispute.

Perhaps most troubling of all, the contextual approach threatens to reopen the problem of relativism. Even if we are clear that we are dealing with incommensurability of values or goods rather than of whole systems of value, it remains, as we have seen, to decide how to rank or trade off those values when they conflict. If the answer is to appeal to a personal or local context, have we not returned, in practice, to a relativist view? For example, how far will we be able to make a case for freedoms of speech and religion in places where the local form of life happens not to accept these as norms?

The problem can arise with the appeal to historical context too. In the final paragraph of 'Two Concepts', Berlin reflects that the values he is defending may be those only of a particular civilization in a specific period of history. 'It may be that the ideal of freedom to choose ends without claiming eternal validity for them, and the pluralism of values connected with this, is only the late fruit of our declining capitalist civilisation' (*L* 217). He goes on to quote Joseph Schumpeter: 'to realise the relative validity of our convictions and yet stand for them unflinchingly is what distinguishes a civilised man from a barbarian'. However, if the basis of our values comes down to a matter of historical contingency, why should we stand for such values unflinchingly? Why should we oppose current attacks on human rights, for example, rather than allow, as sophisticated persons, that such attacks merely signal the arrival of a new historical phase?

Perhaps sensing these problems, Berlin has another suggestion, a 'conceptual' approach. Might it be possible to adjudicate between clashing incommensurables by reference to the concept of value pluralism itself? There is a hint in this direction in 'Two Concepts'. There Berlin writes that if basic values are plural and incommensurable, as he believes,

> then the possibility of conflict – and of tragedy – can never wholly be eliminated from human life, either personal or social. The necessity of choosing between absolute claims is then an inescapable characteristic of the human condition. This gives its value to freedom as Acton conceived

of it – as an end in itself, and not as a temporary need, arising out of our confused notions and irrational and disordered lives, a predicament which a panacea could one day put right.

(*L* 214)

That is, we know that individual freedom is an objective and permanent human value by reflecting on the nature of pluralism. If pluralism is true, then choice among fundamental goods is unavoidable. If so, then the freedom with which to make such choices must itself be a fundamental good. In this way, Berlin points to a conceptual link between pluralism and liberalism.

However, there is a problem with this argument as Berlin presents it. The argument seems to be that freedom of choice is valuable because choice under pluralism is inescapable. But that would appear to be a violation of 'Hume's Law', according to which the derivation of values from facts is a logical non sequitur. In this case, it does not follow from the fact that choice is a necessity that either choice or the freedom to choose is a value we should pursue. Some choices on Berlin's view are tragic and therefore painful – he refers in these cases to the 'agony of choice' (*L* 214). So, it might be argued that we should be relieved of such painful choices by a dictator who will make them for us. From our recognizing choice as inescapable, it does not follow that we should value choices or the freedom to make them.

There is also a conceptual argument for liberalism implicit in Berlin's linking of pluralism with anti-utopianism, but this too is not wholly convincing or complete. To appreciate the plurality and incommensurability of basic values, Berlin teaches, is to accept that there is no final, perfect system of politics that maximizes all such values simultaneously and harmoniously. All political forms are imperfect in the sense that they carry costs as well as benefits. Consequently, pluralism rules out political utopianism – the visions of Plato, Hegel, and Marx, Berlin would argue – and commends those forms of politics that seek only to manage human imperfection and conflict rather than trying to transcend it.

The trouble is that although liberalism would meet this bill, so would conservatism, as Berlin implicitly concedes when he refers to the contextual authority of 'the forms of life of the society to which one belongs' (*CTH* 18). Pluralism does imply anti-utopianism, but anti-utopianism is not sufficient to single out liberalism as a uniquely desirable form of politics.

To summarize this section, Berlin sets out no systematic response to the problem of value pluralism but he offers a range of suggestions. None of these is wholly without merit, but some are stronger than others. The least helpful is the 'psychological' approach, and I will not be discussing this further.[28] Compromise plays an important role in pluralist thought, but it needs normative limits.[29] Little guidance is provided by 'agonism', which ignores the role of context in practical reasoning under pluralism.[30] The three remaining approaches are the most important for my purposes, and these will be the focus of subsequent discussion. These are 'the great goods' (Chapter 2), 'contextualism' (Chapters 3–4), and 'conceptualism' (Chapters 5–8).

Political Implications

Berlin's conceptual arguments from pluralism to freedom of choice and anti-utopianism raise the issue of the political implications of value pluralism. Clearly, he associates pluralism with liberalism. An immediate question is whether that political conclusion does not contradict his own pluralist premise. According to pluralism, no basic value is fundamentally more important than any other, but Berlin's liberalism seems to promote negative liberty to a special status.

That status is not unpluralist, however, because it is not absolutely overriding. Berlin does not claim that negative liberty must outrank all other considerations whatever the situation; that would be a monist position, and Berlin attributes it disapprovingly to laissez-faire forms of liberalism (*L* 38–9). Rather, the claim he makes for negative liberty is qualified in three ways. First, it is appropriate only within a certain historical context – 'the late fruit of our declining capitalist civilisation', as he expresses it at the end of 'Two Concepts' (*L* 217). Second, even within that context negative liberty is emphasized only as a political principle; personal lives may legitimately be based on other ideals, including various senses of positive liberty.[31] Third, even within the political sphere, the kind of liberalism Berlin has in mind balances negative liberty with equality, social justice, and other considerations. He thinks of this as 'New Deal' liberalism, but it aligns with the redistributive 'egalitarian' liberalism of John Rawls and Ronald Dworkin, for example.[32]

But even given the qualified character of Berlin's liberalism, the question remains how he justifies it given his pluralist premises. This is a fraught issue. Sometimes it seems as though Berlin is proposing a logical connection between pluralism and liberalism, as when he refers to 'pluralism, with the measure of "negative" liberty that it entails' (*L* 216). On the other hand, he says elsewhere that, 'I believe in both liberalism and pluralism, but the two are not logically connected' (*CIB* 44). Even within a single series of interviews, he seems to alternate between the two positions. At one time he insists that 'From pluralism to liberalism there is a connection – a direct, not a loose, connection. …Once you allow [pluralism], you can't not be a liberal. Illiberal pluralism doesn't exist'; but later he says, 'There's no logical connection, that's all I'm saying. There is a psychological connection, there's a political connection, but not a logical connection' (*UD* 214, 226). It is hard to avoid concluding that on this point Berlin is simply inconsistent.

To the extent that Berlin's argument is a logical one, it faces the objection from Hume's Law. This was introduced earlier as a problem for Berlin's argument from the necessity of choice to freedom of choice, but might it not be a problem for any attempt to argue from pluralism to liberalism (or any political view) on the ground that pluralism is a set of facts and liberalism (or any political view) a set of values?[33]

One response might be that it is not the concept of pluralism alone that implies a case for liberalism but pluralism together with some set of circumstances.

But what would those circumstances be? Perhaps Berlin means to argue his pluralist case for liberalism by contextualizing it within some set of social or economic or historical conditions. This fits with his reference to 'our declining capitalist civilisation'. If so, he never develops his account. What are the limits of the 'capitalist civilisation' to which he refers, and therefore of the argument in 'Two Concepts'? Even given some set of contextual qualifications, the question remains why liberal values such as negative liberty (or any form of individual liberty) should be emphasized against other plural values.

A measure of the open-endedness of Berlin's arguments is the range of political conclusions drawn from them by his successors. In each case, the fate of liberalism is uncertain at best. Agonism, for example, seems an unlikely basis for liberalism or indeed for any political position that values reasoned justification. Nevertheless, pluralists attracted to agonism have adopted a range of political positions, including Max Weber's demand for an 'ethic of responsibility' in politics, Carl Schmitt's support for fascist dictatorship, and Chantal Mouffe's 'agonistic democracy'.[34]

Nor does the kind of universalism endorsed by Berlin seem promising from a liberal point of view, since it is necessarily accommodating of all or most human societies, including non-liberal ones. An alternative response might be to 'thicken' the universals in question, thus giving a more explicit account of their content and also arming them with more critical teeth. This is one way of seeing the work of Martha Nussbaum, whose 'human capabilities' theory proposes a list of substantial human goods that imply a broadly liberal or social-democratic politics overall (*WHD*, *Caps*). But this move brings its own problems, since the thicker the good, the more controversial will be the claim that it is genuinely universal. Even if the capabilities are genuinely universal, there will still be the pluralist problem of how to rank them when they conflict.

What about Berlin's contextualism? Maybe conflicting political universals – liberty and equality, say – can be ranked within a context. An obvious limitation of this from a liberal point of view is that liberalism will be supported in this way only if liberals can point to a friendly context of liberal values, culture, practices, or institutions; other contexts will indicate different kinds of politics.[35] Indeed, since the contextual approach places so much weight on existing circumstances, it might seem to favor conservative conclusions, as argued by John Kekes (*MP*, 1997, 1998). When the circumstances to be stressed are those of a national culture, the political result may be a form of cultural nationalism, such as that which Berlin finds in Herder (Berlin 2013d: 254–5). Yet the same emphasis on culture has also been turned in a multicultural or multinational direction by pluralist thinkers such as Charles Taylor (1994) and Bhikhu Parekh (2006, 2008). Bernard Williams, who stresses historical context, has linked contextualist thinking with a 'realist' politics associated with a 'liberalism of fear' (*Deed* chs 1, 5, and 6).

Conceptual arguments, too, while often favoring liberalism, have sometimes reached different conclusions. John Gray (2000), for example, links pluralism with a looser, more pragmatic form of 'modus vivendi' politics. Michael

Walzer (1983) argues for a social-democratic 'complex equality' from a pluralist starting point. Richard Bellamy (*LAP*) seeks to connect pluralism with deliberative democracy. Even where pluralist conceptualism is the basis of liberal conclusions, there is disagreement as to what kind of liberalism pluralism supports. The toleration-based 'Reformation' liberalism of William Galston (*LP*, *PLP*), for example, contrasts with my own 'Enlightenment' liberalism grounded in personal autonomy.

Conclusion

Berlin gets us interested in value pluralism, but he leaves us with many questions. To what extent can the pluralist thesis be shown to be true? What exactly are 'the great goods' that form the bedrock of pluralist thought? How far can pluralism be distinguished from relativism? What kind of politics, if any, does pluralism imply? In particular, he leaves us with the problem of value pluralism: how can and should we choose among incommensurable values when they come into conflict?

To this last question, he gives no definitive answer but he does float a number of suggestions. Three of these provide little guidance. 'Psychology' can be set aside as of limited application. Compromise is important but needs normative direction. Agonism ignores people's capacity to rank competing incommensurables in context. It is Berlin's remaining three proposals – appeal to the great goods, contextualism, and conceptualism – that are the most promising.

In the chapters to follow, I examine the ways that some of the most prominent theorists influenced by Berlin have developed these three proposals in particular. Out of these ethical approaches have emerged various political positions: liberal (in different versions), conservative, social-democratic, pragmatist (in the loose sense of those who favor versions of compromise or modus vivendi), and realist. By examining these different responses to Berlin, I aim to formulate a more satisfying overall view.

Notes

1 Most of Berlin's published writings have been gathered into a series of volumes edited by Henry Hardy. These are available in several editions, most recently the set published by Princeton University Press. Berlin's published letters can be found in Berlin 2004, 2009, 2013e, 2015. The leading biography is Ignatieff 1998. The principal book-length critical studies of Berlin's thought are Kocis 1989; Galipeau 1994; Crowder 2004; Dubnov 2012; Cherniss 2013; Gray 2013; Hardy 2018. Notable edited collections discussing Berlin include Ryan 1979; Margalit and Margalit 1993; Dworkin, Lilla, and Silvers 2001; Crowder and Hardy 2007b; Hardy 2009; Baum and Nichols 2013; Cherniss and Smith 2018. See also *The Isaiah Berlin Virtual Library*, a website curated by Henry Hardy (2000–2019), for many Berlin-related materials and references: http://berlin.wolf.ox.ac.uk
2 Berlin discusses Machiavelli in 'The Originality of Machiavelli' in Berlin 2013a. For Berlin's main treatment of Vico and Herder, see Berlin 2013d.

3 See Lukes 1998: 96, 102. Other significant modern formulations of value pluralism, unknown to Berlin, can be found in the work of the American pragmatists Sterling Lamprecht (1920, 1921) and A. P. Brogan (1931). A more complete list of pre-Berlinian expressions of pluralism is available in *The Isaiah Berlin Virtual Library* (Hardy 2000–2019).
4 Compare 'Path', where he says he 'always felt sceptical' about the idealism he describes there: *POI* 8.
5 'Path' is again different on this point because Machiavelli does not feature. There Berlin says it was reading Vico that 'first shook me', and that 'my pluralism is a product of reading Vico and Herder, and of understanding the roots of romanticism': *POI* 8, 15. To the German romantics, Berlin attributes a stress on uniqueness and a 'denial of universal values' (*POI* 12) – although the latter is rejected by Berlin and contradicted by his value pluralism.
6 See, in a pluralist context, John Kekes's distinction between 'primary' and 'secondary' values: *MP* 18–19, 38–44.
7 See similarly *CTH* 12, 19.
8 I owe this point to Henry Hardy.
9 A similar distinction has been drawn by Charles Taylor (2001: 113–4).
10 A weak interpretation might also be identified, which rules out only measurable rankings: see my *LVP* 50–2.
11 See, e.g., Raz 1986: ch. 13; Riley 2000; Moore 2009; Mulligan 2015. Gray seems sometimes to hold this view, as when he refers to choice among incommensurables as 'radical choice – choice without criteria, grounds or principles' (Gray 2013: 97). But elsewhere he appears to agree with the more moderate interpretation of incommensurability discussed next: 'Value-pluralism does not imply that there are not in particular circumstances good reasons for favouring one value, or constellation of values, over others' (Gray 2013: 188).
12 See also *L* 43. Hence, anti-utopianism is a pervasive theme of Berlin's thought. But to say that even the best decisions have costs is not to say that all decisions are, simply, wrong. On the pluralist view, the best decisions are correct but non-ideal.
13 See, e.g., Pollis and Schwab 1980; cp. Donnelly 2003: chs 4–6.
14 See Momigliano 1976; Sandel 1984; Strauss 1989 [1961]; Anderson 1992; Kateb 1999; Sandall 2001; Sternhell 2010.
15 At any rate, Berlin offers no cultural qualifications to his position within the contemporary world. But at the very end of 'Two Concepts', he appears to frame his whole argument within the historical category of 'our declining capitalist civilisation' (*L* 217).
16 The accusation of relativism is leveled at Berlin's interpretation of Vico and Herder by Momigliano (1976).
17 For other attempts to distinguish between pluralism and relativism, see Lukes 2003; Crowder 2004: 114–23; Crowder 2008; Ferrell 2008; Crowder 2017.
18 On the relation between horizon and core, which is controversial, see Crowder and Hardy 2007a; Hardy 2018: 232–4, 240.
19 Most of these are conveniently summarized in *CTH* 17–20.
20 In addition to Walzer, see Galston in *LP* 61–2; Beata Polanowska-Sygulska in *UD* 290–2. There is an exchange in Zakaras 2013a, b; Galston 2013; Crowder 2013b.
21 See Gray 2000; Kekes in *MP*; Parekh 2006, 2008.
22 See, similarly, Lukes 1998: 103.
23 In one place Berlin seems to say that there can be plumping that is 'not irrational' because 'I can give reasons' when I plump: Berlin 2015: 277, n. 4. But that is consistent with there being no *decisive* reason for my choice. It is the absence of decisive reasons for action or judgement that is the essence of agonism.
24 See Nussbaum's account in *LK* ch. 2, and *FG* ch. 10, discussed in Chapter 3. For other explanations of pluralist practical reasoning in the context of an individual

life see Hampshire 1983 and *IE*; Bernard Williams in *ELP*; Kekes in *MP* ch. 5; Richardson 1994; Taylor 1997.
25 Berlin's discussions of the political judgement of individual leaders are examined in Cherniss 2018.
26 See, similarly, *L* 47.
27 The issue of how pluralists should respond to tensions between and within cultural traditions is discussed, in the context of multiculturalism, in Raz 1995; Parekh 2006, 2008; Crowder 2013c, chs 7 and 9.
28 The psychological approach does, however, overlap to some extent with the 'virtues' argument I offer in *LVP* ch. 8. It also has limited affinities with the account offered by Alan Ryan (2013), who argues that Berlin inhabits the personalities of key writers in order to enact 'the history of ideas as psychodrama'.
29 See Chapter 7.
30 Nevertheless, agonism remains an influential view, and I devote two sections to it in Chapter 3.
31 In this respect, Berlin comes close to the 'political' liberalism of Rawls (1993). However, the relation between Rawls's position and Berlin's is a complex matter, and there are important differences between the two. See my *LVP* ch. 7; Crowder 2004: 159–61; Galston in *LP* ch. 4.
32 For Berlin's endorsement of the New Deal, see, for example, *L* 84; Ignatieff 1998: 197, 228; Lukes 1998: 98–9. His general commitment to economic redistribution is documented in Crowder 2013a: 53–7. For the egalitarian liberalism of Rawls and Dworkin, see Rawls 1971, 1993; Dworkin 1985, 2000.
33 See Polanowska-Sygulska in *UD* 295–6; Talisse 2012: 34, 63. I discuss this objection at greater length in Chapter 5.
34 Weber 1948a, b; Schmitt 1996 [1932]; Mouffe 2000, 2005.
35 In this way, John Gray endorses a limited 'agonistic' liberalism, by which he means a case for liberalism that abjures universalism and explicitly limits its claims within an existing liberal cultural context: Gray 1995, 2000.

References

In-text abbreviations are noted in brackets.

Anderson, Perry (1992), 'The Pluralism of Isaiah Berlin', in *A Zone of Engagement* (London: Verso).
Baum, Bruce and Robert Nichols, eds (2013), *Isaiah Berlin and the Politics of Freedom: "Two Concepts of Liberty" 50 Years Later* (New York: Routledge).
Bellamy, Richard (1999), *Liberalism and Pluralism: Towards a Politics of Compromise* (London: Routledge). [*LAP*]
Berlin, Isaiah (1975), 'The End of the Ideal of a Perfect Society', transcribed in Henry Hardy, ed., *The Isaiah Berlin Virtual Library*, http://berlin.wolf.ox.ac.uk
Berlin, Isaiah (1996), *Sense of Reality: Studies in Ideas and Their History* (London: Chatto & Windus).
Berlin, Isaiah (2002), *Liberty*, ed. Henry Hardy (Oxford: Oxford University Press). [*L*]
Berlin, Isaiah (2004), *Flourishing: Letters 1928–1946*, ed. Henry Hardy (London: Chatto & Windus).
Berlin, Isaiah (2009), *Enlightening: Letters 1946–1960*, ed. Henry Hardy and Jennifer Holmes (London: Chatto & Windus).
Berlin, Isaiah (2013a), *Against the Current: Essays in the History of Ideas*, ed. Henry Hardy, 2nd edn (Princeton: Princeton University Press).

Berlin, Isaiah (2013b), *The Crooked Timber of Humanity: Chapters in the History of Ideas*, ed. Henry Hardy, 2nd edn (Princeton: Princeton University Press). [*CTH*]

Berlin, Isaiah (2013c), *The Power of Ideas*, ed. Henry Hardy, 2nd edn (Princeton: Princeton University Press). [*POI*]

Berlin, Isaiah (2013d), *Three Critics of the Enlightenment: Vico, Hamann, Herder*, ed. Henry Hardy, 2nd edn (Princeton: Princeton University Press).

Berlin, Isaiah (2013e), *Building: Letters 1960–1975*, ed. Henry Hardy and Mark Pottle (London: Chatto & Windus).

Berlin, Isaiah (2015), *Affirming: Letters 1975–1997*, ed. Henry Hardy and Mark Pottle (London: Chatto & Windus).

Berlin, Isaiah and Beata Polanowska-Sygulska (2006), *Unfinished Dialogue* (Amherst, NY: Prometheus Press). [*UD*]

Berlin, Isaiah and Bernard Williams (2013), 'Pluralism and Liberalism', in Isaiah Berlin, *Concepts and Categories*, Henry Hardy, ed., 2nd edn (Princeton: Princeton University Press).

Brogan, A. P. (1931), 'Objective Pluralism in the Theory of Value', *International Journal of Ethics* 41: 287–95.

Cherniss, Joshua L. (2013), *A Mind and Its Time: The Development of Isaiah Berlin's Political Thought* (Oxford: Oxford University Press).

Cherniss, Joshua L. (2018), '"The Sense of Reality": Berlin on Political Judgement, Political Ethics, and Leadership', in Joshua L. Cherniss and Steven B. Smith, eds, *The Cambridge Companion to Isaiah Berlin* (Cambridge: Cambridge University Press).

Cherniss, Joshua L. and Steven B. Smith, eds (2018), *Cambridge Companion to Isaiah Berlin* (Cambridge: Cambridge University Press).

Crowder, George (2002), *Liberalism and Value Pluralism* (London: Continuum). [*LVP*]

Crowder, George (2004), *Isaiah Berlin: Liberty and Pluralism* (Cambridge: Polity).

Crowder, George (2008), 'Pluralism and Multiculturalism', *Society* 45 (3): 247–52.

Crowder, George (2013a), 'In Defense of Isaiah Berlin: A Reply to James Tully', in Bruce Baum and Robert Nichols, eds, *Isaiah Berlin and the Politics of Freedom: 'Two Concepts of Liberty' 50 Years Later* (New York: Routledge).

Crowder, George (2013b), 'Justification and Psychology in Liberal Pluralism: A Reply to Zakaras', *Review of Politics* 75 (1): 103–10.

Crowder, George (2013c), *Theories of Multiculturalism: An Introduction* (Cambridge: Polity).

Crowder, George (2017), 'Value Pluralism vs Relativism in Bernard Williams's "Relativism of Distance"', *The Pluralist* 12 (3): 114–38.

Crowder, George and Henry Hardy (2007a). 'Appendix: Berlin's Universal Values – Core or Horizon?', in George Crowder and Henry Hardy, eds, *The One and the Many: Reading Isaiah Berlin* (Amherst, NY: Prometheus Books).

Crowder, George and Henry Hardy, eds (2007b), *The One and the Many: Reading Isaiah Berlin* (Amherst, NY: Prometheus Books).

Donnelly, Jack (2003), *Universal Human Rights in Theory and Practice* (Ithaca, NY: Cornell University Press).

Dubnov, Arie M. (2012), *Isaiah Berlin: The Journey of a Jewish Liberal* (New York: Palgrave Macmillan).

Dworkin, Ronald (1985), *A Matter of Principle* (Cambridge, MA: Harvard University Press).

Dworkin, Ronald (2000), *Sovereign Virtue: The Theory and Practice of Equality* (Cambridge, MA: Harvard University Press).

Dworkin, Ronald (2001), 'Do Liberal Values Conflict?', in Ronald Dworkin, Mark Lilla, and Robert Silvers, eds, *The Legacy of Isaiah Berlin* (New York: New York Review Books).

Dworkin, Ronald (2011), *Justice for Hedgehogs* (Cambridge, MA: Harvard University Press).

Dworkin, Ronald, Mark Lilla, and Robert B. Silvers, eds (2001), *The Legacy of Isaiah Berlin* (New York: New York Review Books).

Ferrell, Jason (2008), 'The Alleged Relativism of Isaiah Berlin', *Critical Review of International Social and Political Philosophy* 11 (1): 41–56.

Galipeau, Claude (1994), *Isaiah Berlin's Liberalism* (Oxford: Clarendon Press).

Galston, William (2002), *Liberal Pluralism: The Implications of Value Pluralism for Political Theory and Practice* (Cambridge: Cambridge University Press). [*LP*]

Galston, William (2005), *The Practice of Liberal Pluralism* (Cambridge: Cambridge University Press). [*PLP*]

Galston, William (2013), 'Between Logic and Psychology: The Links between Value Pluralism and Liberal Theory', *Review of Politics* 75 (1): 97–101.

Gray, John (1995), *Enlightenment's Wake: Politics and Culture at the Close of the Modern Age* (London: Routledge).

Gray, John (2000), *Two Faces of Liberalism* (Cambridge: Polity).

Gray, John (2013), *Isaiah Berlin: An Interpretation of His Thought*, new edition (Princeton: Princeton University Press).

Hampshire, Stuart (1983), *Morality and Conflict* (Cambridge, MA: Harvard University Press).

Hampshire, Stuart (1989), *Innocence and Experience* (Cambridge, MA: Harvard University Press). [*IE*]

Hardy, Henry, ed. (2000–2019), *The Isaiah Berlin Virtual Library*, http://berlin.wolf.ox.ac.uk/

Hardy, Henry (2009), *The Book of Isaiah: Personal Impressions of Isaiah Berlin* (Woodbridge: Boydell Press).

Hardy, Henry (2018), *In Search of Isaiah Berlin: A Literary Adventure* (London: I. B. Tauris).

Ignatieff, Michael (1998), *Isaiah Berlin: A Life* (London: Chatto & Windus).

Jahanbegloo, Ramin (1992), *Conversations with Isaiah Berlin* (London: Peter Halban). [*CIB*]

Kateb, George (1999), 'Can Cultures be Judged? Two Defenses of Cultural Pluralism in Isaiah Berlin's Work', *Social Research* 66: 1009–38.

Kekes, John (1993), *The Morality of Pluralism* (Princeton: Princeton University Press). [*MP*]

Kekes, John (1997), *Against Liberalism* (Ithaca, NY: Cornell University Press).

Kekes, John (1998), *A Case for Conservatism* (Ithaca, NY: Cornell University Press).

Kocis, Robert (1989), *A Critical Appraisal of Sir Isaiah Berlin's Political Philosophy* (Lewiston, NY: Edwin Mellen Press).

Lamprecht, Sterling P. (1920), 'The Need for a Pluralistic Emphasis in Ethics', *Journal of Philosophy, Psychology and Scientific Methods* 17: 561–72.

Lamprecht, Sterling P. (1921), 'Some Political Implications of Ethical Pluralism', *Journal of Philosophy* 18: 225–44.

Lukes, Steven (1998), 'Isaiah Berlin: In Conversation with Steven Lukes', *Salmagundi* 120: 52–134.
Lukes, Steven (2003), 'Must Pluralists be Relativists?', in *Liberals and Cannibals: The Implications of Diversity* (London: Verso).
Margalit, Edna and Avishai Margalit, eds (1993), *Isaiah Berlin: A Celebration* (London: Hogarth).
Momigliano, Arnaldo (1976), 'On the Pioneer Trail', *New York Review of Books*, 11 November: 33–8.
Moore, Matthew (2009), 'Pluralism, Relativism, and Liberalism', *Political Research Quarterly* 62 (2): 244–56.
Mouffe, Chantal (2000), *On the Democratic Paradox* (London: Verso).
Mouffe, Chantal (2005), *On the Political* (London: Routledge).
Mulligan, Thomas (2015), 'The Limits of Liberal Tolerance', *Public Affairs Quarterly* 29 (3): 277–95.
Nagel, Thomas (2001), 'Pluralism and Coherence', in Ronald Dworkin, Mark Lilla, and Robert Silvers, eds, *The Legacy of Isaiah Berlin* (New York: New York Review Books).
Nussbaum, Martha (1990), *Love's Knowledge: Essays on Philosophy and Literature* (Oxford: Oxford University Press). [*LK*]
Nussbaum, Martha (2000), *Women and Human Development: The Capabilities Approach* (Cambridge: Cambridge University Press). [*WHD*]
Nussbaum, Martha (2001), *The Fragility of Goodness: Luck and Ethics in Greek Tragedy and Philosophy*, 2nd edn (Cambridge: Cambridge University Press). [*FG*]
Nussbaum, Martha (2011), *Creating Capabilities: The Human Development Approach* (Cambridge, MA: Belknap). [*Caps*]
Parekh, Bhikhu (2006), *Rethinking Multiculturalism: Cultural Diversity and Political Theory*, 2nd edn (London: Palgrave).
Parekh, Bhikhu (2008), *A New Politics of Identity: Political Principles for an Interdependent World* (London: Palgrave).
Pollis, Adamantia and Peter Schwab (1980), 'Human Rights: A Western Construct with Limited Applicability', in Adamantia Pollis and Peter Schwab, eds, *Human Rights: Cultural and Ideological Perspectives* (New York: Praeger).
Rawls, John (1971), *A Theory of Justice* (Oxford: Oxford University Press).
Rawls, John (1993), *Political Liberalism* (New York: Columbia University Press).
Raz, Joseph (1986), *The Morality of Freedom* (Oxford: Clarendon Press).
Raz, Joseph (1995), 'Multiculturalism: A Liberal Perspective', in *Ethics in the Public Domain* (Oxford: Clarendon Press).
Richardson, Henry S. (1994), *Practical Reasoning about Final Ends* (Cambridge: Cambridge University Press).
Riley, Jonathan (2000), 'Crooked Timber and Liberal Culture', in Maria Baghramian and Attracta Ingram, eds, *Pluralism: The Philosophy and Politics of Diversity* (London: Routledge).
Ryan, Alan, ed. (1979), *The Idea of Freedom: Essays in Honour of Isaiah Berlin* (Oxford: Oxford University Press).
Ryan, Alan (2013), 'Isaiah Berlin: The History of Ideas as Psychodrama', *European Journal of Political Theory* 12 (1): 61–73.
Sandall, Roger (2001), 'The Book of Isaiah', in *The Culture Cult: Designer Tribalism and Other Essays* (Westport, CT: Westview).

Sandel, Michael (1984), 'Introduction', in Michael Sandel, ed., *Liberalism and Its Critics* (Oxford: Oxford University Press).
Schmitt, Carl (1996 [1932]), *The Concept of the Political*, trans. George Schwab (Chicago: University of Chicago Press).
Sternhell, Zeev (2010). *The Anti-Enlightenment Tradition*, trans. David Maisel (New Haven, CT: Yale University Press).
Strauss, Leo (1989 [1961]), 'Relativism', in *The Rebirth of Classical Political Rationalism: An Introduction to the Thought of Leo Strauss*, selected and introduced by Thomas Pangle (Chicago: Chicago University Press).
Talisse, Robert B. (2012), *Pluralism and Liberal Politics* (New York: Routledge).
Taylor, Charles (1994), 'The Politics of Recognition', in Amy Gutmann, ed., *Multiculturalism: Examining the Politics of Recognition* (Princeton: Princeton University Press).
Taylor, Charles (1997), 'Leading a Life', in Ruth Chang, ed., *Incommensurability, Incomparability, and Practical Reasoning* (Cambridge: Cambridge University Press).
Taylor, Charles (2001), 'The Plurality of Goods', in Ronald Dworkin, Mark Lilla, and Robert Silvers, eds, *The Legacy of Isaiah Berlin* (New York: New York Review Books).
Walzer, Michael (1983), *Spheres of Justice: A Defence of Pluralism and Equality* (Oxford: Blackwell).
Walzer, Michael (1995), 'Are There Limits to Liberalism?', *New York Review of Books*, 19 October.
Weber, Max (1948a), 'The Vocation of Politics', in H. H. Gerth and C. Wright Mills, eds, *From Max Weber: Essays in Sociology* (London: Routledge).
Weber, Max (1948b), 'The Vocation of Science', in H. H. Gerth and C. Wright Mills, eds, *From Max Weber: Essays in Sociology* (London: Routledge).
Williams, Bernard (1985), *Ethics and the Limits of Philosophy* (Cambridge, MA: Harvard University Press). [*ELP*]
Williams, Bernard (2001), 'Liberalism and Loss', in Ronald Dworkin, Mark Lilla, and Robert B. Silvers, eds, *The Legacy of Isaiah Berlin* (New York: New York Review Books).
Williams, Bernard (2005), *In the Beginning Was the Deed: Realism and Moralism in Political Argument* (Princeton: Princeton University Press). [*Deed*]
Wong, David (1993), 'Relativism', in Peter Singer, ed., *A Companion to Ethics* (Oxford: Blackwell).
Zakaras, Alex (2013a), 'A Liberal Pluralism: Isaiah Berlin and John Stuart Mill', *Review of Politics* 75 (1): 69–96.
Zakaras, Alex (2013b), 'Reply to Galston and Crowder', *Review of Politics* 75 (1): 111–4.

2 The Great Goods

The idea that there are at least some values that are authoritative universally is one of the key features of value pluralism. But we have seen that Berlin's account of these values and how they relate to one another is sketchy. Two questions stand out. First, which are 'the great goods' to which Berlin refers, and what makes them great – that is, more fundamental and weighty than other goods? It is the great goods that are said to be plural and incommensurable. Yet Berlin's list of goods such as 'liberty', 'equality', and so on looks ad hoc and unjustified. Without a more systematic account, we remain unclear about a basic component of the pluralist idea.

Second, how far do the great goods help us choose among values when they conflict – how far, that is, do they help us answer the problem of value pluralism? This question overlaps the first, since understanding the nature of the great goods should help us to grasp their role in value conflict. If, as Berlin puts it, they 'dominate' the life and thought of most societies, that implies they are more important than other concerns. That in turn suggests that the great goods guide at least some choices. But what is the justification of their dominance; what makes them so important? And even once we have identified and justified the fundamental values, how does that help us when they conflict with one another? Berlin's vagueness about the great goods leaves him with little to say on either score.

How have Berlin's successors handled these issues? In this Chapter, I show that subsequent pluralist writers have developed much more systematic accounts of the universal values that are among the ultimate elements of the pluralist picture. Consequently, they have given us a clearer picture of what the values are, most fundamentally, that value pluralists say are plural and incommensurable.

But I also argue that even the best accounts struggle to explain why the values they nominate as basic and especially important really are basic and especially important. Some approaches are empirical, relying on what actually has been accepted as fundamental by most societies in most periods. The problem with this is that what is universal in these terms – what is common to all actual societies – turns out to be too thin to be normatively significant. By contrast, normative approaches nominate significant values and principles, only to find these difficult to justify as anything more than local or ideological preferences rather than genuinely universal. Moreover, even if the great goods can be identified, that leaves the question of what to do when they conflict with one another. Universality, on its own, does little to solve the problem of value pluralism.

To show this, I discuss the various strategies employed by three pluralists who emphasize the role in pluralist thought of the great goods: Jonathan Riley, Stuart Hampshire, and Martha Nussbaum. All combine empirical and normative approaches in different proportions and with different results. Riley's approach is predominantly empirical, focusing on those values usually thought necessary to the survival of persons and societies, but these turn out to be highly generic and uncritical. Hampshire's account is strongly normative, highlighting the principle of hearing the other side, but on its likeliest interpretation this looks more specifically liberal than universal. Nussbaum's capabilities theory tries to achieve a balance between empirical and normative elements, but these are not combined with complete success. Nevertheless, her view provides the best account available of the universalist framework needed for pluralism.

Survival, Rights, and Decency

Picking up one of Berlin's suggestions, Riley presents an explanation of universal values based on the essentials of personal and social survival.[1] From the values of survival, he derives a set of rights. In Riley's earlier work, these were in turn interpreted as approximating the basic rights of liberalism (Riley 2000). In his later article, 'Isaiah Berlin's "Minimum of Common Moral Ground"' (2013), he retreats to the less demanding claim that the rights in question require only a 'decent' political society. The following discussion is based on Riley's more recent work except where otherwise flagged.

Riley sees himself as interpreting and defending a position already held by Berlin rather than adjusting that position or building upon it. In this spirit, he responds to the familiar concern that Berlin's view is incoherent because his value pluralism contradicts his liberalism. If values are plural in Berlin's sense, then how can he make negative liberty overriding, as he appears to do? One answer has already been given in Chapter 1: negative liberty is not in fact overriding in Berlin's thought. Riley pursues another line of reply.

Riley's basic answer is that Berlin's view is coherent because his pluralism is 'suitably restrained' (*Min* 63). If it were 'unbridled', then no reasoned ranking of values would be possible at all. But Berlin's pluralism is qualified by 'a minimum of common moral ground' or a 'common moral minimum', a set of fundamental and universal moral values that almost always override other concerns (*Min* 62).

According to Riley, Berlin's common moral minimum consists of those values or rules that normal people accept as necessary for the survival of themselves and their society. This echoes Berlin's suggestion that 'there are, if not universal values, at any rate a minimum without which societies could scarcely survive' (*CTH* 19). Such a view, Riley believes, is akin to H. L. A. Hart's 'minimum content of natural law', which identifies a limited range of rules as 'essential for the continuing existence of their society' (*Min* 68). Riley notes approvingly that Hart's minimum content is grounded in basic features of human nature, such as 'human vulnerability, approximate equality (no human is so powerful as to be independent of others altogether), limited altruism, scarce resources, and limited understanding and strength of will'.

Survival values almost always override other concerns. 'Normal people choose many distinct value-systems or ways of life but they also assign moral priority to putative natural laws that they agree are needed for human survival in cases of conflict with other values' (*Min* 68). The only exceptions are 'rare situations where indecent outcomes are the only possible outcomes', such as emergencies of various kinds (*Min* 67, 82).

Except in such rare cases, the common moral minimum thus restrains the effect of value pluralism. 'Normal humans do have an overriding wish to survive. Their choices reveal a universal partial ranking such that the basic value of human survival together with the means necessary to secure it has priority over any competing values'; 'The moral priority of survival is an objective constraint on the way conflicts of values can be reasonably resolved' (*Min* 70). While unbridled value pluralism allows an unlimited variety of conflict resolutions, the common moral minimum puts human survival first.

The goal of human survival includes the means necessary to secure it, and in Riley's interpretation of Berlin, these are principally 'a minimum sphere of individual liberty' and of human rights (*Min* 71–2). The minimum sphere of liberty is identified by Berlin's notion of 'frontiers of freedom which nobody should be permitted to cross' because

> they are accepted so widely, and are grounded so deeply in the actual nature of men as they have developed through history, as to be, by now, an essential part of what we mean by being a normal human being.
>
> (*L* 210)

This minimum sphere of liberty has gone by many names, including 'natural law' and 'natural rights'. Under the modern label of 'human rights', it includes 'rights not to be attacked or murdered, rights to own the fruits of one's labor and investment, and rights that promises and contracts be kept' (*Min* 68).[2]

Those cultures or societies that respect the common moral minimum are 'decent' and those that do not are 'indecent'.

> The threshold of decency may be represented as a boundary line that divides the common moral world into two zones, to wit, a zone of decency above and including the boundary, where human rights are respected, and a zone of indecency below the boundary, where human rights are violated.
>
> (*Min* 72)

Within the zone of decency, Riley argues, the human rights that define it must be 'compossible', or in harmony with one another. Otherwise 'one person's liberty may be rightfully sacrificed for another's. Violations of basic rights would be a permanent feature of everyday life' (*Min* 82).[3]

Below or outside the zone of decency violations of basic rights are indeed a feature of everyday life. Riley spends some time discussing the sense in which Nazi Germany was an indecent society. Since all normal persons are held to prioritize the common moral minimum, the Nazis, who do not, must be 'abnormal' (*Min* 75). More precisely, they are abnormal, in part, because they do want the common moral minimum and its attendant rights and liberties for themselves and certain other approved races, denying these minima to those peoples said to be 'subhuman' (*Min* 79).

Decent societies, then, want human rights for all human beings. Nevertheless, such societies are not necessarily liberal or democratic.

> For [Berlin], decent societies are only required to give moral priority to a minimum of human rights instead of a full set of liberal democratic rights. Normal humans across different social contexts do not agree that rights of democratic citizenship are essential for human survival.
>
> (*Min* 83)

The common moral minimum indicates decency, not necessarily liberalism.[4]

How persuasive is Riley? Recall that the common moral minimum he attributes to Berlin is defined as that set of liberties and rights that normal people recognize as necessary to human survival. The immediate problem is that the values that make up a moral minimum defined in this way are likely to be so thin that they will do little to restrain pluralist choice. Riley's common moral minimum will override those values that come into conflict with it, but few if any will do so.

To see this, note that Riley's definition might be understood empirically or normatively. If the claim is empirical, then those values that are 'necessary to human survival' have been accepted as such by all human societies that have in fact survived for any significant period. By definition, the moral minimum will be common to all viable human societies, so no such society will find its values excluded by this criterion. Almost anything will be permitted because almost anything is compatible with survival.

This initial thought is reinforced when we consider the content of the values that Riley says are essential to human survival in this way, namely liberty and human rights. What kind of liberty is necessary to human survival? Riley nominates Berlin's negative liberty, but how much negative liberty is necessary for a society to survive? Many societies, indeed most, have endured for long periods of time without offering their members much in the way of negative liberty.

Berlin does argue that some degree of negative liberty has been recognized as essential by all societies, but all this amounts to is the minimal non-interference required for moral agency: 'a being prevented from doing anything at all on his own is not a moral agent all' (*L* 207). This, he continues, is far from the insistence on 'a maximum degree of non-interference compatible with the minimum demands of social life' associated with liberals like Mill and Constant. 'The bulk of humanity has certainly at most times been prepared to sacrifice this to other goals'. The negative liberty necessary for social survival is minimal indeed.

Similarly, what 'minimum human rights' are essential to human survival? Again, social systems can survive in which very few rights are recognized, and fewer still of any substance. Riley refers to enslavement and arbitrary killing as two practices ruled out by the basic rights of human survival. But slave-based societies survived for millennia, and the term 'arbitrary' leaves room for a range of culturally endorsed lethal practices. Other examples given by Riley of rights necessary to survival include 'rights not to be attacked or murdered, rights to own the fruits of one's labor and investment, and rights that promises and contracts be kept' (*Min* 68). But these have been observed only unevenly by human societies – theocratic and absolutist political regimes have typically recognized their subjects as having virtually no rights against the divinely authorized ruler.

At this point, Riley might reply that the discussion so far has left out a vital element of his formal definition of a common moral minimum. The common minimum is that set of core survival values recognized not by actual historical peoples but by 'all *normal* persons'. Riley emphasizes that the concept of 'normal' here is not historical or sociological but normative.

> Berlin is not merely making an empirical assertion about what most people in most times and places do in fact accept. Instead, he is making a moral assertion that 'normal' people, with a strong desire for human survival based on their awareness of generic human capacities and vulnerabilities, universally recognize this common moral minimum. The two assertions are consistent if most people in most times and places are 'normal' in this moral sense. But the moral assertion implicitly adds the claim that every human ought to strongly desire human survival and all that is required to forward it.
> (*Min* 74)

This formulation is problematic in several respects. To begin with, it appears to be in tension with Riley's claim elsewhere that Berlin's position is not metaphysical but empirical:

> he is careful to say that the moral priority of certain fundamental rules of decency does not flow from any theological or metaphysical doctrine but instead is grounded on the contingent human desire for survival as confirmed by wide empirical observation of the practices of viable societies.
> (*Min* 71)

On this reading, the nature of human 'normality' seems to be settled by observing what most people in most times and places have in fact thought necessary to their survival. 'Ought' is equivalent to 'is'.

But perhaps the position is more complex. Maybe Riley is saying that Berlin's position is partly empirical and partly normative, that the two components are distinct but connected. This approach would fit with Riley's claim that the human desire for survival is 'confirmed' by empirical observation, implying that the desire has a more permanent or essential status that observation merely reinforces. It would also fit with Berlin's own notion of the features of human nature as having a 'quasi-empirical' character, suggesting again that they partly contingent and partly conceptual (*L* 45, quoted in *Min* 71).

The trouble with this interpretation is that it leaves us with the question of how exactly the essential or conceptual features of human nature relate to the contingent or empirical features. Riley notes, in the passage above, that the two aspects 'are consistent if most people in most times and places are "normal" in this moral sense'. But, as we have seen, most people have not been normal in Riley's moral sense. Although it can be conceded that most people have prioritized their own survival and that of their society, what this has been thought to require morally has varied enormously across different societies. Moreover, most societies have certainly not linked their survival with the liberty and human rights identified by Riley or indeed valued those goods highly for any reason.

So, we are left with a significant gap between the actual-empirical and normative-essential aspects of Riley's idea of the 'normal' human being. In particular, this raises the question of how the normative component is justified. According to Riley, 'every human ought to strongly desire human survival and all that is required to forward it'. We may concede that every human being ought to desire human survival. But again, why should that require minimum liberty and human rights as these are defined by Riley? It is hard to escape the conclusion that his argument is fundamentally circular. For Riley, minimum liberty and human rights are desirable because they are desired by normal people. Which people are normal? Those who desire minimum liberty and human rights.

The notion of 'decency' also raises questions. According to Riley, the recognition of minimum liberties and rights is a threshold that must be met before a society can count as decent. Consequently, there is a boundary between decent and indecent societies, dividing the moral world into two distinct zones. Liberal democracies clearly fall within the zone of decency, Nazi Germany within the zone of indecency.

An initial point is that such a Manichean division of the moral world seems implausible, especially from a pluralist point of view. Are there really two wholly distinct zones when it comes to the moral performance of different societies? Perhaps a more realistic image would be that of a sliding scale or continuum along which different societies are ranged such that their comparative moral performance is more a matter of degree than of meeting or failing to meet a threshold. Even this is too simple, since on a pluralist view there is no single dimension of morality along which to range different societies, but rather multiple dimensions. One society may rank ahead of another when it comes to liberty but lag behind it in terms of equality.

Another problem with Riley's boundary flows from the difficulties already canvassed with the common moral minimum. Decent societies are defined by their acceptance of the common moral minimum, but how is the latter to be understood? The previous discussion brought out two broad possibilities. One is that the common moral minimum requires respect merely for those values necessary for social survival, in which case every viable society has been decent. Alternatively, the rights and liberties said to be required by the common moral minimum can be given more substance, perhaps along liberal lines, in which case no societies have been decent except liberal societies. This latter option was preferred by Riley in his earlier work, where he writes that 'the assumption that decent non-liberal cultures exist is open to serious doubt' (Riley 2000: 121).

Nazi Germany was, of course, both non-liberal and, by most definitions, indecent.[5] But Riley introduces an unnecessary complication by insisting that the Nazis were 'abnormal' as well. He is drawn into this position by his definition of the common moral minimum in terms of what normal people would accept. The Nazis do not accept the common moral minimum, so they must be abnormal.

There are three problems with this. First, if the common moral minimum as Riley defines it really just serves the goal of social survival, then arguably the Nazis did accept it and so were normal. They aimed at survival, and did survive for a significant period, so must, on Riley's view, have been committed to the necessary minimum morality. Second, if Riley insists on their abnormality he is probably in conflict with Berlin, who is inclined to regard the Nazis as ordinary human beings who were terribly misled (*CIB* 38).

Third, Riley brings in still further complexity when he revises his view to say that the Nazis were only partly abnormal because they did recognize the common moral minimum, but only for Aryans and not for 'subhumans'. Against this, it might be said that most societies have discriminated unfairly against some group or other. To the extent that this is true, it suggests that most societies have not extended the common moral minimum to all of their members. If so, then Riley's logic leads once more to the conclusion that there have been few entirely normal (and therefore decent) people except perhaps contemporary liberals. If Riley insists that most societies have accepted the common moral minimum for all of their members in spite of their various unfair discriminations, that suggests once again that the common moral minimum is so thin that almost anyone can accept it.

A final set of difficulties concerns Riley's view that the rights and liberties upheld by decent societies must be 'compossible'. If rights and liberties are compossible, then they harmonize or fit together without conflict. However, that seems to contradict the fundamental picture presented by value pluralism in which conflict is possible even among basic values. Indeed, Riley himself accepted this in his earlier work, where he observed that 'the force of tragic pluralism extends even within liberalism's citadel' and 'that liberal principles themselves cannot be insulated from pluralism', so that 'different basic rights may implicate rationally noncomparable values that clash irreconcilably when the rights conflict with one another' (Riley 2000: 136).

The reason why Riley thinks that a decent society's rights and liberties must be compossible is that otherwise 'violations of basic rights would be a permanent feature of everyday life' and that 'Berlin seems to condone such indecencies only in rare emergency situations' (*Min* 82). But this is an unnecessarily dramatic view. Conflicts of rights *are* an everyday occurrence – for example, free speech vs privacy, religion vs equal treatment, group rights vs individual rights – but the typical response is not the outright rejection of one in order to promote another. More likely the response is a routine compromise. As Berlin puts it, 'collisions, even if they cannot be avoided, can be softened. Claims can be balanced, compromises can be reached' (*CTH* 18). Nor is a compromise among conflicting values the same as wrongdoing or the 'violation' of rights, as I argued in the previous chapter during my discussion of Dworkin.

To summarize, Riley's account of the universals that underpin and constrain pluralism is too thin to provide much critical leverage or even to identify the values concerned. His approach has empirical and normative elements but leans more toward the empirical: a value is part of the common moral minimum if it is necessary for the survival of most societies. But the survival of most societies is compatible with a vast range of different values, and few of these can be singled out as more essential than others. Certainly, very little negative liberty and few individual rights are required. If these are the survival values, then most societies satisfy them. Consequently, these values do little to constrain choice among conflicting incommensurables.

Hearing the Other Side

Stuart Hampshire was a personal friend of Berlin and an Oxford colleague for many years. He was also a fellow-pluralist, noting that 'there is no consideration of any kind that overrides all other considerations in all conceivable circumstances' (*IE* 172). Confronted with the problem of how to choose among conflicting incommensurable values, he gives more than one answer. Here I look at his appeal to universality.

Like Berlin, Kekes, and Riley, Hampshire subscribes to an overarching minimal morality that applies universally and that can be used as a benchmark for judging personal and cultural practices. 'There are obvious limits set by common human needs to the conditions under which human beings flourish and human societies flourish' (Hampshire 1983: 154).

What are those common needs and conditions and consequently the common norms that can be used to assess conduct and culture? Hampshire's initial approach is to consider 'the persisting evils of human life' (*JC* x). People inevitably disagree about the nature of the good life, so conceptions of the good are 'infinitely various and divisive, rooted in the imagination and memories of individuals and in the preserved histories of cities and of states' (*JC* xi). They are much more inclined to agree about the basic evils to be avoided in life, those harms and misfortunes that make life worse for anyone.

> There remain the unchanged horrors of human life, the savage and obvious evils, which scarcely vary from culture to culture or from age to age: massacre, starvation, imprisonment, torture, death and mutilation in war, tyranny and humiliation – in fact, the evening and the morning news.
>
> (*JC* 43)

So, while there is no universal convergence on the great goods, there is widespread agreement about the great evils. Consequently, the most immediate concern of any political system anywhere, before it attempts to secure any particular conception of the good, 'is protection against the perennial evils of human life' (*JC* xi).

However, it might still be asked whether there is not some more positive or affirmative norm that ought to guide morals and politics universally. If the general goal is the prevention of evil, might there not be, at some level, some common means or principle by which this should be pursued? Hampshire identifies the key principle as justice. But he also draws a crucial distinction between 'substantial' and 'procedural' justice.

Substantial conceptions of justice make claims about what is fair that are dependent on particular conceptions of the good. Since people are so deeply divided about the nature of the good, it follows that substantial notions of justice are of little help in resolving deep ethical conflicts such as those between rival ways of life or rival ideologies; they merely reflect such conflicts. For example, rival liberal and socialist accounts of distributive justice are substantial, reflecting, say, opposing liberal and socialist conceptions of the good. To appeal to 'justice' in these terms is to provoke rather than resolve issues of value conflict. In Hampshire's view, appeals of this kind lead to circular arguments, since they merely presuppose a background conception of the good that their opponents do not share.[6]

Procedural justice, on the other hand, is in Hampshire's account genuinely universal, since it is found, in different versions, in all stable cultures, and is therefore dependent on no particular conception of the good to the exclusion of others. The rules of procedural justice 'are in fact understood and applied across many varieties of barriers: across the frontiers of religious belief, across national loyalties, across philosophical and moral barriers' (*IE* 54). It is justice in this procedural sense that holds out the promise of serving as a universal arbiter among clashing incommensurable values.

What, then, is the content of procedural justice? The central principle is *audi alteram partem*, or 'hear the other side'.[7] The most fundamental model of fairness, acknowledged in all cultures, is that when there is a dispute between two parties both should be allowed to state their case.

The basis of the model is a universal norm for how justice is done, and seen to be done, in public institutions such as councils or cabinets, or law courts – *audi alteram partem* is a model for fairness in public debate. The public model then becomes the pattern for what it is for individuals to be unbiased, open-minded, and reasonable in their private judgment. The reasonable person reaches a conclusion only after imagining herself hearing both sides of an issue and weighing these impartially (*JC* 10–11).

Hampshire notes that this reverses the rationalist or 'Cartesian' model, according to which it is the private reasoning of the individual, conceived as mathematical or deductive, that is then to be applied in public. It should be no surprise that the Cartesian model does not work, since ethical and political conclusions cannot be deduced from self-evident axioms. The alternative picture, in which ethical reasoning is modeled on public debate, demystifies the matter.

Moreover, Hampshire believes that he is presenting a philosophical demonstration of the universality of *audi alteram partem*: the principle is implicit in all forms of practical reasoning. The point is 'a kind of transcendental argument. Everyone uses the balancing of pros and cons in his own mind in the pursuit of his own conception of the good, as well as in common prudence, in pursuit of his own interests' (*JC* 42). The universality of practical reasoning implies the universality of the principle of public debate on which it is based.

Procedural justice thus conceived must be not only accepted but also publically institutionalized. Much like the virtues in Aristotelian ethics, the practice of procedural justice must become an ingrained habit if it is to be followed reliably.

> Human beings are habituated to recognize the rules and conventions within which they have been brought up, including the conventions of their family life. Institutions are needed as settings for just procedures of conflict resolution, and institutions are formed by recognized customs and habits.
> (*JC* 54)

This recalls one of Hampshire's lessons of experience that intelligence and education are not enough by themselves to ensure decency.

But Hampshire also notes that procedural justice may be institutionalized in various ways and that these tend themselves to be 'imperfect and not ideal, being the untidy outcome of past political compromises' (*JC* 32). The making of compromises sometimes appears in the value-pluralist literature as if it is desirable unproblematically. Hampshire recognizes that compromises may be either 'smart' or 'shabby' (*JC* 32).[8] The particular form taken by the institutions of procedural justice in a given society may therefore present problems, although that does not undermine the case for procedural justice in itself.

However, what happens when a way of life rejects procedural justice? Hampshire admits that this is a 'bind' for any 'liberal and nonauthoritarian morality'

(*JC* 41). But a way of life that genuinely took this attitude would be taking a very extreme view, since the requirement to hear the other side is 'found in the structure of practical reason itself' (*JC* 42). The rejection of procedural justice would be a very rare case, since it would involve the denial that reason-giving and evidence have any role in justifying ethical beliefs. The great majority of moralities, even highly authoritarian ones, leave at least some room for the idea that evidence gathering, argument, and counter-argument are relevant ethical activities. That is enough to leave an opening, indeed a need, for adversarial debate and negotiation, hence for fair procedures to govern these.

The one case in which Hampshire is confident that he is dealing with a way of life that rejects procedural justice altogether is Nazi Germany. Berlin tended to see the Nazis as upholding a morality of sorts, although one grossly perverted by false beliefs about racial differences, national aspirations, and so on (*CIB* 38). By contrast, Hampshire believes that, uniquely in human experience, the Nazis declared war on even the minimal morality that he identifies as universal. The Nazi regime was a representation of 'pure evil', its aim being 'to eliminate all notions of fairness and justice from practical politics', leaving only a field of naked force and domination (*IE* 67–9). This returns Hampshire to his guiding insight that the political priority is not to pursue the good but to ensure respect for minimal procedural justice in the form of the duty to hear all parties. What happens when procedural justice fails is an appalling 'lesson of recent history' (*IE* 113).

Yet even procedural justice is not overriding in all conceivable cases. Hampshire sometimes gives the impression that it must be, especially when he is emphasizing the importance of fair procedure in the face of disagreements, conflicts, and ultimately, pure evil (*IE* 77; *JC* 32, 79). But the absolute overridingness of any value or principle would not be consistent with his pluralist position. Consequently, he allows that there may be extreme cases of emergency in which procedural justice has to be suspended in order to protect 'some other essential value ... such as the avoidance of widespread misery or the preservation of life' (*JC* 36). In this connection, he notes that Machiavelli exaggerates the need to set aside procedural justice, making that the norm for his prince (*JC* 73–5). The Nazis, of course, go further, trying to eliminate procedural justice entirely. Hampshire's view is that procedural justice is essential to any normal morality and politics, although there may be some exceptional cases where it must yield to some exceptional counter-imperative.

Hampshire's view has attractions and difficulties. In general, he presents a reasonable ethical position that balances the universal – the great evils – with the particular – the immense diversity of human ends, moralities, and ways of life. However, Hampshire's position raises critical questions too.

How universal is the practice of hearing the other side? Hampshire's 'transcendental' argument assumes that it is implicit in any form of intra-personal practical reasoning, but is that true? Some forms of intuitive or faith-based thinking leave little room for the weighing of pros and cons. But perhaps this is a relatively minor difficulty, since it could be that the principle of hearing the other side need not be justified transcendentally, at least in its public application. More straightforwardly, it might be seen as universal in the empirical sense that such a practice has been accepted, in some form, by nearly all legal systems. From there it has entered other areas of institutional life in the form of the concept of 'natural justice'. However, this move becomes problematic when connected with another point, made by John Horton, namely that the notion of 'hearing the other side' can be given a range of interpretations (Horton 2006: 136).

On a weak interpretation, to hear the other side is compatible with a merely formal process in which one's opponents are allowed to speak but are not really listened to. A sadly familiar example is the cynical kind of policy 'consultation' that is practiced in many public and private organizations, amounting to no more than lip service because the decision has already been made. This interpretation of hearing the other side is empirically sound – it makes minimal demands that are easily satisfied in experience – but obviously too empty to be satisfactory. No real listening has taken place, and the process is clearly compatible with the unjust treatment of those 'consulted'.

However, the idea of hearing the other side can be given a stronger interpretation by inserting into it some more demanding norms. One can accept a duty to listen respectfully, to take seriously what is being claimed, to consider the merits of what is being argued, and to do so with an open mind or, more positively still, with a desire to accept as much as possible or to be prepared to learn. A model for this kind of hearing is provided by the deliberative democracy advocated by writers like Amy Gutmann and John Thompson (1996, 2004).[9] Such a procedure does not commit the parties to agreement, since not every claim can be accepted just because it has merits – opposing claims may be more meritorious still. But such a procedure stands a better chance of avoiding unjust outcomes, and of being regarded as fair, because people's views have been given a genuine hearing.

The problem with this stronger interpretation is that it relies on supporting norms that look too specifically liberal to be genuinely universal in the empirical sense now required. For example, the stronger interpretation requires critical 'reflection' (*IE* 39). When we hear the other side, in either public or private, we are involved in reflection or the process of 'stepping back' and questioning our own norms or those of our own society (*IE* 41). This must be so because in considering views other than our own, we are contemplating the possibility that we may be mistaken, that the other side may have it right or partly right, and we may be wrong or partly wrong.

But there are strong links between critical reflection and the characteristically liberal value of personal autonomy. This is noted by Hampshire himself. Reflection, he argues, is an active rather than passive state of mind, in which we pursue 'a line of thought' aimed at our taking control over our goals and values (*IE* 39). Rather than passively accepting the conventions or received norms into which we have been socialized, we review our existing commitments in contrast with alternative possibilities. 'The obvious normative implication is that a person actively directing his or her thought is an autonomous agent, fully responsible for what he or she achieves, and in this respect to be praised' (*IE* 41). The reflective person is most likely to be someone like J. S. Mill's autonomous individual, who is able to take a critical view of prevailing customs and make her own decisions about how to live (Mill 1974 [1859]: ch. 3).

Personal autonomy, however, although celebrated by liberals, is not held in such esteem universally. Bhikhu Parekh, for example, argues that Mill's ideal

> ruled out a wide variety of ways of life, such as the traditional, the community-centred and the religious as well as those that were not grounded in self-knowledge, did not set much store by an energetic and go-ahead spirit, or preferred contentment, weak ambition, humility and self-effacement to their opposites.
>
> (Parekh 2006: 44)[10]

Further, Hampshire sometimes equates hearing the other side with being 'unbiased, open-minded' (*JC* 10). If a majority is obliged not only to hear a minority's view but also to be open-minded about it, then there is less scope for the minority's position to be simply swept aside. The requirement of open-mindedness takes us beyond mere acknowledgment of a different view; it suggests that we also have to weigh that view in some sense equally with our own. This need not require that we accept the opposing view as equal to our own on its merits, but it does suggest that it should be accorded, in Ronald Dworkin's phrase, 'equal concern and respect' (Dworkin 1977: 180).

Mention of Dworkin also suggests that at this point Hampshire's procedural justice is again being made more attractive by injecting into it elements of a substantially liberal outlook. The more demanding reading of hearing the other side imports a notion of impartiality that is more substantial – and more specifically liberal – than the thin proceduralism that Hampshire started with and that he said was necessary in order to provide a universal standard for morals and politics. Moreover, the impartiality imported here is again at odds with universality in the empirical sense Hampshire's argument now requires. Such a principle may be upheld as an ideal in liberal cultures, but it is not in fact approved of everywhere.

Liberal assumptions are present in other parts of Hampshire's position too. What if a society endorses the principle of *audi alteram partem* but applies it only to a certain subset of its population, the 'citizens', to the exclusion of other groups such as slaves, foreign residents, women, ethnic and sexual minorities, and so on? If Hampshire accepts this as consistent with procedural justice, a legitimate local institutionalization, then procedural justice appears again to be seriously defective. On the other hand, if he insists that the principle of hearing the other side apply, say, to all those affected by a decision, then he would seem once again to be importing a liberal presupposition, in this case the equal moral status of all human beings.[11]

A general conclusion follows: Hampshire's account of the universality of hearing the other side is caught in a dilemma. On the one hand, *audi alteram partem* can be interpreted weakly as requiring no more than pro forma consultation. That view may be acceptable as an empirical universal, but it is consistent with injustice. On the other hand, the stronger interpretation requires a commitment to norms – such as critical reflection, personal autonomy, open-mindedness, and human equality of moral worth – that have been endorsed by few other than liberal societies. It is probably the stronger interpretation that Hampshire intends, but that would come at the price of dependence on liberal norms.

Central Capabilities

The capabilities theory of Martha Nussbaum is the last example I consider of universalism as a response to the problem of value pluralism. Berlin does not seem to be a major source for Nussbaum; indeed, she tends to regard him as a representative of the comprehensive kind of liberalism that she rejects in favor of the more constrained 'political' liberalism of Rawls (Nussbaum 2011b). However, Nussbaum may be influenced by Berlin less directly, through the work of Bernard Williams (Nussbaum 2009). Moreover, she is expressly a value pluralist, like Berlin and Williams, holding that the most fundamental human values are plural and incommensurable. Her work occupies an important place in the pluralist canon because she gives the most detailed and systematic account of universal values in a pluralist setting.[12]

For Nussbaum, the most fundamental human values are the 'central human capabilities'. In general, the idea of capabilities addresses questions of quality of life and basic social justice. Responding to these broad issues, the key question asked by capability theorists is, 'what is a person able to and to be?'[13] The basic idea of the capability approach is that levels of well-being or social justice are to be assessed according to the extent that each person is able to function across a plurality of different life dimensions.

Nussbaum and other capability theorists acknowledge alternative understandings of well-being and social justice but see the capabilities framework as superior. Measurement of well-being according to GDP per capita, for example, takes no account of how a nation's wealth, thus measured, is distributed. A citizen of a nation with very high GDP could herself be living in poverty. Capabilities theory addresses this by focusing on the well-being of each individual.

Other accounts of well-being and justice opposed by the capabilities theorists include those based on resources and on cultural tradition or cultural relativism. On the capabilities view, it will not be enough for a person merely to be in possession of 'resources', or money, since it is one thing to possess resources but another to be able to use them.[14] A person could have the money necessary for an education but be prevented from using it by traditional beliefs that discriminate unfairly against people like her on the basis of race or class or gender. A capability in its fullest sense, then, has social and political dimensions.[15] The same example shows that an approach to well-being and justice that was based solely on the authority of cultural tradition would be inadequate. So, cultural relativism is a defective theory from this point of view (*WHD* 48–9).

Similarly, the capabilities approach rules out negative liberty and utilitarianism as adequate standards for public policy. Well-being and justice are not sufficiently appreciated from the perspective of negative or 'formal' freedom alone, since simple non-interference is consistent with the absence of real capacity.[16] Nor is utilitarian satisfaction of preferences sufficient for either well-being or justice, since people's preferences can be 'adaptive' to their circumstances: people can come to accept injustice and a poor quality of life as an inescapable part of the structure of their lives (*Caps* 81–4). In contrast with utilitarianism, capabilities theory regards each person as an end in herself, not merely the instrument of others, and the good of each has to be considered, not only that of groups of which she may be a member.

In public policy terms, the capabilities goal is to ensure that each person has the capacity, within limits, of living a dignified life of her choosing. This involves having the capacity to 'function' well in various ways, although the functioning itself is left as a matter of choice for the individual. Capabilities theory does not enforce any particular conception of the good life; it only insists that people be provided with the capacities to live a range of such lives.

Value pluralism enters at this point. Capabilities theorists are value pluralists because they see human capabilities as irreducibly plural. As Nussbaum expresses it,

> The approach is resolutely *pluralist about value*: it holds that the capability achievements that are central for people are different in quality, not just in quantity; that they cannot without distortion be reduced to a single numerical scale; and that a fundamental part of understanding and producing them is understanding the specific nature of each.
>
> (*Caps* 18–19)

Consequently, the problem of value pluralism is a problem for capabilities theory. On the face of it, there is a myriad of human capabilities. Given that resources are limited, how do we choose which to promote as a matter of public policy? In particular, how do we choose which to promote when they conflict? The immediate answer is that some capabilities are more important to human well-being and justice than others; some will therefore take priority in public policy. The ability to whistle *Yankee Doodle Dandy* while standing on one's head 'is just not very important', Nussbaum writes (*Caps* 28).

But where is the line between the important and the unimportant, and how do we decide this? Different answers are given by the two most prominent capabilities theorists. Amartya Sen leaves the matter to be decided by the political processes of the country in question. Nussbaum, by contrast, is much more prescriptive, proposing an explicit list of 'central human capabilities' that is meant to have moral force globally. The securing of all the items on Nussbaum's list is intended to be an obligation for all governments. 'It ascribes an

58   *The Great Goods*

urgent task to government and public policy – namely, to improve the quality of life for all people, as defined by their capabilities' (*Caps* 19).

Nussbaum's list requires the securing of capabilities in ten areas. In abbreviated form, these are: life; bodily health; bodily integrity; senses, imagination, and thought; emotions; practical reason; affiliation; relations with other species; play; control over one's environment. (I return to some of these below.) These are the most important capabilities in Nussbaum's view, those essential to human well-being and social justice. The implication is that, if these come into conflict with other, lesser capabilities – for example, as rivals for public support – it is these central capabilities that will take precedence.

General features of Nussbaum's list include the following. The list is intended for the modern world rather than as a timeless set of truths (*WHD* 77). Its items are subject to 'multiple realizability' or open to different interpretations in different social and cultural settings. The capabilities do not represent a complete theory of justice; rather, they are 'threshold' or minimal requirements for justice, which is likely to demand more, depending on local circumstances. The list is intended to be 'open-ended and humble', 'a proposal' for discussion and debate rather than a final ruling on the matter (*WHD* 77; *Caps* 36). Consequently, Nussbaum expects the list to be contested by counter-proposals for additions or subtractions. In the former case, she accepts the view of Jonathan Wolff and Avner De-Shalit, who argue that the list should be supplemented by additional concepts, namely 'capabilities security', 'fertile functioning', and 'corrosive disadvantage'.[17]

Note also that Nussbaum does not regard her list of capabilities as amounting to a 'comprehensive assessment of the quality of life in a society' (*Caps* 19). Rather, she sees the list as framed by John Rawls's 'political liberalism', according to which principles of justice are required to be accepted for political purposes only, leaving people free to believe and live according to other values in private. People do not have to believe that Nussbaum's list states the absolute truth in morality, as a 'comprehensive' view claims to do, only that it should be accepted as the basis for a political constitution.

How valuable is Nussbaum's theory from a pluralist point of view? There are two main areas of criticism. First, there is the issue of how the central capabilities are selected. Here Nussbaum gives three different justifications, and they are hard to reconcile with each other (Katzer 2010). One explanation is that the list is formed from an empirical survey of the current and historical beliefs of many different cultures. In particular, Nussbaum claims to have consulted the tragic literature of many different belief systems, which she sees as revealing notions of the worst that can befall human beings (*WHD* 72–3). Like Hampshire, she argues that once we have a picture of what people believe to be life's greatest evils, we can then identify what they regard as life's most fundamental goods. The weakness of this procedure has emerged several times already in this chapter: what is common to all belief systems in this respect is likely to be too thin to possess much critical bite.

An example is the first item: 'Life. Being able to live to the end of a life of normal length; not dying prematurely, or before one's life is so reduced as to be not worth living' (*Caps* 33). The idea of a life of 'normal' length would seem to be highly relative to circumstances, including those of culture and politics. Almost all societies could claim that their citizens live lives of 'normal' length given the resources they are able or willing to expend on looking after their people. This requirement could be satisfied by present-day North Korea, which is prepared to let some of its people starve because its priorities lie with its nuclear weapons program.

On the other hand, Nussbaum's second method of selecting the central capabilities suffers from the opposite problem. This is a more strongly normative procedure, where she derives capabilities from philosophical reflection on a 'core idea' that she says underlies all the items on the list. The core idea is

> of a human being as a dignified free being who shapes his or her own life in cooperation and reciprocity with others, rather than being passively shaped or pushed around by the world in the manner of a 'flock' or 'herd' animal.
> (*WHD* 72–3)

A dignified being, on this view, is a person who is strongly self-determining and who is recognized and treated as such.

The issue that arises here is whether these values have been derived from an ideal of the person that is culturally specific rather than universal – a problem recalling that raised by the stronger interpretation of Hampshire's 'hearing the other side' principle (*Caps* 34). Examples include Item 6, 'practical reason', which consists of 'being able to form a conception of the good and to engage in critical reflection about the planning of one's life', requiring 'protection of the liberty of conscience and religious observance'. Similarly, Item 7 (B), 'affiliation', refers to 'being able to be treated as a dignified being whose worth is equal to that of others'. Item 10 (a), 'control over one's [political] environment', includes 'having the right of political participation, protections of free speech and association'. Nussbaum's capabilities are supposed to be the threshold requirements for any decent conception of human well-being or social justice and are thus intended to be 'cross-cultural' in origin (*WHD* 76). But the capabilities just mentioned involve characteristically liberal or at least post-Enlightenment values that are not shared by some traditional and religious cultures even in the modern world. The point is reinforced by the sources Nussbaum cites for her core idea: Kant and the early Marx (*WHD* 72–3).[18] So, as with Hampshire's hearing the other side, the capabilities might be accused of harboring a liberal proclivity that contradicts their supposed universality.[19]

At this point, Nussbaum has proposed two methods for identifying her central capabilities, respectively empirical and normative, and they exhibit a tension that has been a frequent theme of this chapter. Empirical universalism does no more than report the actual values shared by all or most societies, which yields values that are normatively too thin to provide much critical guidance. By contrast, normative universalism tends to propose values that may be important but which cannot be justified by claiming that they are widely shared. The obvious question is whether there is any way of combining the strengths of both within a single view.

Nussbaum tries to achieve this in her third method of selecting the central capabilities, the idea of an 'overlapping consensus' that she borrows from Rawls (*WHD* 76). On this view, people may accept Nussbaum's list because they regard its items as justified not because of any single conception of the good or of the person, but for various reasons rooted in different systems of belief. Moreover, people may accept the capabilities solely for the purpose of a political settlement, not necessarily because they see them as part of a comprehensive conception of the good that they accept in private. The merit of this idea is that it promises to combine substantial moral commitment to the capabilities, including the more specific or 'liberal' capabilities, with a procedure that is apparently neutral among different conceptions of the good.

Unfortunately, the promise is not fulfilled. Are believers in traditional religions really going to converge with liberals in accepting freedom of religion, even for political purposes? Some may do, but many will not accept this. Perhaps more would do so if they were willing to adopt Rawls's starting point, which is acceptance of the political culture of a 'constitutional democracy' – that is, a liberal democracy. But such a political culture is precisely what is rejected by many traditional beliefs; few positions will overlap on the Rawlsian consensus that are not liberal at heart already. Similarly, few non-liberals will overlap on Nussbaum's more liberal capabilities.

So, it seems that Nussbaum's empirical and normative senses of universality remain in tension. Empirical inquiry yields norms that are plausibly universal but uncritical. On the other hand, important critical norms may be included among the capabilities, but these will not be adequately defended empirically.

The second major objection to Nussbaum's capabilities theory is that even if the central capabilities can be identified, that does little to solve the problem of value pluralism. True, the central capabilities override less important capabilities and so reduce the scope of pluralist choice to that extent. But among the central capabilities themselves (also among the lesser capabilities) the problem of choice remains. Even 'the most important elements of people's quality of life are plural and qualitatively distinct' (*Caps* 18). This

> irreducible heterogeneity of the Central Capabilities is extremely important. A nation cannot satisfy the need for one capability by giving people a large amount of another, or even by giving them some money. All are distinctive, and all need to be secured and protected in distinctive ways.
>
> (*Caps* 35)

No central capability is inherently more or less important than any other; there is no hierarchy among them. So, what is to be done if the central capabilities come into conflict with one another, or when they compete for priority in public policy?

Note that the claim that there is no hierarchy among the central capabilities is not affected by the special status Nussbaum gives to two of them: practical reason and affiliation. These are said to play an 'architectonic' role in relation to the other capabilities, 'pervading' and 'organizing' them (*Caps* 39). Practical reason pervades the other capabilities because it signals the value of choice that runs through the notion of capabilities as a whole; its role in organizing the others is obvious. Affiliation is also part of all the central capabilities because of its close association with respect for human dignity; its organizing role relates to the social aspect of all the central capabilities, which requires attention to relationships. The point to note here, though, is that neither pervading nor organizing means overriding. Practical reason and affiliation play special roles in the overall scheme of capabilities but that does not make them more important or valuable than the other elements of the scheme, each of which has its own unique role to play.

Nussbaum recognizes the problem of choice among colliding capabilities, at least in part. 'Sometimes social conditions make it seem impossible to deliver a threshold amount of all ten capabilities to everyone: two or more may be in competition' (*Caps* 36). For example, in some Indian states children from poor families are deprived of an education because their parents need their labor.

Such a choice situation is seen as 'tragic' by Nussbaum: 'any course we select involves doing wrong to someone' (*Caps* 37). Although she rejects Sen's view that in tragic situations there can be no reasoned ranking of the alternatives at all, she accepts that in such circumstances, even though 'one choice may clearly be better', the tragic quality of the situation means that 'any choice involves wrongdoing' (*Caps* 37).[20]

What, then, should we do in such cases? Nussbaum's answer is that we must strive to prevent such conflicts occurring in the future. 'We do not simply wring our hands: we ask what the best intervention point is to create a future in which this sort of choice does not confront people' (*Caps* 38–9). For example, she describes how the tragic conflict between education and labor in India has been alleviated by programs of more flexible school hours and the provision of a midday school meal that reduces the need for children to work (*Caps* 38).

This response is reasonable as far as it goes, but it does not address the whole problem. In Chapter 1, we saw Berlin make the point that conflicts among plural values can never be avoided entirely, that some such conflicts are inevitable. Nussbaum's assumption is that conflicts of capabilities are due to 'social conditions' that can be adjusted so that the conflicts are removed. But, as Nagel explains, not all conflicts are of this 'contingent' kind. Some are 'noncontingent', inhering in the intrinsic qualities of the values concerned. Take, for example, the inherent tension between work and leisure. It is in the very nature of these activities that the values they represent will conflict in some degree. No amount of forward planning and social reform will remove that conflict altogether. Planning to diminish such conflicts in the future is a good start, but we also need a further strategy – or a further set of skills – when conflicts cannot be avoided.

In spite of these difficulties, Nussbaum's theory of the central capabilities is the best account we have of fundamental values in a pluralist setting. The tension between the empirical and normative aspects of the theory is awkward and not resolved by the move toward Rawlsian political liberalism. However, such a tension is a problem for all the theories I have examined in this chapter. Similarly, the fact that Nussbaum's capabilities theory does not solve the problem of value pluralism shows only that no account of the great goods will solve that problem on its own. To have a picture of the great goods is an essential starting point, but the question of how to choose between them when they conflict is another matter.

The great merit of Nussbaum's view, compared with those of Riley and Hampshire, is the explicitly *plural* account it gives of the fundamental values. It may seem obvious that this is what a pluralist would provide, but for all their insights Riley and Hampshire are oddly single-minded in their understanding of the fundamentals. In each case, there is just one consideration that usually matters more than others: Riley's social survival or Hampshire's hearing the other side. They are not outright monists only because they do not say their chosen value is absolutely overriding but allow the possibility of cases where other concerns take precedence. Nussbaum, by contrast, presents as fundamental a range of incommensurable dimensions of human well-being. Her ten-point list is both far more systematic than anything in Berlin and richer and more vividly pluralist than the arguments advanced by Riley and Hampshire. In the chapters to follow, I shall usually have Nussbaum's model in mind when I think of the nature and content of the fundamental values that are said to be plural and incommensurable.

Conclusion

Berlin makes it tolerably clear that his value pluralism is distinguished from relativism in part by his commitment to a notion of universal values. It is 'the great goods' that are, ultimately, plural and incommensurable. However, he leaves us with two questions. First, what is the content of the great goods? Second, how do we choose among them when they conflict (the problem of value pluralism)?

Berlin's successors make progress toward answering the first question. Nussbaum's capabilities, in particular, provide us with a model of what the great goods may plausibly look like, ranging across various distinct dimensions of human well-being.

However, answering the first question does not, by itself, get us far in answering the second. Riley's survival values are too thin to have any significant critical leverage, since they are satisfied by any society that has, in fact, survived. On the other hand, Hampshire's principle of hearing the other side is, in its most persuasive interpretation, arguably too thick: it depends on a specifically liberal outlook that is not universally accepted. Nussbaum's capabilities may be too thin or too thick, depending on which capabilities are in question.

A general issue is the tension between empirical and normative senses of universality. Each seems to depend on the other for critical heft, yet it is difficult to combine the two. Accounts of ethical universals tend either to emphasize what is empirically accepted universally, leading to a view that is too thin to be critically useful; or they do express a critical norm but at the price of lacking universal acceptability. It is hard to avoid concluding that, while a picture of the relevant universals is a necessary starting point, we need to look further in order to tackle the problem of value pluralism.

Notes

1. Unlike Hampshire and Nussbaum, Riley depends wholly on his universalist argument, rejecting the contextualist approach as 'untypical of Berlin's approach' and not adequately explained (Riley 2000: 129). Neither of these claims is justified. For the former, see my discussion of Berlin's various approaches to 'What is to be done' in Chapter 1. For the latter, see Chapter 3, in which Nussbaum and Kekes are the contextualists discussed.
2. In his earlier work, Riley refers to rights not to be enslaved, or killed arbitrarily, or starved by social and economic institutions: Riley 2000: 140, 141. These more demanding rights do not appear in the 2013 article. See also Riley 2001, 2002.
3. Compare Riley 2000: 136.
4. Compare Riley 2000: 121–2, 139.
5. For other definitions of decency, see Rawls 1999; Margalit in *OC*.
6. See, similarly, Alasdair MacIntyre's explanation of the contest between laissez-faire and egalitarian conceptions of distributive justice as undecidable in the terms used by the opposing parties because these rest on incommensurable conceptions of the good (MacIntyre 1985: ch. 17).
7. Hampshire says that 'Herbert Hart drew my attention to the centrality of this phrase' (*JC* 8).
8. The limits of compromise are discussed in Chapter 7.
9. See, similarly, Richard Bellamy (*LAP*, 2000), discussed in Chapter 7.
10. But later I will argue for the *normative* universality of personal autonomy on the basis of value pluralism: see Chapter 6.
11. The latter option would seem to be favored in Hampshire's discussion of the tendency to be blinded to moral issues by the surrounding culture and the need to overcome this: *IE* 54–62.
12. Nussbaum also provides a significant account of contextual reasoning under pluralism: see Chapter 3.
13. Sen 1992: 37; Nussbaum in *WHD* 71, *Caps* 20.
14. For a leading account of social justice based on resources, see Dworkin 2000.
15. See Nussbaum's concept of 'combined' vs 'basic' and 'internal' capabilities: *Caps* 20–3.
16. The concept of capabilities is developed in terms of freedom by Amartya Sen in particular: Sen 1992: chs 2, 4; 2001; 2009.
17. Wolff and De-Shalit 2007, endorsed by Nussbaum in *Caps* 44–5.
18. Among the most important philosophical influences on her capabilities theory more generally, Nussbaum adds Adam Smith, J. S. Mill, and John Rawls: *Caps* 124. Nussbaum also cites Aristotle, which may absolve her of a thoroughly liberal bias

but she might still be accused of a 'Western' predisposition. She resists this strongly in *WHD* ch. 1.
19 See Linda Barclay (2003), who argues that Nussbaum's position is comprehensively liberal. Nussbaum (2003) denies this.
20 The idea that choice among competing plural values, even if seen as tragic, must involve 'doing wrong to someone' is questionable: see the discussion in Chapter 1 of Dworkin's similar formulation; also my remarks, earlier in this chapter, on Riley's attitude to conflicting rights.

References

In-text abbreviations are noted in brackets.

Barclay, Linda (2003), 'What Kind of Liberal is Martha Nussbaum?', *Sats – Nordic Journal of Philosophy* 4 (2): 5–24.
Berlin, Isaiah (2002), *Liberty*, ed. Henry Hardy (Oxford: Oxford University Press). [*L*]
Berlin, Isaiah (2013), *The Crooked Timber of Humanity: Chapters in the History of Ideas*, ed. Henry Hardy, 2nd edn (Princeton: Princeton University Press). [*CTH*]
Dworkin, Ronald (1977), *Taking Rights Seriously* (London: Duckworth).
Dworkin, Ronald (2000), *Sovereign Virtue: The Theory and Practice of Equality* (Cambridge, MA: Harvard University Press).
Gutmann, Amy and Dennis Thompson (1996), *Democracy and Disagreement* (Cambridge, MA: Belknap).
Gutmann, Amy and Dennis Thompson (2004), *Why Deliberative Democracy?* (Princeton: Princeton University Press).
Hampshire, Stuart (1983), *Morality and Conflict* (Cambridge, MA: Harvard University Press).
Hampshire, Stuart (1989), *Innocence and Experience* (Cambridge, MA: Harvard University Press). [*IE*]
Hampshire, Stuart (2000), *Justice Is Conflict* (Princeton: Princeton University Press). [*JC*]
Horton, John (2006), 'Proceduralism as Thin Universalism: Stuart Hampshire's "Procedural Justice"', in Bruce Haddock, Peri Roberts, and Peter Sutch, eds, *Principles and Political Order: The Challenge of Diversity* (London: Routledge).
Jahanbegloo, Ramin (1992), *Conversations with Isaiah Berlin* (London: Peter Halban). [*CIB*]
Katzer, Matthias (2010), 'The Basis of Universal Liberal Principles in Nussbaum's Political Philosophy', *Public Reason* 2 (2): 60–75.
MacIntyre, Alasdair (1985), *After Virtue: A Study in Moral Theory*, 2nd edn (London: Duckworth).
Margalit, Avishai (2010), *On Compromise: And Rotten Compromises* (Princeton: Princeton University Press). [*OC*]
Mill, John Stuart (1974 [1859]), *On Liberty*, ed. Gertrude Himmelfarb (Harmondsworth: Penguin).
Nussbaum, Martha (2000), *Women and Human Development: The Capabilities Approach* (Cambridge: Cambridge University Press). [*WHD*]
Nussbaum, Martha (2003), 'Political Liberalism and Respect: A Response to Linda Barclay', *Sats – Nordic Journal of Philosophy* 4 (2): 25–44.
Nussbaum, Martha (2009), 'Bernard Williams: Tragedies, Hope, Justice', in Daniel Callcut, ed., *Reading Bernard Williams* (London: Routledge).

Nussbaum, Martha (2011a), *Creating Capabilities: The Human Development Approach* (Cambridge, MA: Belknap). [*Caps*]

Nussbaum, Martha (2011b), 'Perfectionist Liberalism and Perfectionist Liberalism', *Philosophy and Public Affairs* 39 (1): 3–45.

Parekh, Bhikhu (2006), *Rethinking Multiculturalism: Cultural Diversity and Political Theory*, 2nd edn (London: Palgrave).

Rawls, John (1999), 'The Idea of Public Reason Revisited', in *The Law of Peoples* (Cambridge, MA: Harvard University Press).

Riley, Jonathan (2000), 'Crooked Timber and Liberal Culture', in Maria Baghramian and Attracta Ingram, eds, *Pluralism: The Philosophy and Politics of Diversity* (London: Routledge).

Riley, Jonathan (2001), 'Interpreting Berlin's Liberalism', *American Political Science Review* 95: 283–95.

Riley, Jonathan (2002), 'Defending Cultural Pluralism: Within Liberal Limits', *Political Theory* 30: 68–96.

Riley, Jonathan (2013), 'Isaiah Berlin's "Minimum of Common Moral Ground"', *Political Theory* 41: 61–89. [*Min*]

Sen, Amartya (1992), *Reexamining Inequality* (Oxford: Oxford University Press).

Sen, Amartya (2001), *Development as Freedom* (New York: Knopf).

Sen, Amartya (2009), *The Idea of Justice* (Cambridge, MA: Belknap).

Wolff, Jonathan and Avner De-Shalit (2007), *Disadvantage* (Oxford: Oxford University Press).

3 Agonism and Context

A sharper picture of those values that are genuinely universal gives us a better understanding of the nature and content of the fundamental human goods and evils that pluralists say are plural and incommensurable. Such a picture also helps us to respond to the problem of value pluralism by narrowing down choices among incommensurables somewhat: universal values, such as Nussbaum's capabilities, override less important goods. However, we are left with the problem of how to deal with conflict among the universal values themselves. In such cases, the problem of value pluralism is brought into clearer focus but not answered.

Of the various responses proposed by Berlin, I discuss two in this chapter. First, there is 'agonism', according to which choice among incommensurable values must be ultimately non-rational. Thinkers in this category often owe less to Berlin than to Max Weber. The politics associated with this view ranges from the troubled liberalism of Weber himself to the authoritarian dictatorship favored by Carl Schmitt and the 'democratic pluralism' of Chantal Mouffe. I have already pointed to the fundamental difficulty with this view in Chapter 1, namely that it ignores the possibility of contextualism. However, agonism is worth testing further in case there is something more in it to justify its substantial following.

Second, I consider the contextualist approach to the problem of pluralism that is also found in Berlin. Many pluralists reject agonism on the ground that incommensurable values, although not subject to rational rankings that apply in all cases, may still be ranked for good reason in a specific context. But what kind of context are we talking about? At the level of individual decision making, the model is in general that of Aristotle's situated ethics, which is employed in a pluralist setting by Nussbaum and others. Further, such an approach is often backed by an appeal to cultural tradition, suggesting both a wider social or public policy application and also a conservative political bent, a tendency defended explicitly by Kekes.

I argue that while there is good reason for pluralists to accept contextualism in general, there are problems with reading context as tradition, since in modern societies traditions tend to be multiple and conflicting and their merits are disputed. One response is to propose a strong multiculturalism in which all the constituent cultural traditions have a claim on public policy. However, this raises the question of what kind of political framework is suitable for multiculturalism: liberalism is one possibility, but some multiculturalists argue that liberalism is itself too culturally specific for this task.

War of the Gods

The basic idea of agonism is that politics is permanently characterized by conflict that cannot be resolved by rational agreement.[1] One reason for this is the incommensurability of fundamental values. It is assumed that when conflict is among incommensurables, the only response is, ultimately, non-rational. Recall that one of Berlin's more off-the-cuff accounts of how to deal with the problem of value pluralism is that 'you must just plump in some sort of way' (Berlin 1975). In the field of politics, agonists emphasize the permanence of value conflict – and consequently of other kinds of conflict, among interests, classes, ideologies, political parties, and so on – since in the absence of a rational solution there will be no agreement. Of course, political conflicts and disagreements will still have to be managed somehow, but this will be achieved not by reason but by force or coercion or the 'hegemonic' domination of some beliefs by others. The realm of politics is therefore essentially one of conflict and power rather than consensus.

The classic modern statement of agonistic pluralism is found not in Berlin but in Max Weber. While Berlin's reference to plumping is not much more than a throwaway line, an agonistic outlook lies at the center of Weber's political thought. Was Berlin influenced by Weber? He says he was not. 'People often ask me, but surely Weber was the first person, to say this. I answer that I am sure he is, but I had no idea of it' (Lukes 1998: 102).[2] This is easy to believe because apart from the plumping comment there is little of the agonist outlook in Berlin. Any assessment of contemporary agonism as a response to the problem of value pluralism requires us to go beyond Berlin to the work of Weber and those influenced by him.

Weber does anticipate Berlin's basic idea of value pluralism. For Weber, as for Berlin, fundamental human values are incommensurable and prone to conflict with one another. The difference is that while Berlin usually allows the possibility that competing values may be ranked for good reason, at any rate in context, Weber denies that possibility.

The relevant texts are Weber's classic essays, 'Vocation of Politics' and 'Vocation of Science'. In both places, Weber refers to fundamental values as occupying distinct 'spheres' that tend to come into conflict, like the warring gods in Greek polytheism:

> We are placed into various life-spheres, each of which is governed by different laws ... Hellenic polytheism made sacrifices to Aphrodite and Hera alike, to Dionysus and to Apollo, and knew these gods were frequently in conflict with one another.
>
> (Weber 1948a: 123)

Since each god is sovereign in his or her own sphere, and there is no overarching authority, 'the various value spheres of the world stand in irreconcilable conflict with each other' (Weber 1948b: 147). Weber's message is unmistakable: when fundamental values conflict, their conflict is irresolvable by any superior law or rationality.

How, then, should we respond? At the level of personal life, Weber might be happy with Berlin's plumping account, but he is more concerned with the political world. Here he considers three possibilities, respectively three kinds of authority: traditional, rational-bureaucratic, and charismatic (Weber 1964: 328).

The traditional response to the settlement of value conflict is to refer to received customs whose authority is guaranteed by their ancient lineage. But Weber sees this kind of solution as anachronistic under the 'disenchanted' conditions of modernity, in which mystery is replaced by calculation (Weber 1948b: 139). Part of that disenchantment is a widening sense of value pluralism, extending now to a questioning of relations among natural rights (Bellamy 1992: 209). Pluralism invites us to ask why one tradition should take precedence over another, and also why any single tradition should take the shape it does, since any given tradition will itself rank distinct and competing values in a particular way. I return to these issues later in the chapter.

The rational-bureaucratic approach insists on rationally justified solutions, embodied in legal rules typically administered and enforced by a politically neutral bureaucracy. Here the problem for Weber is twofold (Derman 2017: 125–6). First, the growth of bureaucratic rationality is indeed characteristic of the modern world, but it is an anti-liberal development, replacing the freedom of individual judgment with rule-bound, hierarchical forms of organization in which personal creativity is stifled. Second, bureaucratic reasoning is limited from a pluralist point of view. The bureaucrat's authority is confined to 'technical' questions of the best means of achieving a given end. The pluralist question of how to rank or choose among competing ends is beyond him. For that we need the third kind of authority discussed by Weber.

It is only the charismatic kind of authority, Weber argues, that can really provide an adequate response to the problem of value pluralism under modern conditions. Weber defines charismatic authority as 'resting on devotion to the specific and exceptional sanctity, heroism or exemplary character of an individual person, and of the normative patterns or order revealed or ordained by him' (Weber 1964: 328). Charismatic leaders achieve their authority not through custom or appointment by an elite or by reasoned argument but by political conflict, taking the form of a competition for the allegiance of the masses. It is this competition that fits them uniquely for politics. 'What is crucially important is the fact that the only persons with the training needed for political leadership are those who have been selected in political *struggle*, because all politics is essentially struggle' (Weber 1994: 219).

This kind of struggle in turn injects into the system the kind of creative impetus needed to choose not merely among means but among incommensurable ends. While traditionalists remain within immemorial customs and bureaucrats make technical decisions within existing rules, charismatic leaders achieve success by winning a contest for power. In this contest, a country's options are dramatized and its potential leaders take personal responsibility for the choices they make on people's behalf. 'This struggle for personal power, and the resulting personal responsibility, is the lifeblood of the politician' (Weber cited by Bellamy 1992: 203).

The relation between charismatic leaders and their people is vital. In this connection, Weber refers approvingly to 'Caesarism', where the political leader derives his authority not from representatives or experts but directly from the support of the people. Such a leader 'uses the means of *mass* demagogy to gain the confidence of the masses and their belief in his person, and thereby gains power' (Weber 1994: 220). The Caesarist leader appeals over the heads of other elites to the demos: 'the specifically Caesarist instrument is the plebiscite' (Weber 1994: 221).

Critical questions arise, of course. One aspect of Weber's case is an argument by elimination: only charisma and Caesarism respond adequately to the problem of value pluralism because incommensurable values cannot be ranked by reference to tradition or to bureaucratic practice. But is that true? As mentioned earlier, the role of tradition will be discussed later in this chapter, so I postpone it for now. In the case of bureaucracy, it is surely too neat to characterize bureaucrats as following rules and orders that confine them to means rather than ends. There is ample evidence that public administrators are capable of making creative and independent judgments of their own about ends as well as means, even where the ends are incommensurable (*TR* 2004).[3]

There is also a more affirmative dimension of Weber's case: the positive merits of charismatic leadership. Here the obvious worry is whether Caesarism will lead to populist authoritarianism or worse. Will the leader not become a dictator, backed by a majority or plurality, who will ride roughshod over the legitimate claims of minorities? This is, of course, exactly what happened in Germany after Weber's death when the Weimar republic was succeeded by Hitler's Reich. Weber is usually described as a liberal, although often as 'a liberal in despair', who is trying to find a future for liberalism among the harsh realities of the modern world (Mommsen cited by Bellamy 1992: 179). But how is this possible under a regime of Caesarism?

Weber would respond that his position is subject to a series of safeguards, variously liberal and pluralist, institutional and ethical. His model is not the untrammeled dictator but the President of the United States or Prime Minister of the UK. First, the Weberian leader is, as on the American and British models, ultimately accountable to the people through an election. Second, again echoing the Anglophone precedents, Weber sees Parliament as having an important role in upholding civil liberties and other constitutional checks on the leader (Weber 1994: 222).

Unfortunately, there is in each case reason to doubt that Weber's safeguards will achieve their purpose. Weber is ambivalent about them himself. Although he regards the people as 'active' rather than 'purely as passive objects of administration', their activity is limited to responding to the initiative of the charismatic leader (Weber 1994: 220). As for Parliament, while he continues to see it as offering important checks on the power of the leader, he becomes increasingly less confident in its ability to fulfill these functions (Bellamy 1992: 205).

Third, Richard Bellamy argues that Weber's position implicitly contains a philosophical defense of liberalism grounded in value pluralism itself. 'The liberal commitment to an open society derived its rationale, in Weber's view, from the individual's need to affirm the meaning of his or her existence by choosing from amongst numerous competing and often irreconcilable values' (Bellamy 1992: 211). Alert readers will recognize in this the essentials of Berlin's 'conceptual' argument from pluralism to liberalism that I considered and rejected in Chapter 1. The argument begins by pointing out a need to choose and tries to derive from this the value of the open society – that, it violates Hume's Law against deriving a value from a fact.

Finally, and most distinctively, Weber argues that true political leaders will police themselves by observing the distinction between two ethical imperatives. One is 'the ethic of ultimate ends', which bids the leader – for example, 'the convinced syndicalist' – to pursue his goals single-mindedly, even if that means using violence ('the decisive means for politics') (Weber 1948a: 120-1). The other is 'the ethic of responsibility', which invites leaders to consider the realities of human nature, the concrete situation, and the consequences of their actions, especially if these involve violence (Weber 1948a: 121).

One might think that Weber, as a pluralist, would whole-heartedly recommend the ethic of responsibility, which emphasizes the costs of the leader's actions and so draws his attention to values other than his most prominent goals. In fact Weber calls for a balance between the two ethics. Good political leaders must have both head and heart: the ability to weigh costs and risks, and a capacity for conviction. Sometimes leaders must follow their convictions as long as they are prepared to take responsibility for the costs. 'In so far as this is true, an ethic of ultimate ends and an ethic of responsibility are not absolute contrasts but rather supplements, which only in unison constitute a genuine man – a man who *can* have the "calling for politics"' (Weber 1948a: 127).

While it is hard to deny that Weber's vision of the leader who combines the two ethics is an attractive one, it is harder still to be confident that it will actually be observed by the Caesarist leader. Again, Weber sees this himself: 'the problem is simply how can warm passion and a cool sense of proportion be forged together in one and the same soul?' (Weber 1948a: 115). The current President of the United States could well be described as fitting Weber's Caesarist category and to some extent as pursuing an ethic of ultimate ends. But of an ethic of responsibility, there is very little sign.

Is Weber a hopeless idealist after all? For a thinker who places such stress on our need to face up to unpleasant realities, he does seem to leave a very large hostage to fortune if he wants political leaders to be restrained by the ethic of responsibility. Alternatively, his picture of the desirable leader might be seen as underlining the grim reality of politics if it is read as setting out what *would* be necessary for good political guidance to be possible.[4]

Either way – whether Weber is read as an idealist or a realist – the worry about authoritarianism persists. The Caesarist leader will easily become a tyrant unless he is constrained by an ethic of responsibility. Such an ethic is a demanding one.

Antagonism and Agonism

Weber's view of ethical and political conflict as ultimately non-rational and his tendency to an authoritarian response – or a response which may easily lead to authoritarianism – are taken further by Carl Schmitt.[5] Notorious as the 'crown jurist' of Nazism, Schmitt is now celebrated by both conservative and left-wing theorists for his hostility to liberal constitutionalism.[6] Where Weber confronts the problem of value pluralism with charismatic leadership, Schmitt insists on a conception of political dictatorship in which popular support is irrelevant.

Schmitt's starting point is his notion of 'the political', which he defines as dedicated to distinguishing 'friend' from 'enemy'. The most important human institution is the state, and 'the concept of the state presupposes the concept of the political' (Schmitt 1996 [1932]: 19). The distinctive political task is to identify the enemy. 'The specific political distinction to which political actions and motives can be reduced is that between friend and enemy' (Schmitt 1996 [1932]: 26). The enemy is not just any opponent or adversary but 'the stranger', 'existentially something different and alien' (Schmitt 1996 [1932]: 27). Against the enemy, conflict, ultimately meaning war, is always possible. The enemy is not necessarily someone you are at war with all the time, but someone you are prepared ultimately to go to war with if the circumstances require it. Schmitt is not coy about the fact that 'war' means actual physical killing and loss of life. To go to war with the enemy is to be prepared to take the enemy's life and to sacrifice one's own.

Schmitt's principal critical target is liberalism. Liberals do not take the relation of enmity seriously enough. They try to evade the political by treating 'the political concept of battle' as 'competition in the domain of economics and discussion in the intellectual realm' (Schmitt 1996 [1932]: 71). Differences like these can be settled by agreement on the basis of rational discussion, either through trading economic interests or through agreeing on moral principles – hence the liberal love of parliaments, where these discussions take place. Further, liberals see politics as properly constrained by constitutionalism, in which political negotiation and debate is subject to law, itself the product of reasoned agreement.

For Schmitt, the liberal view is ignorant of the true nature of the political, which concerns the deep fissure between friend and enemy, not superficial differences between economic competitors and ethical debaters. Contrary to the facile liberal outlook, the only way of preventing genuinely political enmities from realizing their potential in warfare is to override the conflict by decree from a superior authority. This has become known as the doctrine of 'decisionism': a sovereign authority puts an end to the conflict by issuing a decision to that effect (Hirst 1999; Lilla 2001: 58). There is no discussion, beloved of liberal parliaments, and no reasoned justification. There is simply the sovereign's decision. Nor can the decision be second-guessed on constitutional grounds. On Schmitt's view, the political is not subject to law; rather, law is subject to the political.

Schmitt does not say so explicitly, but the antagonism he describes between friend and enemy can be seen as reflecting the conflict of incommensurable values.[7] Just as enemies cannot agree, so in conflicts among incommensurables, on this view, there is no rational resolution, only permanent disagreement. Indeed, it is reasonable to suppose that enmity is in part caused by the parties' attachment to distinct and conflicting fundamental values. The stranger is alien because he lives by alien norms. But for practical purposes, a decision must be made and this can only be made by an authority whose will is unquestioned and final, otherwise the conflict breaks out afresh.[8] In short, the problem of value pluralism is solved in Schmitt's work by dictatorship.

An immediate objection to Schmitt's view is that his account of liberalism as denying the permanent reality of disagreement and conflict is a travesty. The permanence of social and political disagreement and conflict is in fact a cornerstone of the liberal outlook, going back to the birth of liberalism in the wake of the seventeenth-century wars of religion. It is precisely because people will always disagree about the nature of the human good that liberals argue for mutual toleration and limited government corresponding to the recognition of personal rights and liberties. As Charles Larmore puts it, liberalism 'has taken to heart one of the cardinal experiences of modernity. It is the increasing awareness that reasonable people tend naturally to differ and disagree about the nature of the good life' (Larmore 1996: 122). Liberalism emphatically does not deny the permanence of social conflict; on the contrary, the permanence of social conflict is a condition for liberalism.

Schmitt would reply that liberals do not take their acknowledgment of conflict far enough. Although they recognize the permanence of disagreement in some matters, such as religion, they seek to contain and manage that disagreement with rules, classically the civil and political rights of individuals, on which it is said reasonable people can and should agree. John Rawls, for example, distinguishes between 'conceptions of the good', on which agreement is not to be expected, from 'the right', or the framework of rules on which agreement is possible and desirable (Rawls 1971: 446–9).

Schmitt would respond that not only conceptions of the good but also matters of the right are disputed in modern societies. Moreover, these matters are disputed at the level of antagonism. Again, liberals assume that disagreement about the right is something that can be translated into the language of economic trade-offs or polite debate and so resolvable by rational conversation. But that is not so; these are matters of ultimate, existential difference on which reasoned agreement is not possible.

How can liberals reply? First, it is surely too extreme to assert, as Schmitt does, that the political sphere allows no prospect of reasoned agreement about anything significant at all, including any element of (in Rawls's terms) the right. There is, for example, widespread acceptance of the notion of human rights. While it is true that there is also widespread dispute as to the precise content and implications of human rights – indeed, this is expressly allowed and even encouraged by liberal principles of free speech and inquiry – that does not detract from a significant level of agreement about the right.[9]

Second, Schmitt's insistence that all political disagreement is antagonism is also too extreme. His view of the political is far too narrow. The model seems to be that of conflict between states identified ethno-nationally: something like Hitler's vision of the historic contest between the Teutonic and Slavic peoples. But of course not all politics is like that. Even internationally, many conflicts conform more closely to the liberal model of clashing economic interests or ethical principles – for example, disputes about trade or the fair treatment of refugees. Certainly, domestic politics is hard to fit exclusively within Schmitt's antagonism when it comes, for example, to arguments about taxation or the form to be taken by public services or how to extend greater equality to women or to the disabled or to indigenous groups.

For Schmitt, these arguments are in themselves not properly part of the political; rather, they are liberal dilutions or corruptions of the political by other concerns. But this does no more than win the argument by definition and by an excessively narrow definition. Schmitt may be right that antagonism is part of politics and an ineradicable part. But to claim that it is all of what the political properly amounts to is to impose on politics an impossibly narrow understanding and one that we are better off without.

The reasons for this judgment are in part standardly liberal and in part pluralist. The obvious liberal objection to Schmitt's decisionism is to its evident authoritarianism. For Schmitt, conflicts among antagonists and their values must be managed by political dictatorship. The real-life consequences of this view are amply borne out by his collaboration with the Nazis.

Schmitt has been defended in this connection by Paul Hirst, who argues that Schmitt's dictator is not wholly arbitrary. On this reading, Schmitt endorses dictatorship only as a temporary expedient that is necessary to restore social order. Unlike the Nazis and fascists, for whom sovereignty is completely unlimited, Schmitt introduces the conservative value of stability as a guiding consideration: 'Barbaric excess and pure arbitrary power are not Schmitt's object. Power is limited by a prudent concern for the social order' (Hirst 1999: 12). Seen in this light, liberal constitutionalism is rejected not because it stands in the way of absolutism but because it is not the best way of maintaining or restoring order in a society where order is precarious – the conditions of Weimar Germany in which Schmitt is writing.

The trouble with this move is that it acquits Schmitt of absolutism at the price of undermining his basic argument. That argument is (like Hobbes's) that absolutism is essential in politics because anything less fails to manage those permanent conflicts that arise from antagonism among people and their values. Once the problem has been framed in the extreme terms adopted by Schmitt, only an extreme response will answer to it. If disagreement and conflict are permanent, and permanent in the deep terms of enmity that Schmitt describes, then only the intervention of an absolute sovereign will prevent their consummation in open warfare. That intervention must be final and unquestioned, otherwise conflict will re-emerge. But if there is a higher principle that the sovereign must answer to, such as social order, then there is again an opportunity for that conflict. The parties have space to argue that the sovereign's decision is not, after all, the best way of achieving the overriding goal of order.

There is another problem here, more specifically pluralist. What is the justification for the assertion of social order as the overriding goal to be pursued by the sovereign? On the pluralist view, social order may be an important value but it is on the face of things only one value among others. Why should it be emphasized in the way (according to Hirst) endorsed by Schmitt? The answer cannot be simply that order is endorsed by the sovereign, since that is not necessarily so. An absolute sovereign could pursue any goal. Why pursue social order rather than, say, chaotic cultural revolution or risky imperialist expansion?

If social order is not justified as an overriding goal by the logic of Schmitt's absolutism, then what else could justify it? That question does not seem to have an answer in Schmitt. He leaves us with a choice. Either the sovereign is genuinely absolute, in which case the concern about authoritarian (or totalitarian) politics arises, or the authority of the sovereign is limited by a concern for social order, which has no more than an arbitrary basis. Either way, Schmitt's position leaves serious cause for concern.

I return to the issue of social order and its importance relative to other values in Chapter 4. For the present I turn to a more recent agonist view, that of Chantal Mouffe. Once again the assumption is that there can be no rational resolution of conflicts among incommensurable values. But in contrast with Weber's plebiscitory leader and with Schmitt's dictator, Mouffe proposes a left-wing response she calls 'agonistic democracy'.

Mouffe agrees with both Weber and Schmitt that conflict is a central and permanent feature of human life, in particular political life. Like Weber, she is more explicit than Schmitt in attributing this to the incommensurability of fundamental values. If values are plural in Weber's sense, then they will always conflict and there can be no final, correct answer to the question of how the conflict ought to be resolved. Consequently, conflict will persist and deepen. 'Given the ineradicable pluralism of value, there is no rational resolution of the conflict, hence its antagonistic dimension' (Mouffe 2000: 102).

Again, political conflict is seen as having a depth and permanence beyond the comprehension of liberalism. Liberal deliberation is too 'rationalistic' and too oriented to consensus to accommodate the deep plurality of values and the conflict to which it gives rise. 'Rawls and Habermas', for example, 'want to ground adhesion to liberal democracy on a type of rational agreement that would preclude the possibility of contestation' (Mouffe 2000: 92). That hope is rendered unrealistic by value pluralism.

Unlike Schmitt, however, and rather more like Weber, Mouffe draws back from the prospect of political struggle as always taking the form of antagonism. She insists that she is not advocating 'a total pluralism' and that 'some limits need to be put to the kind of confrontation which is going to be seen as legitimate in the public sphere' (Mouffe 2000: 93). These limits must be political in nature, given the weaknesses of reason and morality in resolving fundamental conflicts.

The key limit is that Mouffe aims at 'defusing' Schmitt's antagonism, 'taming' it into 'agonism' (Mouffe 2000: 101; 2005: 19, 20). Schmittian antagonism is conflict between enemies who seek each other's destruction. But agonism is conflict between 'adversaries' who oppose one another but who also tolerate one another as holding views which, although mistaken, are held legitimately. An adversary is 'somebody whose ideas we combat but whose right to defend those ideas we do not put into question', a 'legitimate enemy, one with whom we have some common ground because we have a shared adhesion to the ethico-political principles of liberal democracy: liberty and equality' (Mouffe 2000: 102). Crucially, adversaries are opponents who tolerate one another. The tendency to antagonism must be acknowledged as permanent, but it can and should be channeled into a less destructive, more tolerant form of political struggle.

The result is Mouffe's 'agonistic democracy'. Political struggle is in itself a condition for democracy, since it is only where partisan political combat is allowed to express itself that the political sphere can be alive and healthy. But antagonistic conflict undermines this, leading to the destruction of one or more of the contending parties. It is when struggle ceases to be antagonistic and becomes agonistic, allowing conflict to be sustained among multiple adversaries, that democracy emerges. Thus, the aim of transforming antagonism into agonism is an 'aim of democratic politics' (Mouffe 2000: 103).

Despite Mouffe's differences with Schmitt, she inherits some of his problems, beginning with Schmitt's one-dimensional understanding of liberalism as ignoring the permanent nature of conflict. To this can be added the fact that Mouffe's response to the problem of pluralism and conflict is itself basically liberal. When she moves from antagonism to agonism, or from enemy to adversary, she does so by accepting 'the ethico-political principles of liberal democracy: liberty and equality' and above all 'liberal-democratic tolerance' (Mouffe 2000: 102). The conversion of the enemy into 'a debating adversary' is precisely the move that Schmitt attributes to liberals and condemns on that account (Schmitt 1996 [1932]: 28). Mouffe claims to oppose liberalism but relies on a liberal move at the heart of her position.

She would reply that the relation between agonistic adversaries is not the same as that between liberal 'competitors'. While competitors are rivals for dominance within the existing 'hegemonic' system, adversaries 'put into question the dominant hegemony' itself (Mouffe 2005: 21). In Rawls's terms, this means that, according to Mouffe, agonistic adversaries are able to question not only conceptions of the good but also those basic rights and liberties of individuals that provide the ground rules within which conflicting conceptions of the good are managed. But liberals can and do raise the same questions. As noted earlier, liberalism allows and even encourages debates concerning the interpretation and prioritization of basic rights. Indeed, liberals are free to question whether there are any such rights at all.

On the other hand, if Mouffe insists that liberalism depends on *some* degree of consensus on fundamental rights, there again it would seem that her own agonistic democracy depends on the same assumption. What sets her view apart from Schmitt's is the acceptance of a set of overarching political values beyond the bare requirement of social order. She concedes that 'a pluralist democracy demands a certain amount of consensus and that it requires allegiance to the values which constitute its "ethico-political principles"' – that is, freedom, equality, and toleration (Mouffe 2000: 103). She adds that this is nevertheless a 'conflictual consensus' in which disputes continue about how the framework principles should be interpreted. But this point, too, can be easily accommodated by liberals, as mentioned above. All things considered, it is hard to see where liberalism ceases and Mouffe's democratic radicalism is supposed to begin.

There are also explicitly pluralist problems with Mouffe's view. How does she justify the emphasis on the values of freedom, equality, and toleration, in contrast with other important goods, that she uses to turn antagonism into agonism? This echoes the pluralist issues that have arisen in the work of the other agonist thinkers discussed here. In the case of Weber, what justifies the singling out of the ethic of responsibility as a check on the charismatic leader? When it comes to Schmitt, why should we accept the stress on the value of social order that supposedly distinguishes the Schmittian dictator from the absolutist leader?

Mouffe's difficulty here is an instance of a more general problem that afflicts all the agonist thinkers. All the agonists, by definition, believe that there can be no reasoned resolution of any conflict of incommensurable values. So, when they are asked why any particular value should be privileged above any other, the answer can only be that the privilege is arbitrary. To recall Berlin's term, all we can do is 'plump' for one option or another. In that case, the agonists seem to be left, necessarily, with no more reason to advance their preferred formulas than any others.

Moreover, the arbitrariness of the agonist formulas brings them into tension with pluralism in another way. Pluralism tells us that there is a wide range of human goods, all of which ought to be taken seriously in our political judgment.

But because agonism imposes an arbitrary selection on the range of goods that might otherwise be pursued, that selection is likely to be unduly narrow.

This is most obvious in the cases of Weber and Schmitt, who rely on a single leader to decide which values will be promoted or permitted in a given society. Conceivably, the leader may enable people to pursue something like the full range of ends possible in the circumstances. More likely, however, leaders of the kind envisaged by Weber and Schmitt will promote their own values and interests, or those of their immediate followers, and not those of other social groups. As Mill reminds us, even well-intentioned leaders find it hard to put themselves in the place of people whose experience and interests are very different from their own (Mill 1958 [1861]: 43–6). Of course, both Weber and Schmitt place some qualifications on the power of the leader, but we have already seen reasons to doubt how effective these will be. For Weber, much depends on how far the leader adheres to the ethic of responsibility; in the case of Schmitt, the sole concern, in the end, is social order.

Mouffe, with her democratic approach, has more of a sense that a greater range of values is likely to be promoted by a greater range of political voices. She takes this further by protecting minority voices through her acceptance of the liberal values of freedom, equality, and toleration. But even in the case of Mouffe, there is cause for pluralist concern in this connection. If political voices are arbitrary in their judgments, then democracy alone, even with liberal protections, will not guarantee that all relevant values are properly considered and weighed. If pluralism invites us to take seriously the full range of human goods, that in turn suggests a commitment to some form of practical reasoning rather than mere bias or sentiment. But a reasoned approach is precisely what is excluded by agonism in whatever form. What form such a reasoned approach might take is a matter I return to later, especially in Chapters 5–7.

Most fundamentally, as already noted in Chapter 1, all the agonist positions make a false assumption and ignore an important possibility. The assumption is that the reasoned ranking of values requires commensuration, so that where values are incommensurable they cannot be ranked for decisive reason. Against this, there is the possibility that, although fundamental values cannot be ranked for decisive reason in the abstract, there may be good reason to rank values in context. On the pluralist view, no single formula exists that successfully ranks values in every case, but the concrete circumstances of particular cases may give us reasons to accept rankings that apply in those cases only. I turn to this 'contextualist' approach to the problem of value pluralism next.

Practical Reasoning in Context

If a reasoned response to the problem of value pluralism is possible in context, how can that be? Jonathan Riley sees it as an objection to the whole contextual approach that it does not explain how context makes reasonable judgment possible (Riley 2000: 129). Is Riley correct, or can some account can be given of how context can generate reasons to rank or trade off competing incommensurable values?

Recall that Berlin refers briefly in this connection to the agent's background conception of the good life: 'When these rules or principles conflict in concrete cases, to be rational is to follow the course of conduct which least obstructs the general pattern of life in which we believe' (*L* 47). Is this an individual or collective 'we'? Is Berlin proposing a subjective standard or one based on a shared cultural tradition? Here, as so often, he is not explicit.[10]

In the context of an individual life, the classic account of contextual decision making in ethics is Aristotle's. For Aristotle, practical wisdom (*phronesis*) is the art of judging the right action to perform in a given situation. Ethics is too complex a field to be reducible to one or a few abstract rules. Rather, the person of practical wisdom (*phronemos*) addresses the concrete circumstances and tailors his action accordingly. Experience helps: we have a better chance of deciding well if we have been in comparable situations before and seen the consequences of different kinds of response. The experience of other people can help too, since we can receive valuable guidance from those more experienced than we are. All that experience can be in a certain sense codified in the form of 'virtues' or settled dispositions to act well in different dimensions of life. The classical virtues celebrated by Aristotle are courage, self-control, justice, as well as practical wisdom itself.

Is Aristotle a value pluralist? Clearly, he does not think of himself in these terms, but might he still qualify as holding a pluralist position *avant la lettre*? Berlin would tend to say no, identifying Aristotle, along with Plato, as a monist theorist of the 'contemplative life as the highest that a man can lead' (*L* 295).[11] Hampshire would agree, so far as he associates Aristotle with the idea of a hierarchy of elements within the soul (*IE* 23–38), although his overall view of Aristotle has much more to it.[12] Charles Larmore (1996) would also classify Aristotle as a monist on the ground of his doctrine of the unity of the virtues.

However, Nussbaum interprets Aristotelian practical wisdom as essentially a response to value pluralism.[13] In Chapter 2, Nussbaum was mentioned as favoring an approach to pluralist conflict of, essentially, avoidance. Once fundamental incommensurables are in conflict, we are in a tragic situation to which there is no solution. The best response to this problem is to try to arrange our affairs so as to prevent it arising. But this is Nussbaum's more recent view of pluralist conflict. In her earlier work – in particular in *The Fragility of Goodness* (2001: first published in 1986) and *Love's Knowledge* (1990) – she presented a more optimistic account of reasoned choice among incommensurables by way of a highly sympathetic interpretation of Aristotelian practical wisdom.

According to Nussbaum in her earlier writings, Aristotle reacts against Plato's 'scientific' view of ethics. Plato's model is characterized by an impersonal 'god's-eye' perspective and by an attempt to formulate universal and dispassionate rules based on the commensuration of values in a single, absolute system. By contrast, the Aristotelian approach is non-scientific, taking as its criterion for correct action not a system of rules but the example of the person of practical wisdom. Such a person possesses a capacity for 'perception' or 'complex responsiveness to the salient features of one's situation' (*LK* 55). The person of practical wisdom makes ethical judgments by attending and responding intuitively (although with some assistance from rules and principles) to the particulars of the situation in which she finds herself.

For my purposes, two features of Nussbaum's account of Aristotle are especially important. First, Nussbaum sees one of Aristotle's critical targets as the widespread view, exemplified by Plato, that a rational account of right action requires a 'science of measurement'. Ethical choices tend to throw up a bewildering variety of considerations. On the 'science of measurement' view, this apparent heterogeneity can and should be overcome by finding in it 'some single standard of value' that commensurates all others, so that the choice 'can be recast as a matter of maximizing our quantities of that value' (*LK* 56).

According to Nussbaum, the pluralist reply to be found in Aristotle is that there is no such single master-value. The leading candidate, pleasure, is itself plural: there is no single 'pleasure' but many different kinds of pleasure. More generally, and again contrary to Plato, there is no single, unitary 'Good' but rather an irreducible plurality of distinct goods. Across the wide range of things deemed to be good by human beings, there is no one feature common to them all that accounts for their goodness. Instead, 'what we pursue or choose when we deem each of these things choiceworthy is something distinct, peculiar to the item in question' (*LK* 58). The good human life is 'a life inclusive of a number of different constituents, each being defined apart from each of the others and valued for its own sake'; to understand and value each of these constituents properly entails 'recognition of its distinctness and separateness from each of the others' (*FG* 296). In short, 'the values that are constitutive of a good human life are plural and incommensurable' (*LK* 294).

How can we choose rationally among such values when they come into conflict? To do this would seem to involve comparing or weighing them, but how is that possible without reference to some single value that will serve as a common standard? Once a science of measurement has been ruled out, it may seem that we must abandon the possibility of rational choice in ethics.

Nussbaum replies that when the question is put in this way it presents a false dichotomy, suggesting that 'deliberation must be either quantitative or a shot in the dark' (*LK* 60). But our ordinary experience with ethical questions shows that there is another alternative: that deliberation can be qualitative and no less rational for that. Indeed, to be rational here requires that we attend to the distinct qualities of the values in play rather than treating them as commensurable. Does this mean that the values cannot be weighed against one another? The 'weighing' metaphor does suggest some quantitative standard by which 'weight' is measured. But might it not be possible to 'weigh' goods or options against one another in the looser sense that we consider their relative force within some context?

This brings in the second principal feature of Aristotelian practical reason on Nussbaum's reading: its emphasis on particularity. For Aristotle, the primary focus of practical reason is not on universal principles deduced from an impersonal, scientific understanding (*epistēmē*), as on Plato's model, but on 'ultimate particulars' that must be 'grasped with insight through experience' (*FG* 299; *LK* 68). Fixed rules or laws cannot capture correct choice adequately because 'practical matters' are too complex: 'mutable', 'indeterminate', and 'particular' (*FG* 302–3; *LK* 70–1).

Rather, the key to good deliberation is 'perception', which is 'a faculty of discrimination that is concerned with the apprehending of concrete particulars, rather than universals' (*FG* 300). The person of practical wisdom deals with a choice situation not simply by applying a preconceived rule, but by responding intuitively to the situation, taking into account all its relevant details. She has 'the ability to recognize, acknowledge, respond to, pick out certain salient features of a complex situation' (*FG* 305). This calls for 'ethical flexibility' – illustrated by Aristotle with the analogy of the good architect, who measures a fluted column not with a straight ruler but with the curved 'Lesbian Rule' (*LK* 70). It also calls for experience (*nous*): the capacity for perception 'is gained only through a long process of living and choosing that develops the agent's resourcefulness and responsiveness' (*LK* 305).

Does this picture amount to a mere 'rootless situational perspective that rejects all guidance from ongoing commitments and values' (*FG* 306)? Nussbaum denies this. First, the person of practical wisdom has the guidance of good character – that is, a settled disposition to act in accordance with general values and virtues such as justice, courage, moderation, friendship, and generosity. Second, it follows that some general rules will still be useful, although as 'rules of thumb' or 'summaries of wise decisions' rather than as decisive authorities in their own right (*FG* 301, 304; *LK* 69, 73, 93).

Third, the person of practical wisdom will therefore seek something of a balance between particulars and rules, on the one hand using rules as guides in imagining possible responses to the situation, on the other hand attending to the particulars of the situation to judge the applicability of the rules, or even to revise the rules themselves. There will be an 'interplay of the general and the particular in Aristotelian choice' (*LK* 94).

> In ethical terms, what this means is that the perceiver brings to the new situation a history of general conceptions and commitments, and a host of past obligations and affiliations (some general, some particular), all of which contribute to and help to constitute her evolving conception of good living.[14]

However, the contextual approach to pluralism as explained so far suffers from a more serious limitation: its personal character. Nussbaum uses Aristotelian practical reasoning to show how an individual can judge how to respond to conflicting incommensurables within the context of his or her own life. But personal conceptions of the good may lead individuals in many different directions. What about judgments at the public level of politics and public policy, where some degree of convergence is typically sought and needed?

Cultural Tradition

The answer is that contextual judgment may also be presented as having a social or cultural dimension. On this view, conduct is justifiable by the way it accords with rules or practices that fit into a shared, not just a personal, way of life. This may be true even where the judgment is that of an individual concerning her own life: what is right for her may reflect a norm that is not merely hers but that of her society. Recall the ambiguity in Berlin's phrase, 'the general pattern of life in which we believe' (L 47). The 'we' here may refer either to our own life and or to the life we share with others, or both.

If we are talking about shared norms, these are typically embodied in a cultural tradition. In the pluralist literature, the role of cultural tradition is most strongly emphasized by the work of John Kekes, most notably *The Morality of Pluralism* (1993). 'The vast majority of conflicts we encounter', writes Kekes, 'occur within particular traditions or within particular people' (MP 24). In both cases, it is usually possible to resolve matters by reference to 'a system of values in the background in whose maintenance the disputants have a vested interest'. In the case of conflicts among people who share a social or cultural tradition, the background system of values is clearly that tradition. But even in the case of value conflicts faced by a single person, Kekes's account makes tradition determining in the end. On that basis, he goes on to draw out political implications that are not liberal, like Berlin's, but conservative.

When it comes to intra-personal value conflicts, Kekes's starting point is that individuals resolve these by appeal to their own conception of the good life. 'In the case of conflicts occurring within people, the system of values [to which they appeal to resolve the conflict] is the conception of a good life of the agent who faces the conflict' (MP 24). Individual conceptions of the good are, of course, multiple and variable among different people. However, in order to count as reasonable an individual conception of the good must observe certain limitations, including the 'primary values'. This is Kekes's version of the great goods: basic goods that are part of any account of human well-being, hence essential to any sensible conception of the good life. Primary values are contrasted with secondary values, which are not essential to all conceptions of the good.

Another limitation is that individual conceptions of the good are drawn from a surrounding social or cultural tradition. The judgments that resolve value conflicts rest on 'conceptions of a good life regarded as acceptable in the surrounding tradition' (MP 77). Individuals construct their conceptions of the good by being committed, in varying degrees, to a selection of the conventions of which the overarching tradition is comprised.

In Kekes's view, every tradition comprises conventions, which are the habitual practices of individuals. 'Deep' conventions are those which protect or express primary values and also those secondary values that specify or give local form to the essential primary values. 'Variable' conventions deal with other secondary values, those more purely local concerns that do not reflect any primary matters. Deep and variable conventions mark off, respectively, required and permissible elements of individual conceptions of the good. All conceptions of the good must comply with a tradition's deep conventions, but its variable conventions constitute a palette of permissible activities and practices from which a person can select.

People can be committed to the conventions of their traditions in varying degrees. A 'basic' commitment is the strongest level, where a person's identification with the convention is at its most profound. In a 'healthy' tradition, people will have a basic commitment to the tradition's deep conventions because these are essential to any conception of the good they may have (*MP* 86). 'Conditional' commitments are appropriate to 'day-to-day obligations that attach to our jobs and to our roles as parents, children, spouses, lovers, friends, colleagues, and citizens' – significant commitments that may nevertheless 'be defeated by sufficiently strong countervailing considerations' (*MP* 88). 'Loose' commitments are the weakest, dealing with lesser norms such as tact and politeness. Individual conceptions of the good consist of various patterns of basic, conditional, and loose commitments to the deep and variable conventions of the relevant tradition.

These discriminations among different strengths of commitment are important, Kekes argues, because they help people to resolve conflicts among plural and incommensurable values. Basic commitments override conditional commitments, which in turn override loose commitments. But what happens when conflicts arise within rather than among these categories? Kekes proposes two criteria, 'fecundity' and 'balance': 'One is to opt for the value whose realization would make it more likely to contribute to the possession of other equally or more important values. Another is to try to strike a balance between the values' (*MP* 89).[15]

Such issues arise, however, within the boundary of a tradition, and this remains a crucial emphasis throughout Kekes's thought. In the picture he presents, individual conceptions of the good are formed, on the whole, not through challenges to tradition but by people committing themselves, in varying degrees as appropriate, to the conventions that constitute a given tradition. Kekes does recognize certain countervailing thoughts that I discuss in a moment, but by and large respect for tradition is the norm.

From the norm of respect for tradition, Kekes constructs a political case for conservatism. In *A Case for Conservatism* (1998), he argues that conservatism is the most rational response to the problem of value pluralism. Pluralism means that fundamental values must be ranked in context, which means ranked in accordance with people's background conceptions of the good, which in turn are formed within a tradition. Consequently, people can best resolve the deep value conflicts with which they are faced by 'following the historical practices of the traditions in which they participate' (Kekes 1998: 66–7).[16]

Kekes does acknowledge that his framework has limitations, but he denies that these damage his basic case. He admits that the contextualized practical reasoning he describes will not always reach clear and unequivocal conclusions, but he responds that this is simply in the nature of practical pluralist reasoning realistically conceived. He concedes that not everyone will be persuaded by the kind of reasoning he outlines, because people will not invariably be reasonable – for example, they sometimes reject the authority of the primary values. He replies that persons and traditions that deny the primary values will not survive long. But the thinness of the values that are necessary for social survival has already been noted during the discussion of Riley's view in the previous chapter.

Another question for Kekes is how far can tradition be the bottom line of practical reasoning, given that traditions themselves can be subjected to critical questioning? Kekes sees this issue himself, allowing that traditions can be more or less 'healthy' (*MP* 82, 84). For one thing, it may be asked whether a tradition adequately protects the primary values: does it have 'concrete and specific forms' that properly interpret and support the primary values, and to what extent does it endorse these compared with alternative traditions (Kekes 1993: 81)? Further, a sign of a healthy tradition is that its members have strong ('basic') commitments to its deep conventions and conditional or loose commitments to its variable conventions. But 'traditions can go wrong' when this order is reversed – in effect, when people lose sight of which values are objectively more important and begin to subordinate what should be their core morality to matters of secondary or trivial importance (*MP* 84).

To the extent that Kekes concedes the possibility of traditions being questioned, the political implications of the picture start to look less conservative and more liberal. The liberal side of Kekes is also strongly apparent in his discussion of 'the possibilities of life' under pluralism, where he presents the pluralist outlook in positive, inspirational terms (*MP* 27–31, and ch. 6). There he lists three conditions for good pluralist decision making: a tradition that makes 'available a sufficiently rich supply of possibilities from which we may select some as choiceworthy'; 'a sufficiently developed imagination to enable us to form an adequate notion of the nature of our possibilities'; and

> the enlargement of our freedom. For the more numerous are the available possibilities and the better we appreciate the nature of these possibilities as possibilities we may try to realize, the greater will be our freedom to make for ourselves what seem to us like good lives.
>
> (*MP* 28)

The emphasis here is less on the standard conservative picture of a good life as the following of a tradition than on the liberal idea of choosing one's own way of life for oneself – or at least on a tradition that makes that possible, that is, a liberal tradition.[17]

Elsewhere, however, it seems that Kekes would be unwilling to endorse the criterion of a tradition with liberal content. In the last chapter of *The Morality of Pluralism* and again in *Against Liberalism* (1997), Kekes argues that liberalism is necessarily at odds with value pluralism because it holds that some fundamental goods outrank others in all cases, while of course pluralists reject that view. 'Liberals do regard some values [freedom, equality, human rights] as overriding. And the reason why that matters is that pluralists deny that there are any overriding values' (*MP* 202).[18]

To this it may be replied that liberalism does not depend on the claim that any values are absolutely overriding. On the contrary, it is possible to construct a case for liberalism within the contextual terms that pluralism allows. We have already seen that Berlin wraps his defense of negative liberty in three layers of context: negative liberty is especially prominent as a political value, not necessarily in personal life; even within politics it has to be balanced by other important goods, depending on the situation; and the whole position is framed by the historical context of 'our declining capitalist civilisation'. This contextual approach to the defense of liberalism is taken up by Bernard Williams in particular, whose work will be discussed in the next chapter.

A final issue begins with the observation that, under modern conditions at any rate, traditions are not only contestable but multiple and conflicting within the same society. As Rawls (1993) points out, Western societies have hosted a plurality of religious traditions since the Reformation at least. Multiple ethical strands coexist within the moral outlook of such societies, as Alasdair MacIntyre (1985) observes. In recent times, heightened levels of international migration have brought different ways of life face to face within the same social structures on a scale hitherto unknown.

Given all this, how far does it make sense to point to 'tradition' as the focal point for resolving conflict among plural and incommensurable values? Kekes acknowledges that his approach assumes that there is a shared tradition among those with an interest in the conflict, and he concedes that this may not always be the case. He replies that such cases 'are bound to be rare' (*MP* 26). Moreover, even if the parties to an inter-personal or inter-group conflict come from completely different traditions, they can fall back on their common humanity and the authority of the primary values.

These responses are not convincing. The absence of a shared tradition – shared unproblematically by a whole society – is not a rare occurrence in the modern world for the reasons already given. As for the primary values of a shared humanity, these are too thin or generic to offer much guidance for the reasons examined in Chapter 2. Kekes concedes this point when he accepts the need for primary values to be given more specific secondary form in each tradition. The secondary interpretations of the primary values will vary among traditions, 'since a wide array of reasonable answers' is possible to the question of how to interpret any primary value (*MP* 81–2). The appeal to shared primary values leads quickly to disagreement at the level of secondary values.

So, conflict among different traditions is a given under modern conditions. One response is to insist that, despite the presence of multiple traditions in a society, it is appropriate, perhaps on majoritarian or historical grounds, for one or a small combination of these to maintain a position of dominance in that society. One version of this response is more conservative, demanding or seeking the assimilation of minority or subordinate traditions to the dominant view. Kekes would usually seem to be committed to such a view. This course brings with it a number of practical and ethical difficulties, but from a pluralist point of view the question is why it should not be regarded as simply arbitrary. Why is one such value ranking better than another? Perhaps the answer is historical, raising issues I pursue in the next chapter.

Alternatively, a tradition's claims to dominance may be qualified by toleration of its rivals: they are not officially endorsed but neither are they assimilated or interfered with. This is the classical liberal solution, going back to John Locke's *Letter Concerning Toleration* (1991 [1689]), and so would immediately represent a departure from the conservatism recommended by Kekes.[19] But again there is reason to question its adequacy from a pluralist perspective. On a pluralist view, alternative ways of life are not just second-bests, and they have the positive value imparted to them by their constituent goods. Consequently, the pluralist outlook implies pressure not just to tolerate multiple traditions but to celebrate them as possessing positive value.

The response that goes beyond toleration and enters the territory of positive celebration and recognition is that of multiculturalism. This, too, can take more than one form, depending on the strength and shape of multiculturalist policy. Is this largely rhetorical or substantial? Does it accord limited special rights to minorities or does it go further and endow them with aspects of sovereignty?

It is important to note that the link between value pluralism and multiculturalism is not entirely straightforward. It might be thought that if fundamental values are incommensurable, it follows that whole systems of value, such as cultures, must also be incommensurable.[20] So, this argument goes, in the same way that fundamental values are, so to speak, on a moral par, so ethical parity must obtain among cultures. Pluralism, therefore, implies multiculturalism in the sense in which it is popularly understood, as equivalent to cultural relativism.[21]

That view was rejected in Chapter 1. There it was shown that the incommensurability of values does not imply the incommensurability of cultures. On the pluralist view, the values that are plural and incommensurable are the most fundamental goods, the universals or 'great goods'. If there are universal values, then these must be shared by all cultures. Hence, different cultures overlap on the great goods and cannot be wholly incommensurable. Value pluralism is the idea that it is values that are incommensurable, not systems of value, such as cultures. So, pluralism does not support the kind of multiculturalism popularly equated with cultural relativism.

Another, similar attempt to connect pluralism and multiculturalism should be accepted only with qualification. This is the idea that pluralism suggests that we should promote a diversity of values, so it follows that we should also promote a diversity of cultures. If there are many different values, we should respect and pursue them; hence, we should respect and promote many different cultures, since these are vehicles for values.

Later I shall argue that the premise of this argument should be accepted: that value pluralism implies that we should promote a diversity of values.[22] However, it does not follow that we should promote a diversity of cultures in the same way and to the same extent. The reason is that not all cultures are themselves equally accommodating of value diversity: some are hostile to the pursuit of more than a narrow range of values, whether within the cultural group or outside. If the goal is value diversity, then pluralists cannot be enthusiasts for cultures that are hostile to that goal. Value diversity does not support a case for cultural diversity without inquiry into the nature of the cultures concerned.

This point does not entirely invalidate a link between pluralism and multiculturalism, but it qualifies that link. It emphasizes that the diversity that is primarily endorsed by value pluralism is *value* diversity, not cultural diversity. There is still a pluralist case to be made for cultural diversity, but this is instrumental to the case for value diversity: value pluralism supports the promotion of a diversity of cultures to the extent that these are themselves supportive of a diversity of values. Value diversity is the primary concern; cultural diversity is secondary.

In political terms, the argument implies that value-pluralist multiculturalism will be multiculturalism within the limits of liberalism.[23] This will recognize traditional identities, norms, and practices, but subject to a prior concern for fundamental liberal values such as civil and political rights. Such a position is exemplified by the work of Will Kymlicka (1995) and Joseph Raz (1995).

To this, critics like Bhikhu Parekh (2006) object that no form of liberalism is culturally neutral enough to be an adequate container for multiculturalism. But then the critics are themselves hard put to describe a framework for multiculturalism that goes beyond liberalism without abandoning important rights and liberties (Crowder 2013: ch. 5). Some of those liberal values are attractive for distinctively pluralist reasons. I discuss these connections in Chapters 5 and 6.

Conclusion

The identification of the great goods leaves us with the problem of how to rank them when they conflict. Agonists reply that there can be no rational ranking of incommensurables; rather, we must respond politically. Weber proposes charismatic leadership subject to plebiscitory support and an ethic of responsibility; Schmitt advocates decisionist dictatorship for the sake of social order; for Mouffe the answer is democratic pluralism limited by the standard liberal values of freedom, equality, and toleration. The problem common to the agonists is that all of these formulas can only be arbitrary given their assumption that incommensurable values cannot be ranked for good reason.

That assumption is challenged by the contextualist approach, under which reasoned ranking is possible in concrete situations. Different writers emphasize different kinds of context. The context of an individual life is the focus of Aristotle's classic account of practical reason and of the pluralist version of that account found in Nussbaum. This may seem limited from a political point of view, but it soon emerges that part of what frames personal context in these explanations is a background conception of the good which includes a shared cultural tradition. It is easy to see how this view can be interpreted in a politically conservative direction, as it is by Kekes. However, in modern societies cultural traditions are clearly disputed, multiple and conflicting, reopening the question of choice among pluralities. The multiculturalist response looks plausible but itself raises the question of what the appropriate political framework should be. So far, the appeal to the richer field of contextual thinking looks like an advance on the impasse of agonism, but its direction is uncertain.

Notes

1. See Mouffe 2000, 2005, 2013; Connolly 2002, 2005; Wenman 2003; Fossen 2008.
2. See also Lukes 1998: 96.
3. See Chapter 8.
4. The model here is Judith Shklar's interpretation of Rousseau in Shklar 1969.
5. Mark Lilla (2001: 69) sees Schmitt as 'deeply indebted' to Weber in his understanding of leadership, and Bellamy (1992: 209) notes 'a close affinity' between the two views. However, this is denied by Derman 2012: 190. See also Colliot-Thélène 1999 for a balanced although obscure account of the similarities and differences between Weber and Schmitt.
6. For both an account of Schmitt's collaboration with the Nazis and an explanation of his current appeal to the left, see Lilla 2001.
7. Here I follow Mouffe's interpretation: Mouffe 2000: 102. See also Berlin's association of Schmitt with the plumping response to conflicts of plural values: Lukes 1998: 103.
8. On this point, Schmitt is influenced by Hobbes: Schmitt 1996 [1932]: 52, 65, 67.
9. There is, however, a further question of how reliable commitment to rights will be, especially in the face of terrorist fears and populist enthusiasms, and especially if it relies on democratic institutions alone. I discuss this problem in Chapter 8. My point against Schmitt is that political agreement on rights is possible, not that it is infallible or even entirely trustworthy on its own without the support of strong constitutional institutions including judicial review.
10. For other references to the contextual approach in Berlin, see *L* 42; *CTH* 19; Berlin and Williams 2013: 326–8.
11. See also *CIB* 32 and 56 (where Aristotle is explicitly described by Berlin as a representative of monism). On the other hand, Aristotle is listed among the pluralist 'foxes' in Berlin's famous essay 'The Hedgehog and the Fox': see Berlin 2008.
12. See his Aristotelian account of practical reasoning in Hampshire 1983 and *IE*.
13. This is controversial: Larmore 1996, 163–7. But even if Nussbaum's account is not accepted as an accurate interpretation of Aristotle, it can still be advanced and assessed as her own independent account of practical reason. Similarly, Aristotelian responses to value pluralism can be found in Hampshire 1983 and *IE*; Bernard Williams in *ELP*; Kekes in *MP*; Richardson 1994; Taylor 1997.
14. In this connection, Nussbaum draws a parallel between practical reason and artistic improvization. The improvizing jazz musician is not bound by a score or conductor, but neither is her performance (if it is done well) wholly subjective or irresponsible. On the contrary, 'she will be more responsible than the score-reader, not less, to the unfolding continuities and structures of the work': *LK* 94.
15. 'Fecundity' is akin to the notion of 'diversity' that I develop in Chapter 5. 'Balance' is a notion that recurs at several places in later chapters, in particular Chapters 5, 6, and 8.

16 See also Kekes 1998: 62–3; *MP* 22–4, 77–9.
17 The possibility of a liberal tradition is allowed by Gray in his 'agonistic' liberalism: Gray 2000.
18 See also Kekes 1997: ch. 8; Moore 2009. This was a position I held myself at one time: Crowder 1994.
19 For contemporary expressions of liberalism emphasizing toleration, see Barry 2001; Galston 2002; Kukathas 2003.
20 See Gray 2013: 80; Hardy 2018: 179.
21 See, e.g., Paul Scheffer's comment that 'multicultural thinking represents a continuation of cultural relativism by other means': Scheffer 2011: 197.
22 See Chapter 5.
23 For more detailed treatments of the relation between value pluralism and multiculturalism, see Crowder 2002: 236–46; 2008; 2013: ch. 7.

References

In-text abbreviations are noted in brackets.

Barry, Brian (2001), *Culture and Equality* (Cambridge: Polity).
Bellamy, Richard (1992), *Liberalism and Modern Society* (University Park, PA: Pennsylvania State University Press).
Berlin, Isaiah (1975), 'The End of the Ideal of a Perfect Society', transcribed in Henry Hardy, ed., *The Isaiah Berlin Virtual Library*, http://berlin.wolf.ox.ac.uk
Berlin, Isaiah (2002), *Liberty*, ed. Henry Hardy (Oxford: Oxford University Press). [*L*]
Berlin, Isaiah (2008), *Russian Thinkers*, ed. Henry Hardy and Aileen Kelly (London: Penguin).
Berlin, Isaiah (2013), *The Crooked Timber of Humanity: Chapters in the History of Ideas*, ed. Henry Hardy, 2nd edn (Princeton: Princeton University Press). [*CTH*]
Berlin, Isaiah and Bernard Williams (2013), 'Pluralism and Liberalism', in Isaiah Berlin, *Concepts and Categories*, ed. Henry Hardy, 2nd edn (Princeton: Princeton University Press).
Colliot-Thélène, Catherine (1999), 'Carl Schmitt versus Max Weber: Juridical Rationality and Economic Rationality', in Chantal Mouffe, ed., *The Challenge of Carl Schmitt* (London: Verso).
Connolly, William (2002), *Identity/Difference: Democratic Negotiations of Political Paradox*, expanded edition (Minneapolis: University of Minnesota Press).
Connolly, William (2005), *Pluralism* (Durham, NC: Duke University Press).
Crowder, George (1994), 'Pluralism and Liberalism', *Political Studies* 42: 293–305.
Crowder, George (2002), Liberalism and Value Pluralism (London: Continuum). [*LVP*]
Crowder, George (2008), 'Pluralism and Multiculturalism', *Society* 45 (3): 247–52.
Crowder, George (2013), *Theories of Multiculturalism: An Introduction* (Cambridge: Polity).
Derman, Joshua (2012), *Max Weber in Politics and Social Thought: From Charisma to Canonization* (Cambridge: Cambridge University Press).
Derman, Joshua (2017), 'Max Weber', in Ewa Atanssow and Alan S. Kahan, eds, *Liberal Moments: Reading Liberal Texts* (London: Bloomsbury).
Fossen, Thomas (2008), 'Agonistic Critiques of Liberalism: Perfection and Emancipation', *Contemporary Political Theory* 7 (4): 376–94.
Galston, William (2002), *Liberal Pluralism: The Implications of Value Pluralism for Political Theory and Practice* (Cambridge: Cambridge University Press). [*LP*]

Gray, John (2000), *Two Faces of Liberalism* (Cambridge: Polity).
Gray, John (2013), *Isaiah Berlin: An Interpretation of His Thought*, new edition (Princeton: Princeton University Press).
Hampshire, Stuart (1983), *Morality and Conflict* (Cambridge, MA: Harvard University Press).
Hampshire, Stuart (1989), *Innocence and Experience* (Cambridge, MA: Harvard University Press). [*IE*]
Hardy, Henry (2018), *In Search of Isaiah Berlin: A Literary Adventure* (London: I. B. Tauris).
Hirst, Paul (1999), 'Carl Schmitt's Decisionism', in Chantal Mouffe, ed., *The Challenge of Carl Schmitt* (London: Verso).
Kekes, John (1993), *The Morality of Pluralism* (Princeton: Princeton University Press). [*MP*]
Kekes, John (1997), *Against Liberalism* (Ithaca, NY: Cornell University Press).
Kekes, John (1998), *A Case for Conservatism* (Ithaca, NY: Cornell University Press).
Kymlicka, Will (1995), *Multicultural Citizenship* (Oxford: Oxford University Press).
Kukathas, Chandran (2003), *The Liberal Archipelago* (Oxford: Oxford University Press)
Larmore, Charles (1996), *The Morals of Modernity* (Cambridge: Cambridge University Press).
Lilla, Mark (2001), *The Reckless Mind: Intellectuals in Politics* (New York: New York Review Books).
Locke, John (1991 [1689]), *A Letter Concerning Toleration*, ed. John Horton and Susan Mendus (London: Routledge)
Lukes, Steven (1998), 'Isaiah Berlin: In Conversation with Steven Lukes', *Salmagundi* 120 (Fall): 52–134, at 96.
MacIntyre, Alasdair (1985), *After Virtue: A Study in Moral Theory*, 2nd edn (London: Duckworth).
Mill, J. S. (1958 [1861]), *Considerations on Representative Government*, ed. Currin V. Shields (Indianapolis: Bobbs-Merrill).
Moore, Matthew (2009), 'Pluralism, Relativism, and Liberalism', *Political Research Quarterly* 62 (2): 244–56.
Mouffe, Chantal (2000), *The Democratic Paradox* (London: Verso).
Mouffe, Chantal (2005), *The Political* (London: Routledge).
Mouffe, Chantal (2013), *Agonistics: Thinking the World Politically* (London: Verso).
Nussbaum, Martha (1990), *Love's Knowledge: Essays on Philosophy and Literature* (Oxford: Oxford University Press). [*LK*]
Nussbaum, Martha (2001 [1986]), *The Fragility of Goodness: Luck and Ethics in Greek Tragedy and Philosophy*, 2nd edn (Cambridge: Cambridge University Press). [*FG*]
Parekh, Bhikhu (2006), *Rethinking Multiculturalism: Cultural Diversity and Political Theory*, 2nd edn (London: Palgrave Macmillan).
Rawls, John (1971), *A Theory of Justice* (Oxford: Oxford University Press).
Rawls, John (1993), *Political Liberalism* (New York: Columbia University Press).
Raz, Joseph (1995), 'Multiculturalism: A Liberal Perspective', in *Ethics in the Public Domain* (Oxford: Clarendon Press).
Richardson, Henry. S. (1994), *Practical Reasoning about Final Ends* (Cambridge: Cambridge University Press).

Riley, Jonathan (2000), 'Crooked Timber and Liberal Culture', in Maria Baghramian and Attracta Ingram, eds, *Pluralism: The Philosophy and Politics of Diversity* (London: Routledge).

Scheffer, Paul (2011), *Immigrant Nations*, trans. Liz Waters (Cambridge: Polity).

Schmitt, Carl (1996 [1932]), *The Concept of the Political*, trans. George Schwab (Chicago: University of Chicago Press).

Shklar, Judith N. (1969), *Men and Citizens: A Study of Rousseau* (Cambridge: Cambridge University Press).

Taylor, Charles (1997), 'Leading a Life', in Ruth Chang, ed., *Incommensurability, Incomparability, and Practical Reasoning* (Cambridge: Cambridge University Press).

Thacher, David and Martin Rein (2004), 'Managing Value Conflict in Public Policy', *Governance* 17 (4): 457–86. [*TR*]

Weber, Max (1948a), 'The Vocation of Politics', in H. H. Gerth and C. Wright Mills, eds, *From Max Weber: Essays in Sociology* (London: Routledge).

Weber, Max (1948b), 'The Vocation of Science', in H. H. Gerth and C. Wright Mills, eds, *From Max Weber: Essays in Sociology* (London: Routledge).

Weber, Max (1964), *The Theory of Social and Economic Organization*, trans. A. M. Henderson and Talcott Parsons, ed. Talcott Parsons (New York: Free Press).

Weber, Max (1994), 'Parliament and Government in Germany under a New Political Order', in Peter Lassman and Ronald Speirs, eds, *Political Writings* (Cambridge: Cambridge University Press).

Wenman, Mark (2003), '"Agonistic Pluralism" and Three Archetypal Forms of Politics', *Contemporary Political Theory* 2 (2): 165–86.

Williams, Bernard (1985), *Ethics and the Limits of Philosophy* (Cambridge, MA: Harvard University Press). [*ELP*]

4 Realism and History

Agonism, although it may capture some extreme cases, is in general a normative dead end and untrue to much experience of reasoned decision making under pluralism. That experience points to the validity of the contextualist approach according to which incommensurable goods can often be ranked for good reason in particular circumstances. Much, however, is left to be desired by the accounts of context inspected so far. The context of a personal life has obvious limitations for public policy, and cultural traditions are contested, multiple, and conflicting.

In this chapter, I remain within the general framework of a contextual approach to conflict under value pluralism, but look at two different explanations of what that context might be. First, I consider the context of politics, focusing on the 'realist' interpretation of the political, which emphasizes social order over other values such as justice. Second, I look at the historical context.

Conveniently, both of these tendencies are present in a single pluralist thinker, Bernard Williams. A close personal friend of Berlin, Williams combines a deeply pluralist sensibility with a concern for the effect of history on thought and argument, and an attraction for realist ideas in contrast with the excessive 'moralism', he finds in contemporary political theory.

Another dimension of Williams's thought is his liberalism, and this too becomes an issue as it is for Berlin. What is the relation between Williams's liberalism and his realism, and how far is it possible to defend liberal values in historical context? How, ultimately, is liberalism compatible with value pluralism?

I begin by tracing the idea of value pluralism in Williams's work and connecting it with the general shape of his ethical and political thought. Williams's realist and historical arguments are then discussed in turn. I argue that Williams's realism is deeply at odds with his value pluralism and that his defense of liberalism in historical context, while consistent with pluralism, is incomplete. The latter can be reinforced, but history alone is not enough to justify liberalism or to resolve the problem of value pluralism more generally.

Pluralism, History, and Realism

Williams's ethical theory cannot be reduced to that of Berlin, but he does accept the essentials of Berlin's value pluralism, beginning with the attack on monism.[1] In his introduction to Berlin's *Concepts and Categories*, Williams writes,

> Again and again, in these essays and elsewhere, Berlin warns us against the deep error of supposing that all goods, all virtues, all ideals are compatible, and that what is desirable can ultimately be united into a harmonious whole without loss.
>
> (Williams 2013: xxxv)

The ethical reality concealed or ignored by monism is a field of complexity, diversity, and conflict – the world of value pluralism. As it is for Berlin, the key feature of this pluralist picture for Williams is the idea of the incommensurability of fundamental values. Our most basic ethical considerations are 'genuinely different', not merely instances of a super-value or rungs in a hierarchy. More precisely, values are incommensurable when either there is 'no one currency in terms of which each conflict of values can be resolved', or there is no independent value to appeal to that will resolve the conflict, or none of the conflicting values themselves can (by itself) bring about a resolution (Williams 1979: 227). Fundamental values such as liberty and equality, or Nussbaum's capabilities, are intrinsic goods, each of which speaks with its own unique voice, none of which can be subjected to a rule for ranking that applies in all cases.

Williams thus follows Berlin in accepting the key components of value pluralism: the irreducible multiplicity of fundamental values, their potential for conflict, and their incommensurability. This is not to say, however, that Williams and Berlin approach pluralism in wholly the same way. For one thing, the two address different problems: while Berlin's dominant concern is political, Williams's pluralism connects most immediately with his view of ethics.

As is well known, Williams is a fierce critic of what he sees as the leading tendencies of modern moral philosophy.[2] He argues that both utilitarianism and Kantianism are instances of 'the morality system', in which the sphere of ethics is portrayed in terms of universal and abstract rules – for example, utility maximization or the categorical imperative – that are claimed to apply in any situation. For Williams, the universality and abstraction of the morality system detach us from our actual ethical experience, which is deeply embedded in our social and historical situation. Rather than the thin rules of morality, it is the 'thick' concepts of our own social setting – notions such as specific virtues – that we really live by and that motivate us (*ELP* 140). Our ethical life is lived from the inside, not according to abstract blueprints.

However, although Williams is more interested in the morality system than in the political authoritarianism that worries Berlin, there is a similar pattern in the way they link their respective concerns with monism. Just as Berlin traces authoritarian politics to ethical monism, so Williams finds monist assumptions in the morality system. The oversimplifying idea of the single super-value has already been mentioned. In addition, the morality system is defined by another level of monism: the idea that a single *kind* of norm subsumes or outranks all others. This is moral obligation – indeed, a particularly demanding kind of moral obligation, achieving its 'purest, deepest, and most thorough representation' in Kant but present in all forms of the morality system (*ELP* 174). In that system, the dominant considerations are obligations that amount to inescapable duties, such that if we fail to perform those duties we deserve blame. 'Blame is the characteristic reaction of the morality system' (*ELP* 177). There is an oppressiveness about this system that corresponds to the political oppression identified by Berlin, and both originate in a narrow, monistic understanding of value.

Of course, the alternative to monism is pluralism, and this brings us up against the problem of ranking irreducibly plural and incommensurable values when they come into conflict. This is especially acute when it comes to political issues. Like Berlin, Williams is a liberal and faces the same difficulty in defending the values constitutive of liberalism – that is, the particular interpretations of individual liberty, equality, and justice that are characteristic of the liberal canon. Why should we not opt for some other set of values, such as the contrasting interpretations of equality and social justice typical of socialists, or the caution and loyalty to tradition that mark conservatism?

Williams's dominant response is the same as Berlin's: the appeal to context. Indeed, Williams endorses that response in the article he co-authored with Berlin, first mentioned in Chapter 1 (Berlin and Williams 2013). The plurality of values, they concede, does rule out the possibility that value conflicts can be resolved by a single rule that applies in all cases. However, this is consistent with allowing that there is a decisive reason for favoring one value over the other in certain circumstances. Value pluralism rules out absolute rankings or measurements of value, but not judgments made in concrete situations and not the idea that some situated judgments make more sense than others.

But how far does this advance the defense of liberalism? It may seem that the possibility of contextual judgment under pluralism rules out irrationalism but opens up a problem of relativism. If Berlin and Williams are saying that conflicts among incommensurable values can be settled by reference to the surrounding context of political culture, then that view is hard to distinguish from cultural relativism. The ultimate ethical authority is the de facto culture. At the level of politics the liberal values to which Berlin and Williams are committed – fundamental human rights and liberties – will be justified only so far as the surrounding culture happens to endorse them. If so, we are almost back to square one, since it seems that liberalism has no more to recommend it, ultimately, than its ideological opponents, so far as these have cultural support.

However, Williams rejects cultural relativism in the orthodox sense that value judgments apply only within the boundaries of a particular cultural community and that cross-cultural judgment can never be valid. For Williams, it is always either 'too early or too late' for this kind of relativism: too early when one culture has not yet confronted another, so the issue of their relation has not yet arisen; too late when the two have met because their very meeting forces the parties 'to see beyond their existing rules and practices' (*ELP* 159).[3] Cultural contexts cannot be clearly separated if they are contemporary, Williams believes, especially in a modern world of globalization where 'we' overlap so much with 'them' (*Deed* 68–9).

Instead, Williams accepts what he calls 'the relativism of distance': some belief systems are 'related to our concerns too distantly for our judgements to have any grip on them' (Williams 1981: 142). Appraising such distant systems of belief – or elements of them, or conduct in accordance with them – is impossible or pointless or irrelevant, because they are too remote from us for our judgments on them to be serious or substantial. The remoteness in question is less likely to be geographical than historical. It is those societies that are historically remote from our own that we have least in common with and that consequently we are least likely to be able to appraise.[4]

Williams's relativism of distance implies a strong commitment to the framing of political judgment within historical context. If regimes and societies can be appraised only by those standards that are historically appropriate to them, then that implies that there are many such standards depending on the historical circumstances. Different historical conditions give rise to different ethical criteria, hence different social and political ideals.

In particular, liberalism is, historically, only one legitimate political form among others. If liberalism were eternally valid, as some of its defenders suppose, they would need to provide a 'theory of error' to explain why pre-liberal societies and individuals got it so wrong (*Deed* 66). So far, no such theory of error has been forthcoming.[5] The more plausible view is that liberalism was not an appropriate or conceivable form of political legitimacy in those historical circumstances that obtained in the remote past. It is neither necessary nor relevant nor helpful to upbraid past non-liberal societies for not being liberal.

However, Williams argues that liberalism is valid under current historical circumstances; indeed, liberalism is the only valid form of political legitimacy 'now and around here' (*Deed* 8). This last phrase is not defined and looks ambiguous. It may refer narrowly to contemporary liberal democracy, in which case Williams's claim amounts to a truism.[6] More probably it refers more widely to 'modernity' as interpreted by social thinkers such as Weber and Habermas (*Deed* 9). Liberalism, that is, is peculiarly suited to modern social conditions marked by the decline of traditional authority, pluralism of culture and belief, individualism, critical reflection, and rational, bureaucratic forms of social control (*Deed* 9, 38, 42). Williams summarizes his view in the slogan, 'LEG [legitimacy] + Modernity = Liberalism' (*Deed* 9). By and large it is only liberalism that is appropriate for modernity, at any rate 'now and around here'.

Note that Williams's argument here, if it succeeds, provides a further reply to Kekes's complaint (mentioned in the previous chapter) that liberalism is necessarily at odds with pluralism. According to Kekes, liberals claim that their values

– for example, negative liberty – override others in all circumstances, which is precisely what pluralism denies. Already in Chapter 1, we saw that this is not true in the case of Berlin, who insists that negative liberty is not overriding but contextual. Similarly, Williams offers a defense of liberalism that is not absolute but expressly limited by political and historical context, the latter being the context of modernity.

If we go on to ask what kind of liberalism fits best with modernity, Williams is especially drawn to Judith Shklar's 'liberalism of fear' (*Deed* ch. 5). This is an austere, self-consciously anti-utopian liberalism whose focus is the prevention of the worst evils rather than the pursuit of higher ideals and more ambitious social goals, as in the 'liberalism of natural rights' whose ancestor is John Locke, or the 'liberalism of personal development' associated with J. S. Mill (*Deed* 55). The central aim of the liberalism of fear is to secure freedom in the most basic sense: 'from the abuse of power and the intimidation of the defenceless' (*Deed* 54). Its focus is again on the most universal of political concerns: 'power, powerlessness, fear, cruelty, a universalism of negative capacities' (*Deed* 59). Consequently, Williams argues, the liberalism of fear has genuinely global application in the modern world, although he expresses a wariness of global agendas in practice.

The liberalism of fear links with another aspect of Williams's political thought, one that emerged in some of his last work, namely his realism.[7] The context here is that of politics or 'the political'. At its broadest, the idea of the political refers to the essence or heart of political experience. What is it that is most distinctive about political affairs in contrast with other aspects of human affairs – for example, the personal, the cultural, and so on? To this question, many answers have been given. It follows that the role that might be played by the political in resolving conflicts among plural and incommensurable values depends on the particular account of the political in play. Some of these are more plausible than others.

One account is the classical view according to which the political is the field in which the state enforces or makes possible the best possible life for its citizens. Aristotle, for example, defines political association as 'the most sovereign of all', therefore aiming at 'the most sovereign of all goods' (Aristotle 1946 [n.d.]: 1). The good life possible at the level of the polis is the highest form of human life, in which citizens relate to one another as fully ethical beings, governed by their reason. This contrasts with subordinate levels of social life, the family and household, in which less exalted ends are pursued.

Clearly, however, the classical view can be ruled out as a guide for contemporary pluralist politics straight away, for two reasons. First, such a hierarchy among basic ends is denied by pluralism. Second, we have noted already (Chapter 3) that reasonable disagreement about the content of the good life is pervasive within modern societies. The political cannot now be conceived as the pursuit of a unitary conception of the highest human good. At best it might be imagined, as on the liberal model of Rawls (1971, 1993) and others, as an agreed framework of rights and obligations within which divergent conceptions of the good may coexist peacefully.

At the opposite end of the spectrum from classical perfectionism, the political has often, especially in the modern world, been conceived as a sphere ultimately dominated not by any idealistic conception of the good life but by the brutal reality of power. Hobbes, for example, sees the state as holding back what would in its absence be a state of nature that amounts to a state of war. The anarchical power of competitors in the state of nature is replaced by the orderly power of the sovereign, who is capable of settling disputes by force. The sovereign's title to rule is based on its sheer capacity to do so, and the moment that power is lost the sovereign's privileges disappear. The realm of politics thus aims at no higher good than order. It does not matter how disputes about the good life are determined, only that they be determined effectively.

Among pluralists, the agonists would tend to fall into this latter category. If fundamental values are like Weber's warring gods, then power rather than the good life is indeed the keynote of politics, since fundamental conflicts can only be managed by the use of political power, not reasoned agreement. But the limitations of this view have been seen already. None of the agonists, not even Schmitt, is willing to endorse the use of power without some kind of ethical constraint, but none of them can give an account of this that is not arbitrary. Moreover, the underlying assumption that there can be no reasoned ranking of fundamental goods, even in context, is untrue to lived ethical experience.

Somewhere between the idealism of Aristotle and the arbitrariness of the agonists lies the territory of realism. This has a long lineage that includes thinkers such as Machiavelli, but in the recent political-theory literature realism has two principal aspects. First, realists are united by the view that the 'high liberalism' of Rawls, Dworkin, and others 'represents a desire to evade, displace or escape from politics' (Galston 2010: 386). Focusing on the justification of broad principles through systems of abstract reasoning, the high liberals (the realists say) ignore the real stuff of politics, which is less to do with principles, ideals, and reasoned agreement, and more to do with power, interests, and various forms of conflict.

Second, most current realist writers – at any rate those 'prescriptive' realists who have some course of political action or attitude to recommend (Freeden 2012: 1) – nevertheless have normative principles of their own. 'If conflict is ineliminable', Galston writes, 'it is natural to see the ordering and channelling of conflict as the core of politics from which the rest radiates' (Galston 2010: 397). Consequently, the dominant normative commitment of realists is to the achievement and preservation of social and political order: 'preventing the worst is the first duty of political leaders, and striving for far-reaching social improvement makes sense when doing so does not significantly increase the odds that some previous abated evil will reappear' (Galston 2010: 394). Realists tend to value social order above other goods, such as justice, liberty, equality, and so on.

Williams embraces both of these aspects of realism. On the one hand, he emphasizes the distinctiveness of the political sphere. In this respect, he condemns much of the existing body of Anglo-American moral and political philosophy for its 'moralism', referring to 'views that make the moral prior to the political' (*Deed* 2). Rawls is Williams's chief critical target in this respect. In both his earlier and later work, Rawls holds political decisions and institutions to account at the bar of justice. For Williams, this denies the distinctiveness or autonomy of political thought and action, the unique realm of 'the political', which he hopes to restore. Berlin is also a moralist according to Williams's definition. Williams might also have mentioned, but does not, Berlin's comment that 'political theory is a branch of moral philosophy, which starts from the discovery, or application, of moral notions in the sphere of political relations' (*L* 168).

On the other hand, Williams accepts that part of what is distinctive about the political is that it has its own ethic. The political generates its own values, and paramount among these is social order. Williams's account of the normative content of the political begins with what he calls 'the "first" political question', namely how to secure the fundamental goods of 'order, protection, safety, trust, and the conditions of cooperation' – Hobbes's question (*Deed* 3). This mirrors Williams's framework notion of the universal evils, 'power, powerlessness, fear, cruelty' (*Deed* 59) and implies his parsimonious conception of the most basic human rights that address those evils. The first priority of a political system is to uphold those rights and thereby prevent the evils they are intended to combat. It does so by instituting a state that is prepared to use force and coercion to secure order.

However, Williams adds that the state must also be legitimate. The political system that is intended to guarantee order must not do so in a manner that amounts to a new tyranny – as it arguably does in the case of Hobbes's sovereign. Rather, the system must be in some sense legitimate – it must be entitled to the allegiance of its people – rather than a regime of sheer force: 'might is not, in itself, right' (*Deed* 23).

In Williams's terminology, the system must meet the 'basic legitimacy demand (BLD)' (*Deed* 4). The key feature of the BLD is that its precise terms in any particular case must be 'acceptable' to all those – 'every subject' – over whom the state exercises its authority (*Deed* 4, 6). The terms are acceptable when they are actually accepted by most of those concerned, subject to a 'critical theory principle' that acceptance is not valid if it is 'itself produced by the coercive power which is supposedly being justified' (*Deed* 6).

Crucially, the precise content of the BLD is subject to historical context, which returns us to the historical dimension of Williams's political thought. Political legitimacy may take a number of different forms depending on the historical circumstances. Hence, the BLD may be met in different ways under different historical conditions. Under the conditions of modernity, however, the BLD is satisfactorily met only by liberalism.

To sum up: Williams endorses the central features of Berlin's value pluralism, and so is confronted by the same problem of value ranking, in particular when it comes to the defense of liberalism. His dominant response is also like that of Berlin: contextualism. In the case of Williams, however, the key context is not that of cultural tradition. Rather, he focuses on two kinds of context, political and historical. Within the context of politics, a realist approach points toward the liberalism of fear. Within the context of history, liberalism can be justified in the circumstances of modernity. I now consider Williams's treatment of these two contexts in greater detail, beginning with realism.

The Realist Context

How far can Williams's realist emphasis on order and legitimacy be maintained consistently with his value pluralism? While realism seems to make order and legitimacy overriding, or at any rate answers 'the first political question', pluralism denies that any value can have that status. While the two aspects of Williams's thought can be reconciled to a degree, a tension between them cannot be dispelled altogether. To the extent that Williams advances a realist stress on order, his pluralism is under pressure; to the degree that he follows the imperatives of his pluralism, his position ceases to be distinctively realist.

In one important respect, there is no problem. Williams's realist theme of the distinctiveness of political values is in keeping with the pluralist insight that there are different kinds of values and norms. This in turn connects with Williams's theme of the complexity of ethics and his hostility toward the monist simplifications of modern moral philosophy. The 'untidiness' of lived normative experience has been noted as a theme shared by Williams and his fellow-realist Raymond Geuss (Hall and Sleat 2017: 281). Normative untidiness – the interplay of multiple values of different kinds – is a pluralist theme too.

Further, it might be thought that Williams does not violate value pluralism because he does not claim that any value overrides all others in all circumstances. It was noted earlier that Berlin's defense of negative liberty is subject to multiple political and historical conditions. Williams holds a similar position. To begin with, it is only within the context of the political that Williams sees order and legitimacy as values to be emphasized. In the private sphere, it may be that personal integrity, for example, is the weightiest consideration for an individual agent, as Williams famously argues against the utilitarians (Williams 1973: 108–18).

Indeed, Williams does not claim that order and legitimacy are overriding even within the political context. Again, his view parallels Berlin's treatment of negative liberty according to which that value, although usually dominant in liberal politics, sometimes defers to other considerations. Similarly, the best word to describe Williams's view of the political value of order and legitimacy is 'emphasis': the weighting he places on these values as opposed to others is a matter of emphasis rather than an absolute ranking, even assuming the realm of politics. Order and legitimacy are usually to be regarded as politically weightier than other values, but not necessarily always. There may be occasions where they have to be balanced against other concerns, and there may even be exceptional situations where such rival concerns outrank them. It is not hard to imagine revolutionary circumstances where values such as liberty or justice may have stronger claims at least for a time.

Such an approach seems to be more in line with Williams's general ethical outlook than a more rigid insistence that order and legitimacy are political absolutes. If this is right, then Williams's position on the claims of order and legitimacy is not once but twice removed from value monism. The primacy of order and legitimacy is not only contextualized by politics, but even within that sphere it is a matter of emphasis rather than an absolute.

However, it may still be asked whether, within the political context, Williams's highlighting of order and legitimacy is justified, even as a matter of emphasis. After all, other values are often advanced in politics. Why should these be regarded as less worthy of emphasis than order and legitimacy?

The most obvious alternative candidate is justice. What, for example, of Rawls's claim that 'Justice is the first virtue of social institutions, as truth is of systems of thought' (Rawls 1971: 3)? 'Laws and institutions', writes Rawls, 'no matter how efficient and well-arranged must be reformed or abolished if they are unjust'; 'an injustice is tolerable only when it is necessary to avoid an even greater injustice'; justice (along with truth) is 'uncompromising' (Rawls 1971: 3, 4).

It seems from these remarks that in the context of politics Rawls regards justice as not merely of equal importance with other values, including order and legitimacy, but overriding.[8] I do not mean to defend that contention, but Rawls's position does raise a significant issue that pluralists would be inclined to take seriously. Many people would agree with Rawls that justice is at least a fundamentally important value in politics on a level with order and legitimacy and that the proper relation among all these values is one of balance. Why should we accept Williams's view that in politics order and legitimacy must be emphasized and that justice should take a back seat?

Williams's basic answer is that social order and political legitimacy are fundamental to politics in a way that justice is not. The answer is not that order and legitimacy have a universality that justice lacks. Williams acknowledges justice, at least in a bare, 'primitive' sense, to be a universal concern in ethics, although this is too thin an idea to tell us much (Williams 1995: 138, 143). He takes much the same view of order and legitimacy, as I explain in a moment. These may be values present universally in politics, but they mean little until they are shaped by politics in its specific, local form.

So, in what sense does Williams claim that order and legitimacy are more fundamental to politics than justice is? His answer is that, unlike justice, order and legitimacy are 'inherent' in the political. Justice is a universal moral value that is extended or projected onto politics. But order and legitimacy are concerns generated from within politics. Unlike some realists, Williams does not deny that the political is an ethical sphere, since it includes the restraints of order and legitimacy as required by the BLD. But the BLD 'does not represent a morality which is prior to politics'; rather, 'it is a claim that is inherent in there being such a thing as politics' (*Deed* 5). The first political question is how to achieve social order, and the answer is basically state coercion. But state coercion must be legitimate in order not to be part of the problem, so the political is not a realm of power alone but a combination of power and legitimacy. Given a starting point in the nature of politics thus understood, the BLD is internal to politics rather than a prior morality.

Some critics have argued that Williams's political ethic is not wholly internal to politics but depends on an external morality, and so should count as moralist after all (Freeden 2012; Larmore 2013). The objection runs as follows. Supposing that the BLD is inherent in our understanding of politics, as above, one can still ask, what is Williams's justification of politics? His answer refers to 'the first political question' of how to secure the basic goods (order, etc.). But the basic goods are not themselves inherent in politics; rather, they are prior to politics, which is a response to the question of how to secure them (Larmore 2013: 291).[9] So, on this view, Williams's whole argument is driven by goods external to politics and is therefore moralistic.

However, does this interpretation of Williams mistake the basic shape of his argument? Edward Hall would say it does:

> rather than beginning with an antecedent moral view that is applied to politics, [Williams] begins by looking at the existent character of political rule and asks if we can extract an internal ethic from it, hence his suggestion that the BLD "is implicit in the very idea of a legitimate state, and so is inherent in any politics".
>
> (Hall 2015: 468–9)

Hall sees Williams's whole argument as starting from the de facto practice of politics, from which ethical constraints are then derived, a neat reversal of the standard moralist move from ethical standards to forms of politics. On this view all the norms in Williams's argument are internal to the actual practice of politics. Such a view seems to fit with Williams's fondness for Goethe's maxim, 'In the beginning was the deed' (*Deed* 14, 24).

The critics reply, however, that the actual practice of politics, considered universally, is consistent with such a variety of norms that it hardly supports Williams's values of order and legitimacy at all. If the 'primitive core' of justice is too thin to indicate any substantial ethic, the primitive core of the political is too thin to indicate any substantial form of politics. There are forms of politics in which order is not highly valued, at least the state-centered order that Williams assumes. Even if, contrary to their stereotype, most anarchists do advance a vision of order in society, this will not be the kind of order that is imposed by the state.[10] In the case of legitimacy, Michael Freeden objects that such a norm is not 'inherent in any politics', because politics is not necessarily legitimate: 'Politics can, contra Williams, also include terrorism and acts that would be very hard to regard as legitimate' (Freeden 2012: 6). If politics is not necessarily legitimate, then the norm of legitimacy does not derive from politics itself but is external to it. Consequently, Williams's position would be, again, moralist.

Between these opposed readings, a reasonable via media might be formulated as follows. *Some* notion of order and legitimacy is indeed inherent in any politics – even anarchists want order (without the state) and terrorists usually try to justify their actions. However, it is a further question whether the particular versions of order and legitimacy advanced by Williams are inherent in all conceptions of politics. His account of legitimacy, in particular, looks distinctly liberal. Its reliance on notions of acceptance or acceptability invokes the classical liberal criterion for legitimacy, namely the consent of the governed. This is only one way of understanding legitimacy, another being the notion of Divine Right of Kings that was dominant in Western political thought before liberalism. So, has Williams not imported his preferred criterion for legitimacy from some source external to the practice of politics as such?

Williams would respond that the practice of politics must always be considered in historical context. The primitive core of the political is indeed too thin to provide much guidance, so we must look to local practices. When it comes to local or historically specific attitudes to legitimacy, Williams notes that, of course, the liberal version of legitimacy has been only one among others. However, liberal legitimacy is the only form that is valid 'now and around here'. That kind of legitimacy is internal to any politics under current historical conditions.

This is still problematic. As noted earlier, the phrase 'now and around here' is ambiguous. If it is interpreted to mean 'contemporary liberal democracies', then Williams's liberal criteria are indeed inherent in politics, but only because he has stipulated a context that makes his claim true by definition. He is then telling us very little. On the other hand, if, as seems more likely, 'now and around here' refers to the wider notion of modernity, then on the face of it Williams's claim is untrue. Modernity has included many non-liberal strands of politics, so liberal legitimacy does not seem to be obviously inherent in modernity as such.

Perhaps, though, Williams would argue that liberal legitimacy is something like the fullest expression of distinctively modern politics, non-liberal forms being only anachronistic leftovers of previous epochs. If so, his argument is incomplete, needing a more detailed account of modernity in which the special link with liberalism is confirmed. I return to this issue later.

Let us suppose that the values of social order and political legitimacy are inherent in the political sphere of life, subject to the qualification that particular forms of legitimacy (and order) vary with historical context. How does this settle the question of emphasis between order and legitimacy on the one hand and justice on the other? That question remains open because it remains open to the defenders of justice to assert the equal (or incommensurable) claims of that value in balance with order and legitimacy.

They might do this in either of two ways. First, they might argue that justice is no less inherent in politics than are order and legitimacy – Rawls's assertion.

Could this be refuted? One way of doing so would be to argue that justice is an inappropriate imposition on politics from a wholly alien sphere. This might use the model developed in Michael Walzer's *Spheres of Justice* (1983), which proposes that there are distinct spheres of life, each of which has a set of internal norms that is appropriate to that particular sphere, but inappropriate, indeed 'unjust', when applied to other spheres.[11] Surely, however, this would be going too far in the case of Williams's view of the application of justice to politics. His claim is not that justice is wholly inappropriate in politics, rather that justice is somehow less fundamental than order and legitimacy. But again, fundamental in what sense?

Perhaps Williams means that order and legitimacy are distinctively public concerns, while justice is really a private matter that is applied to politics only by some kind of metaphorical extension. This is the view of Friedrich Hayek, for example, who argues that justice is properly a matter of fair dealing between individuals and that the notion of 'social justice' as an attribute of a whole society is misplaced (Hayek 1976). But again, Hayek would be a strange bedfellow for Williams, who does believe in the coherence and possibility of social justice (Jubb 2015: 923).

Further, why should Willams believe that justice is imported from private to public rather than the other way round? The opposite view is advanced by Hampshire, who argues that the way justice is done in public, through open debate in which each party hears the other side, is the model for private, intra-personal impartiality (*JC* 6–12). My point is not that Hampshire is right about this, only that his view issues an implicit challenge to Williams's. Why should Williams suppose that the origins of justice are any less inherent in politics than the origins of order and legitimacy? He does not say.

Defenders of justice might argue against Williams in a second way. Even if we suppose that order and legitimacy are in some sense more inherently political than is justice, it is not clear what follows from this. Those who want more from their politics than bare order and legitimacy (nearly everyone) will still be inclined to appeal to notions of justice. Or to put it another way, most people will be inclined to expand the idea of the political to include some notion of justice. Even if order and legitimacy possess an inherently political character that justice does not, the following propositions may still be true: (1) justice is still an important concern in politics; (2) justice is indeed *no less* important a concern in politics than are order and legitimacy; (3) compared with order and legitimacy, justice is sometimes *more* important to political actors.

At this point Williams has produced no convincing argument to support the greater emphasis he places on social order and legitimacy, compared with justice, within the political sphere. It may be true that the values of order and legitimacy are inherent in any politics and, more controversially, that liberal readings of these are inherent in any modern politics. But it can then be replied that justice is no less inherent in politics or that, even if justice is less inherent, it is no less important in that sphere than order and legitimacy.

Order as a Precondition

Perhaps, though, Williams's realist norms should be conceived not as values in competition with other values but as preconditions for the enjoyment of any value. Along these lines, Galston describes realists as holding 'that civil order is the *sine qua non* for every other political good' (Galston 2010: 408).[12] So, we could say that order and legitimacy are preconditions for justice in the sense that we need order and legitimacy before justice can become a practical proposition. This is not the same as saying that order and legitimacy are more valuable than justice, so it avoids the problem of ranking under pluralism altogether.

To clarify, we can distinguish two senses of 'priority'. On the one hand, priority may be evaluative or normative, so that 'X is prior to Y' means that 'X is more valuable than Y'. On the other hand, there is a sequential sense: X can be prior to Y in the sense that X has to be achieved before Y is practicable. Priority can be sequential without being evaluative or normative. A builder has to build the foundations of a house before its roof, but that does not mean the foundations have greater value than the roof; both contribute in different ways to the house overall.

If Williams is claiming that order and legitimacy are preconditions for other values, then he is claiming only a sequential rather than evaluative priority for order and legitimacy. He is not saying that order and legitimacy are weightier or more important goods than justice and liberty, only that order and legitimacy must be achieved first in order to make justice and liberty practicable. In that case, his position is thoroughly consistent with his value pluralism because he is not ranking these values normatively at all.

But then it becomes questionable whether Williams should still be counted as, distinctively, a realist. On the precondition account, he is no longer saying that order and legitimacy must be ranked above rival values, even as a matter of emphasis and even within the context of the political. In what, then, does his realism consist? Crucially, is he saying anything that could not be said by a so-called moralist? It seems to me that the answer is no: the claim that order and legitimacy are preconditions for other values can also be made by a moralist.

Rawls, for example, supposedly the arch-moralist, can agree – does agree – that security must be established before his theory of justice as fairness can apply. To see this, consider his distinction between 'general' and 'special' conceptions of justice. The familiar Rawlsian formula for justice as fairness involves a 'lexical' order according to which the first principle, the equal distribution of basic rights and liberties, overrides the constrained social and economic inequalities permitted by the second principle. This is Rawls's 'special conception' of justice, and its application assumes that the basic rights and liberties of the first principle can be enforced, that there is sufficient security (order and legitimacy) for the primacy of liberty to be effective. When that is not the case, 'when social conditions do not allow the effective establishment of these rights', the special conception is replaced by the general conception (Rawls 1971: 152). The general conception omits the lexical order, requiring an equal distribution of all 'social values', including the basic rights and liberties, but allowing an unequal distribution if that is 'to everyone's advantage' (Rawls 1971: 62). In effect, Rawls is saying that security is crucial: it is an essential precondition for the kind of justice he wants to defend, namely the special conception.

The positions held by Williams and Rawls are not identical, but they are closer than Williams's hostility to Rawls would lead us to expect. Rawls also says that where there is insufficient security his position reverts to the general conception, so that *some* notion of justice applies to social institutions in any situation. He does not quite say, as it seems Williams would, that security is a precondition for the application of any kind of justice. Still, it is only a short step from Rawls to Williams. Rawls acknowledges the possibility of a society that lacks security (order and legitimacy), and he recognizes that a lack of security influences which other social values can reasonably be aspired to. More specifically, he allows that without security we can aspire only to a less demanding, looser form of justice, the general conception. It is no great distance from there to Williams's view that in the absence of adequate security it is unrealistic to hope for any kind of social justice. That further step is especially plausible if we emphasize practicality. Even Rawls's general conception of justice requires the equal distribution of social values as a default position. Without security, that will not be practicable.

This interpretation of Williams fits with recent work arguing that the gap between Rawls and Williams is narrower than the latter claims (Jubb 2015; Thomas 2017). Robert Jubb, for example, notes that in Rawls's later work his theory of justice as fairness is framed by an understanding of politics that overlaps Williams's to a significant degree. Among other things, both take seriously 'Isaiah Berlin's claim that there is no social world without loss' – that is, value pluralism (Jubb 2015: 925). Rawls's 'political' liberalism is made necessary by the 'fact of reasonable pluralism' that has been characteristic of modern societies since the Reformation. This in turn is based on the 'burdens of judgement', some of which are basically formulations of pluralism, a point confirmed by Rawls's explicit referencing of Berlin.[13]

Jubb sees Williams as taking value pluralism more seriously than Rawls, since 'for Williams the comparatively unified account of political values Rawls hopes for is impossible because of the extent of conflict between values' (Jubb 2015: 925). It may be true that Rawls expects more agreement in the face of pluralism than does Williams. Rawls maintains his case for justice as fairness on the basis of an 'overlapping consensus' among different comprehensive moral doctrines.

Still, there is a case for seeing Williams and Rawls as overlapping to a greater extent even than that allowed by Jubb. Williams's value pluralism does not prevent the possibility of reasoned choice among competing values in context, so to that extent it does not rule out the possibility of agreement. For his part, Rawls, like Williams, constructs his argument within a series of nested contexts. His starting point, like Williams's, is historical, in the modern fact of reasonable pluralism. Second, Rawls applies his argument only to the 'public political culture' of 'constitutional democracies', equivalent to the narrow reading of Williams's 'now and around here' qualification. Third, even within that political-cultural context, Rawls argues that justice as fairness need apply only for public purposes, not necessarily as a comprehensive moral doctrine to which people need be committed in private. This aligns with Williams's conception of the political as an autonomous realm generating its own distinctive values, although in Rawls's case the values in question include a conception of justice.

Rawls's overlapping consensus may be too optimistic, but his contextual method is similar to that used by Williams. Both are conscious of the rival claims of incommensurable ideals, and both seek to address these within an explicitly historical, cultural, and political context, or a nested series of contexts. Both see order and legitimacy as preconditions for other values. Both allow that justice is one of those values. Seen in this light, the supposedly realist Williams and the allegedly moralist Rawls would seem to have little between them.

In the end, Williams's political thought can be reconciled with his value pluralism, but only at the cost of distancing him from a distinctively realist position. If his argument were the characteristically realist one that social order is always paramount over other ethical concerns, then that claim would clearly be contradicted by his pluralism. But Williams does not go that far. At most he claims only that order has especially strong normative claims in the context of politics, and even then that its significance is a matter of emphasis rather than overridingness. Nevertheless, pluralism still prompts us to ask for a justification of that normative emphasis, especially against the apparently equally strong claims of justice. To this question, Williams produces no convincing reply. His view might then be reinterpreted as the claim that order is not normatively but only sequentially prior to other values: a precondition rather than a superior value. Thus restated, his position is wholly consistent with pluralism. However, the price for that consistency is that his position is no longer distinctively realist, since it can be held by so-called moralists like Rawls.

LEG + Modernity = Liberalism

The realist aspect of Williams's response to the problem of value pluralism may be unsatisfactory, but what about his stress on history? Recall that his general claim is that competing incommensurables can be ranked in historical context. More specifically, a characteristically liberal ranking is justified, and uniquely so, under the conditions of modernity. How far is that true?

As noted in Chapter 1, there are traces of such a view in Berlin. In the last paragraph of 'Two Concepts', he seems to place the argument of the essay within the historical framework of 'our declining capitalist civilisation' (*L* 217). Nevertheless, Berlin continues (quoting Schumpeter), the fact that our beliefs are historically bounded should not make us any less devoted to them: 'to realise the relative validity of one's convictions and yet stand for them unflinchingly is what distinguishes a civilised man from a barbarian'. Part of what it means to have developed fully as a human being is to understand that our beliefs are conditioned by history.

What does this historical contextualism mean for political ideas? Michael Sandel gives one answer:

> Although Berlin is not strictly speaking a relativist – he affirms the ideal of freedom of choice – his position comes perilously close to foundering on the relativist predicament. If one's convictions are only relatively valid, why stand for them unflinchingly? In a tragically-configured moral universe, such as Berlin assumes, is the ideal of freedom any less subject than competing ideals to the ultimate incommensurability of values? If so, in what can its privileged status consist? And if freedom has no morally privileged status, if it is just one value among many, then what can be said for liberalism?
>
> (Sandel 1984: 8)

On this view, the historical contextualization proposed by Berlin is too wide. It is consistent with multiple different rankings of competing incommensurable values, depending on one's historical perspective. Any such perspective could have been otherwise, so why should our own perspective carry more conviction with us than any other?

Berlin's answer seems to be that we are committed to our liberal values simply because they are ours.

> In the end, men choose between ultimate values; they choose as they do because their life and thought are determined by fundamental moral categories and concepts that are, at any rate over large stretches of time and space, and whatever their ultimate origins, a part of their being and thought and sense of their own identity; part of what makes them human.
>
> (*L* 217)

But that reasoning would apply to any set of values. If our values happened to be fascist or communist (as might well have been the case if crucial historical events had turned out differently), then we would be just as committed to them. So far, the appeal to history, in support of liberalism in particular, has generated little justificatory weight.

Does Williams's historical case for liberalism fare any better? A good place to start is his essay, 'Philosophy as a Humanistic Discipline' (2006). There Williams says that what we are looking for in general is the 'vindication' of our beliefs and values (e.g., liberal values of liberty and equality) – that is, their justification against the alternatives (Williams 2006: 190). Might we possess vindicatory arguments that justify liberal values and refute those of non-liberal or pre-liberal regimes?

Unfortunately, what history tells us, Williams argues, is that there are no such vindicatory arguments. History explains how the values that are dominant for us have come to be dominant. It shows that liberal value rankings have prevailed – at least in some parts of the world. But they have prevailed not as a result of arguments being won. For an argument to be won, our opponents have to come round to accept our point of view. But the intellectual representatives of pre-liberal regimes had too little in common with liberals for that to happen. Rather, the transition from pre-liberal to liberal value rankings was 'propelled by many crises ... of confidence or of legitimacy' (Williams 2006: 191). History shows not that pre-liberal thinkers eventually accepted the arguments of their liberal opponents but that they gradually, or through a series of sudden jolts, lost confidence in the force of their own ideas. It is not arguments that drive historical change in the field of values but crises of confidence that have various origins and characters.

Might we say, then, that history vindicates our values not by indicating winning arguments but by narrating a vindicatory story? Perhaps it is the explanation of historical change itself that vindicates change: history might demonstrate a certain pattern that shows our current ideas to be superior to those of the past. Williams rejects this too, associating it with the discredited historicism of Hegel and Marx. Current philosophical understandings do not favor such historicist outlooks; we do not believe that history automatically vindicates the present.

And yet, Williams adds, we do need some kind of historical account that helps us to vindicate our beliefs. We need this

> if we are to know what reflective attitude to take to our own conceptions. For one thing, the answer to the question whether there is a history of our own conceptions that is vindicatory (if only modestly so) makes a difference to what we are doing when we say, if we do say, that the earlier conceptions were wrong.
>
> (Williams 2006: 191)

We need to assess our own values and value rankings, and this has to be done within some kind of historical perspective.

Williams's conclusion in 'Philosophy as a Humanistic Discipline' seems to be, very much like Berlin's in 'Two Concepts', that our current values are, if not vindicated, at any rate *ours*. When we learn from history that our liberal values are contingent on various accidents and crises that might have turned out otherwise, we are apt to be disappointed. But we should not be.

> Precisely because we are not unencumbered intelligences selecting in principle among all possible outlooks, we can accept that this outlook is ours

just because of the history that has made it ours; or, more precisely, has both made us and made the outlook as something that is ours.

(Williams 2006: 193)

History explains how we and our values have developed together. We cannot help identifying with our own values.

For all Williams's sophistication does this amount to saying much more than whatever history gives us has to be accepted? Admittedly, the results of history are not justified, on Williams's view, since vindication has been ruled out. Instead, we are told that history makes us who we are, and therefore our values along with us. One immediate problem is that we may be divided as to what our values are, or ambivalent about them. Presumably Williams would reply that, if so, that is our identifying inheritance and we must make the best of it. More disturbingly, we can imagine the contingencies of history turning out very differently from the way they have. Nazi Germany might have prevailed in the Second World War or the Soviet Union in the Cold War. Would we then have to say of our resulting totalitarian values that, in Williams's phrase, 'this outlook is ours just because of the history that has made it ours'?

Williams takes a different and perhaps more promising approach in 'Realism and Moralism in Political Theory' (in *Deed*). There he seems to use history not only to vindicate liberal values but to do so by means of a vindicatory argument. This is the argument outlined earlier in the chapter. The form taken by political legitimacy depends on historical conditions. These do not necessarily favor liberalism; indeed, in the broader context of human history they have seldom done so. Under modern conditions, however, liberalism is the only valid form of legitimacy.

> Now and around here the BLD together with the historical conditions permit only a liberal solution; other forms of answer are unacceptable. In part, this is for the Enlightenment reason that other supposed legitimations are now seen as to be false and in particular ideological.
>
> (*Deed* 8)

Williams's view is encapsulated in his slogan 'LEG + modernity = liberalism' (*Deed* 9).

These passages invoke three different criteria for the unique contemporary validity of the liberal form of legitimacy. First, liberal legitimacy is said to be required 'now and around here'. The ambiguity of this expression has already been noted, along with its justificatory problems in either case. If it refers to contemporary developed societies, then the claim is a truism; if it embraces all societies in modernity, then it is false.

Indeed, Williams's second criterion for legitimacy, the authority of the Enlightenment, cuts across the first criterion and links with the point just made. Liberalism is, of course, closely connected to the Enlightenment, but other views are consistent with the Enlightenment too, such as socialism. Perhaps socialism is among those views Williams would say is now regarded as false and ideological, but he does not explain why. The political failure of state communism in Europe and its de facto transformation in China do not exhaust the intellectual resources of socialism as a whole. Social democracy, for example, remains a significant force both intellectually and politically, although perhaps Williams would say that this kind of socialism is liberal at heart.

Third, the authority of liberal legitimacy is said to be in keeping with 'modernity'. Williams's most substantial statement on this link is

> the basically sociological point, that the legitimations appropriate to a modern state are essentially connected with the nature of modernity as the social thought of the past century, particularly that of Weber, has helped us to understand it. This includes organizational features (pluralism, etc., and bureaucratic forms of control), individualism, and cognitive aspects of authority (*Entzauberung*).
>
> (*Deed* 9)

Elsewhere he remarks that 'modernity is marked by the decline of traditional patterns of authority, and by secularization' (*Deed* 42).

The best one can say of this account of how modernity requires the politics of liberalism is that it is incomplete. Williams himself confesses that this is 'a very general sketch at a very high level of generality' (*Deed* 15). He adds that the picture he sketches has been satisfactorily elaborated by Weber and Habermas but he does not explain in what way. Suppose we accept that Williams has correctly identified the salient features of modernity. One may argue that pluralism (meaning Rawlsian de facto pluralism of conceptions of the good) and individualism rule out as inappropriate extreme forms of authoritarianism such as fascism and state communism – although someone might complain that these have both made plausible claims to represent certain aspects of the spirit of modernity. But neither these nor the remaining features – secularization, bureaucracy, and rationalist forms of authority – are enough to support a unique recommendation of liberalism.

For example, the features of modernity to which Williams draws attention seem compatible with such notably non-liberal political forms as the authoritarian capitalisms of East Asia and Russia. As John Gray writes, 'In China, and perhaps in parts of the post-Soviet world, market institutions may exist, and flourish, in combination with non-democratic regimes, for generations' (Gray 1995: 84). What makes this possible, in Gray's view, is the continuation under modern conditions of cultural forms that prioritize values other than personal autonomy. The East Asian experience in particular appears to show that modern economic development is compatible with an emphasis on 'the maintenance of social consensus and communal harmony' in preference to individual rights and liberties (Gray 1995: 83).[14] If that is the case, then Williams cannot make a case for liberalism simply by pointing to the historical context of modernity.

Freedom Rising

Williams does not satisfactorily link modernity with liberalism, but that does not mean that such a link cannot be made. A more complete account can be given if Williams is supplemented by the recent work of Christian Welzel. In Welzel's *Freedom Rising* (2013), there is a well-developed narrative not only of how liberalism has in fact emerged in modernity but of how liberalism is better suited than alternative forms of politics to the conditions that modernity has thrown up.

Welzel's basic theme, like that of Williams, is that liberal values and institutions emerge, and are justified, under certain historical conditions. For most of human history, ordinary people have struggled just to survive, and so have had little interest in the freedoms at the center of liberalism. 'Under existential pressures freedoms have little utility, so people place little value on them' (Welzel 2013: xxiv). What they want instead is security and order, the 'survival values' (Welzel 2013: 40), which are adequately supplied by authoritarian social and political systems. Those regimes are appropriate for those circumstances.[15]

However, the Scientific and Industrial Revolutions, by making it possible for people to meet their material needs so much more efficiently, made it possible for them to look beyond mere survival to a more liberal ethos. 'Fading existential pressures increase the utility of universal freedoms, and people begin to value those freedoms accordingly' (Welzel 2013: xxiv). Released from the struggle for survival, people begin to 'prioritise freedom over security, autonomy over authority, diversity over uniformity, and creativity over discipline' (Welzel 2013: xxii). In short, the 'emancipative' values and ultimately the institutions of liberalism become valuable and justified under the conditions of modernity.

Welzel's schema is both descriptive and normative. Clearly, it is a description of the development of liberal democracy in the wake of the Scientific and Industrial Revolutions, and a distillation of the elements of that account into a set of social-science propositions. Those propositions are subjected by Welzel to extensive testing using empirical data from sources such as the World Values Surveys. But his account is normative too, since it amounts to a contextual justification of liberal democracy. Given the resources provided by the Industrial Revolution, Welzel is saying, the emancipative values of liberalism, backed by the civic guarantees of liberal institutions, maximize human utilities – that is, they make the best use of human potentialities. Authoritarian political forms were rational in the pre-industrial world, when freedom had little utility and security came first. But in the industrial and post-industrial world, freedom has more utility and authoritarianism less.

Indeed, under modern conditions authoritarianism becomes a constraint: 'oppressive systems are unable to harness people's intrinsic motivations [their emancipative values], and this disables them to mobilize human intellect at its full scope' (Welzel 2013: 50). Authoritarian systems can, of course, mobilize their human resources to a degree, achieving rapid industrialization in the cases of the Soviet Union and Maoist China. But there are limits to what can be achieved beyond this. Welzel cites the instances of Soviet Russia and Nazi Germany, which he sees as experiments: 'Can one achieve technological leadership and global dominance while continuing people's disempowerment? With unfathomable human costs, the failure of both experiments suggests that one cannot' (Welzel 2013: 55).

Welzel goes on to question whether contemporary China's 'ambition for technological leadership will ... materialize unless it begins to empower its people' (Welzel 2013: 55). In this way, he provides a reply to Gray's 'East Asia' objection. The authoritarian model of modernity is likely to come up eventually against the drive for empowerment that is generated by the model's own success at creating material prosperity.

However, the East Asian case remains troubling. To take the central example of China, it may be that some progress toward liberalization and democratization has been made and that liberalism and democracy will be achieved in the future. But the stubborn reality remains that at present individual rights and liberties are restricted to such a degree in China that hopes for liberalization or democratization can only be described as speculative.

As just one indication of the direction China is taking, consider leadership succession. 'How a country manages the transfer of power at the very top sends an unmistakable signal to all levels below', John Thornton wrote in 2008, and he proceeded to argue that on such a test China was showing promising signs (Thornton 2008: 21). But in 2018 the President of China, Xi Jinping, was able to extend his power indefinitely when the National People's Congress abolished the presidential term limits in the constitution. That move does indeed send an unmistakable signal, but not one that will make liberals optimistic.

This is to say, once again, that 'modernity' is too broad a notion to provide anything like a vindicatory argument, or narrative, for liberalism. The modern world is perfectly capable of enabling deeply illiberal regimes and societies to exist and flourish. Modernity is compatible with multiple rankings of fundamental political values, some liberal, some not.

The same must be said of 'history', more generally. History ranks competing incommensurables only in the sense that historical circumstances place very broad constraints on what is possible or desirable at any particular time. As Welzel argues, for example, only at a certain level of economic development does the desire for individual liberty become capable of shaping a society. But as the East Asian case shows, that value may be offset by other fundamental goods that are also attractive under the same economic conditions, at least to people with a cultural background in which those goods are highlighted. Historical context is a framework, not a formula. Modernity is a necessary but not a sufficient condition for liberalism.

So, if we are looking for the justification of a characteristically liberal ranking of fundamental values under pluralism, we have not found it yet. History helps us to frame the argument within the conditions of modernity, but it does not supply the argument itself. For that, we need a different approach.

Conclusion

Two contexts within which conflicting incommensurables may be ranked are the political and the historical, and both are explored by Bernard Williams. In the case of the political, Williams advocates a realist understanding, according to which the values of order and legitimacy are given a special weighting. Even if this claim is a matter of emphasis only, the questions arises of whether it is consistent with value pluralism. May justice, in particular, not have as good a claim to political priority? Williams's response is ultimately unconvincing. Simply to establish that order and legitimacy are inherent in the political does not show that they must outweigh justice. Alternatively, Williams might abandon any claim to the normative priority of the realist values and present them as practical preconditions for the enjoyment of any value. But to take that line would be to jettison what is normatively distinctive about the realist position.

Williams's attention to historical context is to some extent harder to fault. He is right to argue that a characteristically liberal ranking of values, for example, makes sense only in a particular set of historical conditions rather than eternally. More specifically, liberalism can be justified only under the conditions of modernity. This thesis is fleshed out by the work of Christian Welzel, who shows how modern levels of economic development make it worthwhile for people to pursue 'emancipative values'. However, the argument becomes less persuasive when it turns into the stronger thesis that under modern conditions *only* liberalism is vindicated. Modernity is too broad a category to indicate liberalism as its sole legitimate political expression. To make a case for liberalism against its modern rivals, we need more than history.

Notes

1 For Williams's main treatments of value pluralism, see Williams 1979; *ELP*; 2001; 2013; Berlin and Williams 2013.
2 On Williams's ethics in general, see Altham and Harrison 1995; Jenkins 2006; Thomas 2007; Callcut 2009.
3 See also Williams 1981; *Deed* 69.
4 See also *ELP* 162; *Deed* 68–9. I question some aspects of the relativism of distance from a pluralist point of view in Crowder 2017.
5 But see the discussion in Tsai 2013.
6 For this narrow reading of the phrase, see Jubb 2015: 922.
7 Williams's political realism is examined by Flathman 2010; Frazer 2010; Galston 2010; Bavister-Gould 2011; Forrester 2012; Freeden 2012; Larmore 2013; Sleat 2013; Hall 2014, 2015; Jubb 2015; Sagar 2016.
8 Another qualification is that 'the circumstances of justice' must apply; that is, questions of justice arise only where there is 'moderate scarcity' giving rise to conflict over resources: Rawls 1971: 128. I discuss further Rawlsian preconditions for justice later.
9 See also Jubb 2015: 923.
10 For an account of how the classical anarchists believe that social order is possible without the state, see Crowder 1991.

11 This 'segregation' approach is critically examined from a pluralist perspective in Chapter 3.
12 Endorsed by Jubb 2015: 921.
13 Rawls 1993: 56–7. The value-pluralist elements of the burdens of judgment are identified in my *LVP*: 165–71 and in Galston's *LP*: 46.
14 Gray extends this point to 'Asian immigrants, whose cultural traditions do not valorize autonomy' but who are no worse off than those who do: Gray 1995: 213. He is responding to Joseph Raz, who argues that the central liberal ideal of personal autonomy is appropriate, even unavoidable, for all societies under 'the conditions of the industrial age and its aftermath with their fast changing technologies and free movement of labour': Raz 1986: 369.
15 This recalls the problem facing Riley in Chapter 2: substantial rights and liberties are not necessary for mere survival.

References

In-text abbreviations are noted in brackets.

Altham, J. E. J. and Ross Harrison, eds (1995), *World, Mind, and Ethics: Essays on the Ethical Philosophy of Bernard Williams* (Cambridge: Cambridge University Press).
Aristotle (1946 [n.d.]), *The Politics*, trans. Ernest Barker (Oxford: Oxford University Press).
Bavister-Gould, Alex (2011), 'Bernard Williams: Political Realism and the Limits of Legitimacy', *European Journal of Philosophy* 21 (4): 593–610.
Berlin, Isaiah (2002), *Liberty*, ed. Henry Hardy (Oxford: Oxford University Press). [*L*]
Berlin, Isaiah and Bernard Williams (2013), 'Pluralism and Liberalism', in Isaiah Berlin, *Concepts and Categories*, ed. Henry Hardy, 2nd edn (Princeton: Princeton University Press).
Callcut, Daniel, ed. (2009), *Reading Bernard Williams* (London: Routledge).
Crowder, George (1991), *Classical Anarchism: The Political Thought of Godwin Proudhon, Bakunin and Kropotkin* (Oxford: Clarendon Press).
Crowder, George (2002), *Liberalism and Value Pluralism* (London: Continuum). [*LVP*]
Crowder, George (2017), 'Value Pluralism vs Relativism in Bernard Williams's "Relativism of Distance"', *The Pluralist* 12 (3): 114–38.
Flathman, Richard (2010), 'In and Out of the Ethical: The Realist Liberalism of Bernard Williams', *Contemporary Political Theory* 9 (1): 77–98.
Forrester, Katrina (2012), 'Judith Shklar, Bernard Williams and Political Realism', *European Journal of Political Theory* 11 (3): 247–72.
Freeden, Michael (2012), 'Editorial: Interpretative Realism and Prescriptive Realism', *Journal of Political Ideologies* 17 (1): 1–11.
Frazer, Elizabeth (2010), 'What's Real in Political Philosophy?' *Contemporary Political Theory* 9: 490–507.
Galston, William (2002), *Liberal Pluralism: The Implications of Value Pluralism for Political Theory and Practice* (Cambridge: Cambridge University Press). [*LP*]
Galston, William (2010), 'Realism in Political Theory', *European Journal of Political Theory* 9 (4): 385–411.
Gray, John (1995), *Enlightenment's Wake: Politics and Culture at the Close of the Modern Age* (London: Routledge).
Hall, Edward (2014), 'Contingency, Confidence, and Liberalism in the Political Thought of Bernard Williams', *Social Theory and Practice* 40 (4): 545–69.

Hall, Edward (2015), 'Bernard Williams and the Basic Legitimation Demand: A Defence', *Political Studies* 63 (2): 466–80.
Hall, Edward and Matt Sleat (2017), 'Ethics, Morality and the Case for Realist Political Theory', *Critical Review of International Social and Political Philosophy* 20 (3): 278–95.
Hampshire, Stuart (2000), *Justice Is Conflict* (Princeton: Princeton University Press). [*JC*]
Hayek, Friedrich (1976), *The Mirage of Social Justice* (London: Routledge).
Jenkins, Mark P. (2006), *Bernard Williams* (Montreal and Kingston: McGill-Queen's University Press).
Jubb, Robert (2015), 'Playing Kant at the Court of King Arthur', *Political Studies* 63 (4): 919–34.
Larmore, Charles (2013), 'What Is Political Philosophy?' *Journal of Moral Philosophy* 10 (3): 276–306.
Rawls, John (1971), *A Theory of Justice* (Oxford: Oxford University Press).
Rawls, John (1993), *Political Liberalism* (New York: Columbia University Press).
Raz, Joseph (1986), *The Morality of Freedom* (Oxford: Clarendon Press).
Sagar, Paul (2016), 'From Scepticism to Liberalism? Bernard Williams, the Foundations of Liberalism and Political Realism', *Political Studies* 64 (2): 368–84.
Sandel, Michael (1984), 'Introduction', in Michael Sandel, ed., *Liberalism and Its Critics* (Oxford: Oxford University Press).
Sleat, Matt (2013), *Liberal Realism: A Realist Theory of Liberal Politics* (Manchester: Manchester University Press).
Thomas, Alan, ed. (2007), *Bernard Williams* (Cambridge: Cambridge University Press).
Thomas, Alan (2017), 'Rawls and Political Realism: Realistic Utopianism or Judgement in Bad Faith?', *European Journal of Political Theory* 16 (3): 304–24.
Thornton, John L. (2008), 'Long Time Coming: The Prospects for Democracy in China', *Foreign Affairs* 87 (1): 2–22.
Tsai, George (2013), 'An Error Theory for Liberal Universalism', *Journal of Political Philosophy* 21 (3): 305–25.
Walzer, Michael (1983), *Spheres of Justice: A Defence of Pluralism and Equality* (Oxford: Blackwell).
Welzel, Christian (2013), *Freedom Rising: Human Empowerment and the Quest for Emancipation* (Cambridge: Cambridge University Press).
Williams, Bernard (1973), 'A Critique of Utilitarianism', in J. J. C. Smart and Bernard Williams, eds, *Utilitarianism: For and Against* (Cambridge: Cambridge University Press).
Williams, Bernard (1979), 'Conflicts of Values', in Alan Ryan, ed., *The Idea of Freedom: Essays in Honour of Isaiah Berlin* (Oxford: Oxford University Press).
Williams, Bernard (1981), 'The Truth in Relativism', in *Moral Luck: Philosophical Papers 1973–1980* (Cambridge: Cambridge University Press).
Williams, Bernard (1985), *Ethics and the Limits of Philosophy* (Cambridge, MA: Harvard University Press). [*ELP*]
Williams, Bernard (1995), 'Saint-Just's Illusion', in *Making Sense of Humanity and Other Philosophical Papers* (Cambridge: Cambridge University Press).
Williams, Bernard (2001), 'Liberalism and Loss', in Ronald Dworkin, Mark Lilla, and Robert B. Silvers, eds, *The Legacy of Isaiah Berlin* (New York: New York Review Books).

Williams, Bernard (2005), *In the Beginning Was the Deed: Realism and Moralism in Political Argument* (Princeton: Princeton University Press). [*Deed*]

Williams, Bernard (2006), 'Philosophy as a Humanistic Discipline', in A. W. Moore, ed., *Philosophy as a Humanistic Discipline* (Princeton and Oxford: Princeton University Press).

Williams, Bernard (2013), 'Introduction' to Isaiah Berlin, *Concepts and Categories*, ed. Henry Hardy, 2nd edn (Princeton: Princeton University Press).

5 Diversity and Liberalism

The problem of value pluralism remains, at this stage, largely unresolved. We have seen that the great goods provide some guidance, but they are subject to such a wide range of legitimate interpretation, and they are so prone to conflict with one another, that the guidance they provide is limited. Similarly, the appeal to context is important but accounts of context – personal, cultural, historical, political – are various and conflicting. The historical framework of modernity does indicate a pluralist case for liberal democracy, but seems also to admit the legitimacy of authoritarian alternatives.

In this chapter, I begin to consider a different approach, one that seeks to identify norms by reflection on the concept of value pluralism itself. Hence, this may be called a conceptual or logical approach. May there not be features of the idea of value pluralism that suggest appropriate choices, or fields of choice, among conflicting incommensurable goods? Berlin, it is recalled, hints at such a move when he tries to link the concept of pluralism directly with the value of freedom of choice. That argument, I concluded, does not succeed, but may there not be another such conceptual move that would be more convincing?

The argument I want to consider first can be labeled the 'diversity' argument. It begins with the concept of pluralism, which is shown to imply a norm of value multiplicity. This is qualified by the need for some degree of coherence among multiple values in practice. These notions of multiplicity and coherence together constitute the idea of 'diversity' I am proposing.

Further, I argue that the pluralist norm of value diversity has political implications. It counts against the authoritarianism that is left in play by arguments based on historical context alone. Instead, it supports a case for liberalism as a uniquely desirable form of politics under modern conditions. The overall claim is that liberalism allows or enables a maximum diversity of goods to be pursued and enjoyed within a modern society. Considerations of context are not abandoned entirely, because the norm of value diversity commends the promotion of as great a range of values as possible in the circumstances, which brings in historical, economic, and other situational factors. But the initial driver of the argument is the concept of pluralism itself.

I begin by setting out the diversity argument, breaking it down into two main steps: from pluralism to diversity, then from diversity to liberalism. In the first step, I emphasize that pluralist diversity should be understood as including aspects of coherence as well as multiplicity and that different degrees of coherence are appropriate at levels of individual and social life. In the second step, I argue that coherence at the political level, under normal modern conditions, should be understood on a model of 'balancing' competing values and that this requirement is best met by liberalism, in particular egalitarian or redistributive forms of liberalism. In the remaining two sections, I respond to the leading objections to the diversity argument that have emerged in the literature.

From Pluralism to Diversity

In Chapter 4, we saw Bernard Williams approach the problem of value pluralism on the basis of two different kinds of context: political (his realist account) and historical (his modernist defense of liberalism). But Williams has another response to the problem, deriving liberal political norms from the concept of pluralism itself. In his Introduction to Berlin's *Concepts and Categories*, he writes,

> There is the obvious point that if there are many and competing genuine values, then the greater the extent to which a society tends to be single-valued, the more genuine values it neglects or suppresses. More, to this extent, must mean better.
>
> (Williams 2013: xxxvii)

Roughly speaking, it is better that a society embrace a greater rather than lesser multiplicity of values. In Nussbaum's terms, a society whose members enjoy more human capabilities is superior to one whose members enjoy fewer. Moreover, it is better still, at least prima facie, if a society can offer its members, or leave space for its members to propose, multiple interpretations of those capabilities.

Why should a society promote, or at least not impede, more values rather than fewer? The basic reason appeals to the concept of pluralism itself. On the pluralist view, there is a wide range of intrinsic human goods or distinct components of human well-being. Because these goods contribute to human well-being, we have reason to pursue or promote them. Moreover, we have reason, prima facie, to promote them equally. None of the basic human goods is intrinsically more or less valuable than any other. All possess an equal status in that sense; each has, prima facie, an equal claim on us. Consequently, in the abstract, we have reason to pursue all of these goods equally – that is, we have reason to pursue a multiplicity of basic goods.

This conceptual, prima facie commitment to the norm of multiplicity has to be qualified by an empirical observation: in the circumstances of real life, it will not be possible to pursue the entire range of human goods and interpretations of those goods simultaneously and to the maximum extent conceivable. The concrete circumstances in which we find ourselves will suggest reasons for narrowing down that range for practical purposes. Hence, the pluralist norm of value multiplicity is best expressed as a presumption: to recognize the plurality of values is to recognize a commitment to pursue all of them equally until we have a contextual reason to select some rather than others. Pluralists should endorse the pursuit of as many genuine human goods as possible. A good society will enable its members to pursue the widest possible range of ends subject to good reasons, governed by the practical situation, for narrowing that range.

One such reason for narrowing the range of ends in the case of a particular society is a low level of economic development. Pre-modern societies, for example, simply did not have the resources to enable the pursuit of more than an elementary range of values or dimensions of well-being. Further, even assuming modern conditions of more advanced development, a narrower focus may be justified, or imposed, by exceptional circumstances – situations of war or natural disaster, for example. In such cases, where the physical survival of many people is at stake, or the cultural or political survival of a whole society, a wider range of considerations has to be suspended in favor of the immediate and overriding goal of survival. But in more routine circumstances, people have an interest in other aspects of well-being.[1] Thus far, assuming modern circumstances of relative affluence, pluralism raises a presumption in favor of attention to a greater multiplicity of values, a presumption that is rebuttable only in exceptional circumstances, such as those of the emergencies mentioned.

A modern society will also have to narrow its value-focus in a more routine way: even normal circumstances require us to qualify the multiplicity of values we pursue with some consideration for their coherence. The basic idea connects with the 'conflict' aspect of value pluralism. If diversity were entirely a matter of 'more is better', it would often be self-defeating, since, as Berlin emphasized, plural goods frequently come into conflict with one another.[2] This is recognized by Williams when he adds to his initial imperative in favor of maximal multiplicity

> the important qualification that not all values *can* be pluralistically combined, and that some become very pale in too much pluralistic company. There are logical, psychological and sociological limits on what range of values an individual can seriously respect in one life, or one society respect in the lives of various of its citizens.
>
> (Williams 2013: xxxvii)

So, it may be that a numerically greater set of values will result in a lesser overall range of goods enjoyed by an individual or group if many of the values come into conflict and negate one another. Conversely, a numerically smaller set may be greater in overall range if it is more coherent.

Issues of coherence among conflicting incommensurable values can arise at different levels. At the level of the individual, Kekes makes the point that different goods may pull us in different directions, so that if we try to pursue all of them our efforts become 'too scattered' to be successful: 'the attractions of many possibilities are perceived but too few of them are realized' (*MP* 97). Consequently, there is a certain pressure toward coherence within individual lives, although this is perhaps more often honored in the breach, at any rate under modern conditions. Whole societies experience a similar pressure that is in some measure connected with the felt need for shared norms that will unite and identify the group. The anxiety experienced by relatively young countries like Australia over the perceived need for a national identity is a case in point (Stokes 1997). At the political level, too, there is in most societies a perception that some set of mutually consistent principles, rules, and institutions is desirable.

It is important to distinguish these levels of coherence because there is reason to believe that coherence should not be pursued to the same degree or in the same way in every case. The general issue is how we should respond to the tension between multiplicity and coherence. At each level, there is a range of possibilities.

Within an individual life the scattered, contradictory existence has been noted. While such a life does not usually violate any obligation to others, there is, as Kekes suggests, something unsatisfactory about it from a pluralist point of view. There is a sense that no particular value is taken entirely seriously; hence, it may be thought that the spectrum of values is underestimated overall. An alternative pattern is proposed by Aristotle in his picture of the 'rounded and balanced' life (as Hampshire puts it: *IE* 28) – that of the person who exhibits all of the major virtues in a harmony imposed by practical reason.

Although the rounded and balanced life takes seriously the plurality of goods that constitute human well-being, most pluralists would be inclined to see it as too optimistic about the prospects of combining all the virtues within a single life and of harmonizing them through the application of reason. Thus, Hampshire enters a plea for the 'eccentric or lopsided' lives of people who focus their energies on some relatively specialized field and who consequently develop only the virtues that go with that field to the neglect of other goods and virtues – for example, the single-minded artist or sportsperson or captain of industry (*IE* 28). This seems right. The circumstances of a single person are limited in a number of ways – talent, ambition, opportunity, and so on. A reasonable pluralist will take this into account and will not expect every person to exhibit every virtue.

Matters are different at the social level, however. Here the equivalent of the lopsided individual life is the society that is structured around a single, substantial conception of the good, exclusive of alternative conceptions or value rankings. Again, there are circumstances where this is only to be expected, notably in pre-modern conditions where realistic options are narrowed by economic constraints and traditional beliefs. Under modern conditions, however, which have opened up many more possible ways of life, such limitations are unrealistic. This point is captured in part by Rawls's notion of 'the fact of reasonable pluralism', or the presence in modern societies of multiple conceptions of the good, none of which can be demonstrated conclusively to be superior to the alternatives (Rawls 1993).

Lopsidedness is consequently an implausible or undesirable response to value multiplicity at the social level under normal modern conditions. On the other hand, the concern about its opposite, scatteredness, does translate to the social level. A scattered society is one in which so little is held in common that disintegration is a real possibility – one might think of the Ik tribespeople studied by Colin Turnbull (1973) or parts of New Orleans in the wake of Hurricane Katrina in 2005. As in the case of the scattered individual, the scattered society is self-sabotaging and likely, ultimately, to offer a narrower range of ends than its more coherent rivals.

At the social level, therefore, assuming normal modern conditions, the more realistic and desirable range of responses to pluralist multiplicity of value will fall somewhere between the extremes of scattered anarchy and lopsided devotion to a single, narrow conception of the good. Further, pluralists cannot pursue social coherence on the model of Aristotle's well-rounded ideal, since that assumes a picture of seamless inclusion and harmonization that is impossible on the pluralist view. The best that can be hoped for is a tolerably coherent package of social values within which conflicts can be managed before they become destructive of the whole. Balance is still an appropriate guiding image, but this will be an imperfect balancing of selected elements in conflict, leaving open the precise content of the elements selected (or inherited) and the precise balance to be struck. I realize that this picture is irritatingly vague, but I shall try to clarify it when I discuss value coherence at the political level, which I come to shortly.

What I want to underline immediately is that 'diversity', for my purposes, is equivalent not to multiplicity alone but to a combination of multiplicity and coherence. The goal of sheer multiplicity should be tempered by some attention to the content of the goods pursued and how well or badly they fit together within a coherent project, given the understanding of coherence just explained. The logic of value pluralism itself, revealing as it does the great range of genuine human goods, always pushes us toward the pursuit of multiplicity. But the circumstances in which we find ourselves introduce considerations of coherence. At the individual level, these count against the desirability of the scattered life and permit or even recommend (depending on individual circumstances) the lopsided existence of the single-minded person or the specialist. At the social level, lopsidedness makes less sense, since it translates into the demand that all members of a society adopt a single, exclusive conception of the good, which is unrealistic under modern conditions. Indeed, it should be frankly admitted that coherence among values at the social level under modern conditions will be limited. On the other hand, scatteredness to the point of anarchy is no more attractive. Moral and social conflicts are inevitable; the only question is how to prevent them from becoming damaging. Much will depend on the kind of coherence that can be achieved at the political level, to which I now turn.

From Diversity to Liberalism

The second step in the diversity argument is from diversity to liberalism. Here the basic claim is that the value diversity commended by pluralism is best enabled at a political level (under modern conditions and except in emergencies) by liberal values, principles, and institutions. Liberal norms do not purport to resolve all the conflicts raised by the plurality of values, but only to provide a political framework within which such conflicts can be debated in a way that does justice to all the considerations at stake. Within the space enclosed by that framework, incommensurable values still collide and hard choices continue to arise, but these conflicts and choices will be contained and managed by the framework. Moreover, there will be conflict among the constituent parts of the framework itself; the liberal settlement is always provisional and revisable, never absolute.

Let us consider this case in more detail, starting with the general question: what does diversity involve at the political level? In general, to speak of the political level is to invoke systems by which personal and group norms can be accommodated and enabled by enforceable rules. So, the issue is, to what extent and in what ways can the diversity outlined in the previous section be protected and promoted by rules and institutions backed by the legitimate use of force?

Recall that diversity incorporates elements of multiplicity and coherence, making both scattered and lopsided social values undesirable or impossible. Consequently, diversity will rule out both scattered and lopsided *political* settlements. The multiplicity element militates against authoritarian political systems that severely narrow the range of goods allowed as legitimate in a society: politics based on the enforcement of a single religious, cultural, nationalist, or even cosmopolitan orthodoxy, such as theocracy, absolutist monarchy, Fascism, state communism, or strong communitarianism. On the other hand, the coherence requirement counts against political forms that pay insufficient attention to the need for minimal unity in a political framework. In this category belong the politics of postmodernism and of radical multiculturalism, in which no set of norms can legitimately claim priority over any others.[3]

The case of authoritarian politics is especially important, since this emerged in the previous chapter as a plausible alternative to liberalism from the perspective of historical context. Williams's thesis that liberal values must be prioritized under the conditions of modernity was confronted by the counter-example of modern East Asia (and Russia) in which liberal values are rejected. Modernity seems to be compatible with both liberalism and its authoritarian rivals.

The diversity thesis enables pluralists to argue for liberalism and against authoritarianism in a way that is not viable by appeal to historical context alone. How is this possible? It has to be conceded that the promotion of value diversity by an authoritarian political system is a logical possibility if we imagine an idealized version of an eighteenth-century enlightened despot. President Xi's wisdom could be such that his policies will succeed in balancing maximal multiplicity of values with their coherence.

This is a logical possibility but an empirical improbability. More likely, authoritarian leadership will serve the interests and values of the leaders and their followers only, leaving those of dissenters, and even of the general populace, to one side. Mill's observation has been noted that people cannot rely on their interests being protected adequately by leaders whose circumstances are far removed from their own (Mill 1958 [1861]: 43–6).[4] Circumstances are indeed different where there are huge disparities of political power. The smaller the governing group the less likely it is that their judgments will maximize the potential value multiplicity. A narrower range of judgment may result in increased coherence, but not even that can be counted on where checks and balances are lacking.

Moreover, authoritarianism is likely to rely heavily on the use of violence, and from a pluralist point of view this is a dubious policy instrument. In the absence of concern for rights or consensus, violence will be necessary to overcome dissent and resistance. Again, it is possible that the costs of violence will be outweighed by gains in the values it serves. But Berlin makes the point that the costs of violence are apt to be both severe and unpredictable.

> Revolutions, wars, assassinations, extreme measures may in desperate situations be required. But history teaches us that their consequences are seldom what is anticipated; there is no guarantee, not even, at times, a high enough probability, that such acts will lead to improvement.
>
> (*CTH* 18)[5]

Bearing all this in mind, it is safe to conclude that pluralist diversity points not to an authoritarian or lopsided form of politics, but once again to a 'balanced' form. Plurality and conflict will be acknowledged as inevitable and permanent, perhaps even salutary in some cases, but contained and managed by a framework of enforceable principles, rules, and institutions. Such a framework will be accommodating of a multiplicity of values and conceptions of the good, but it will not be so open-ended that it will disintegrate in the face of the conflicts among those values and conceptions that will inevitably occur. Roughly speaking, it will allow or enable as much multiplicity as possible consistent with the minimum degree of coherence necessary to maintain social cohesion under modern conditions. The presumption will be in favor of multiplicity, but this can be rebutted by the need for that degree of coherence required in the circumstances.

This general schema points strongly toward liberalism. On the side of multiplicity, liberal values and institutions emphasize various dimensions of individual liberty, which open up paths to the pursuit of other goods and conceptions of the good. On the side of coherence, the resulting variety of legitimate goods and ways of life is contained within a political framework whose constituent elements – values such as rights, liberties, equality and justice, and institutions such as constitutionalism, responsible government, an independent judiciary, and a free press – are tolerably coherent.[6]

To describe liberal values and institutions as 'tolerably' coherent is, first, to acknowledge that a liberal political order is not free from tensions and disputes – far from it. This is obviously true within the civil society that the liberal political framework protects and regulates, but conflicts will also break out within the liberal political framework itself. Liberty will sometimes pull apart from equality, or different conceptions of liberty from each other, and the independence of the courts will sometimes come into collision with the liberties of the media or the popular accountability of the legislature. Anti-liberal pluralists such as John Gray regard this as a fatal problem for liberalism (Gray 1995: 107–10; *IB* 181–3).

But liberals are well aware of this phenomenon and not helpless in the face of it; such conflicts can be controlled and managed before they become destructive of the society as a whole. How is that possible? The key idea, touched on above, is balance. The liberal political solution accepts conflict, even within the principles and institutions of liberalism themselves, as normal and inevitable rather than an aberration to abolish or transcend. On the other hand, liberalism also accepts the task of managing such conflicts rather than allowing their consequences to fall where they may. Competing values are respected but conflicts among them are contained. The upshot is the holding of rival goods and interests in a dynamic equilibrium subject to revisable judgments about where exactly the necessary compromises and trade-offs should fall.

Contrary to those critics, like Mouffe and Gray, who see liberalism as a theory of moral and political absolutes, the balancing process is never final; it is always contested and provisional. Liberals are guided by their overarching (but not absolutely overriding) emphasis on certain goods – again, principally, individual rights and liberties – as conduits for the enjoyment of other goods. That emphasis constitutes, as Hampshire puts it, 'a kind of case law of moral assumptions from which arguments can start and to which principles can be critically applied' (*IE* 62). But like a case law, the assumptions of liberalism can themselves be revised in the light of experience.

Balance in this sense is a persistent theme in liberal political thought. For example, the need to strike a balance between liberty and equality, and between different interpretations of these, is well attested.[7] But the theme of balance is especially prominent when applied to institutions in classical liberal discussions of constitutionalism. Jeremy Waldron describes how, in the eighteenth century, the constitution is seen as 'a machine with weights, springs, ratchets, ballasts, escapements, and centrifugal governors' (*PPT* 278).[8] The story begins with Locke's separating out of the different functions of kingship into the distinct tasks of legislature, executive, and judiciary. From a value-pluralist perspective, one might see these as each connected with a particular range of values – respectively, representation and deliberation, administrative efficiency, and impartiality in legal judgment and enforcement. These functions are then recombined so that each checks and balances the other.

A similar view is found in other liberal or proto-liberal writers. Montesquieu, for example, writes, 'To form a moderate government, it is necessary to combine the several powers, to regulate, temper, and set them in motion; to give, as it were, ballast to one, in order to enable it to counterpoise the other' (Montesquieu 1949 [1748]: 62). Along the same lines there is Madison's argument, in the *Federalist Papers*, that the best safeguard against factionalism becoming dangerous in the new American republic is to allow factions to multiply so that a balance will be maintained.

Once again, the plurality and conflict accommodated by liberal balancing are not confined merely to the social space facilitated by the constitutional framework; plurality and conflict are explicitly acknowledged as entering into that framework itself. As Waldron writes, American constitutional design in particular was deliberately 'untidy and pluralistic, setting out to *house* rather than reconcile the pursuit of competing and incommensurable values' (*PPT* 283). Liberal constitutionalism, more broadly, has always maintained 'a provisional and uneasy equilibrium, in need of repair'. Although 'a product of reason', it is also a product 'of many reasons sitting uneasily with one another'. But it is in this way that liberal constitutionalism meets the requirements of pluralist diversity: by imposing on value multiplicity no more than a tolerable coherence, sufficient to sustain a minimal social unity without trying to transcend the reality of plurality and conflict.

This is not to deny that liberal constitutionalism often employs a rhetoric that sounds more 'absolute' than the account just given. Liberals have often spoken in terms, for example, of 'rights as trumps' (Dworkin 1984) or (in Berlin's case) minimal 'frontiers of individual liberty' (*L* 52; see also *L* 210). But the familiar problem of conflicting rights shows that such claims, although exceptionally weighty, cannot be absolute in the most literal sense. Rather, basic liberal rights such as freedom of speech are better thought of as raising strong presumptions that may be rebutted under limited circumstances. What exactly those circumstances are is a subject of continual dispute, negotiation, and compromise. To see the fundamental principles of liberalism in this way is consistent with the basic value-pluralist insight that no value or narrow selection of values is always overriding.

Can we go further and link pluralist diversity not only with liberalism in general but also with a particular kind of liberalism?[9] For example, does diversity point more firmly toward the classical liberalism of the unrestrained market or toward the egalitarianism of state redistribution? I believe that we have good reason to see diversity as better promoted by the egalitarian stream of liberal thought. Again, this looks like the more balanced position. In classical liberalism, one particular form of liberty, namely negative liberty (non-interference), is very strongly emphasized to the point that in some versions, such as Robert Nozick's, it becomes completely overriding (Nozick 1974). Although this does open up 'formal' opportunities for people to pursue a range of other goods, it is consistent with people's lacking any real capacity to do so because they lack the necessary material resources or (in Nussbaum's sense) capabilities. Pluralists should see this as an imbalance. Thus, Berlin acknowledges 'the evils of unrestricted laissez-faire' (*L* 38). Similarly, Michael Walzer writes that 'a radically *laissez-faire* economy would be like a totalitarian state, invading every other sphere, dominating every other distributive process' (Walzer 1983: 119). Classical liberalism is essentially a form of monism.

In egalitarian liberalism, by contrast, negative liberty is balanced or supplemented by other considerations, such as effective freedom and a more-than-merely-formal equality of opportunity. One classic statement is that of T. H. Green in his reference to freedom as not merely negative but also 'a positive power or capacity' (Green 1991 [1881]: 21). Another is Rawls's formulation of his two principles of justice as fairness, in which the negative liberty enshrined in the first principle is supplemented by the fair equality of opportunity and special concern for the least advantaged that characterize the second principle (Rawls 1971).

Further, the liberalism that best answers to value diversity will go beyond the traditional realm of toleration and enter the territory of multiculturalism, where minority cultures are celebrated for the positive value that they bring to a society, and where that celebration is in turn translated into public policy. Liberal multiculturalism balances a multiculturalist valuation of a range of human cultures with a liberal concern for the rights and liberties of the individual. This view was touched on in Chapter 3 and will be discussed further in the next chapter.

To sum up: the diversity argument links value pluralism and liberalism in two steps. First, pluralists have good reason to demand that their society enable its members to pursue a diversity of human goods, understood as combining considerations of multiplicity and coherence. Second, the goal of diversity is most likely to be achieved or approximated at a political level by a settlement in which value multiplicity is strongly encouraged, but qualified by considerations of coherence in the moderate sense of 'balancing' competing values. This goal is best satisfied by a liberal form of political culture and more specifically by an egalitarian form of liberalism.

Does Pluralism Commend Diversity?

The diversity argument has been criticized on a number of grounds. I now review what I see as the most important of these, beginning with the first phase of the argument, from pluralism to diversity.

An initial objection can be dealt with quickly. This is that the diversity argument is really a monist maneuver because it makes a single value, namely 'diversity', overriding (Moore 2009: 251). The central claim of value pluralism is, of course, precisely that no single value, or narrow range of values, can be overriding. However, the idea of value diversity, as used here, is not a single value or subset of values but rather a shorthand for the desirability of promoting a multiplicity of distinct values subject only to the limitations of circumstances and the coherence condition.[10]

A more challenging objection has been advanced to the effect that the diversity argument breaches 'Hume's law' against deriving normative statements from factual statements. The objection is that value pluralism makes a claim of fact, about the nature of values, from which the diversity argument then illicitly deduces a value judgment, that we ought to promote a diversity of values. Value pluralism tells us only that fundamental values are plural and incommensurable. It does not tell us what those values are or which values we should pursue. Therefore, it cannot tell us that we ought to promote value diversity.

This objection is most forcefully (and repeatedly) expressed by Robert Talisse.[11] Referring to 'the barrenness' of value pluralism, Talisse writes that pluralism 'entails nothing about what we ought to do' (Talisse 2015: 1070). Pluralism, he continues, 'is a thesis about *the nature of value* rather than one about *what is of value*'. The pluralist 'recognizes a plurality of objective incommensurable values'. But that is consistent with the possibility of a 'tyrannical value pluralist' who rejects the promotion of value diversity and instead upholds 'things such as power, control, domination, hegemony, and the humiliation of others'. Such a pluralist may be mistaken, but if so she is mistaken about 'what is of value', not about 'the nature of value'. Value pluralism itself does not entail a normative commitment to value diversity.[12]

In Chapter 1, I accepted that the is-ought objection applies to Berlin's attempt to ground the value of freedom of choice in the necessity of choice. It is hard to see that argument as any other than a proposal to derive a value directly from a fact. The problem is that the argument begins by focusing narrowly on a single aspect of pluralism which looks like a bare datum of pluralist experience – namely, the inescapability of hard choices if values are incommensurable.

However, the argument from pluralism to diversity is a different matter. The starting point of the argument is not a single aspect of pluralism but the whole concept, which we have seen to be complex. Some aspects of pluralism, such as the necessity of choice, do indeed look more like claims of fact. Others, however, have normative qualities. It is the normative components of the idea that enable pluralists to argue for normative conclusions.

Along these lines several replies to Talisse are possible.[13] First, he assumes a narrow, strictly descriptive understanding of pluralism that differs from the partly normative understanding employed by most value pluralists. For most pluralists, to explain the plurality of values involves saying something about the content of the values that are said to be plural. Berlin, Hampshire, Kekes, Williams, Nussbaum, and others all claim not only that there are plural and incommensurable values but also that those values have a certain content, although they give various accounts of what that content is.

Indeed, it is hard to make the first claim, about the plural nature of value, without being drawn into the second, about what the plural values are. If someone says, 'there are plural and incommensurable values', a natural response would include the question, 'Well, then, what are they?' It makes little sense to insist that the second kind of claim, about content, is wholly separate from the first, about nature. A fully explained pluralist position is one that fleshes out, at least to some extent, the values that are said to be plural.

If that is so, then pluralism is a partly normative view. And if *that* is so, then the diversity argument does not violate Hume's injunction against deriving ought from is, since the pluralist starting point is itself, in part, an ought. The diversity argument does not pass from is to ought but from ought to ought. The starting point of the argument is not a claim of fact about what people happen to value, but a value judgment to the effect that certain generic goods (and more specific local expressions of these) contribute, in distinct ways, to human well-being. Nussbaum's human capabilities, for example, are norms rather than statements of fact. Consequently, the diversity argument as reconstructed here does not violate Hume's law because it does not move from fact to value but from value to value.

This view is supported by Kekes, who writes,

> pluralism is an evaluative theory, because it is not an uncommitted analysis of the relations among various types of values involved in good lives but a theory motivated by a concern for human beings actually living good lives. Consequently, pluralism is at once descriptive and evaluative. It offers a description of some conceptual and factual features relevant to good lives, but it also undertakes to evaluate these features on the basis of their contribution to good lives.
>
> (*MP* 10)

Pluralists, that is, are usually motivated by an interest in the way multiple and diverse values contribute to human well-being, not in values conceived as disembodied Platonic entities conceived in abstraction from any substantial notion of well-being.

Again Kekes writes,

> It may be asked whether [pluralism] is an ethical or a meta-ethical theory. It is arguable whether this distinction is tenable, but if it is, then the answer is that pluralism is both. For it is concerned both with first-order moral phenomena, such as various values and their relation to each other, and with the second-order analysis, justification, and criticism of the judgements we make about the first-order moral phenomena.
>
> (*MP* 13)

Two points are being made here. First, as already noted, the issue of what kinds of things values are (meta-ethics) is inextricably connected with the issue of what values there are (ethics). Pluralism concerns both, since in dealing with the relations among values, it necessarily deals with the content of those values. Second, ethics involves not only first-order prescriptions – for example, 'lying is wrong' – but also second-order reflection on those prescriptions – for example, 'is that prescription always correct?' Second-order reflection can be assisted by meta-ethical description. Pluralism is relevant to both prescription and reflection.

This second point can be illustrated from Talisse's own observation that value pluralism, if correct, falsifies utilitarianism. 'Whatever pluralism is', he writes, 'it had better be something that utilitarians must reject' (Talisse 2012: 10). Pluralism, if it means anything, must mean the rejection of ethical monism, or the idea that one value or ethical formula is overriding in every case. Utilitarianism advances such a super-value or formula: that in every case utility (however conceived) is an overriding consideration. Therefore pluralism must oppose utilitarianism. But utilitarianism is a first-order ethical prescription: it tells us what we ought to do – maximize utility. So, pluralism (if true) falsifies a first-order ethical prescription. On Talisse's own account pluralism is not prescriptively barren: it rules out a substantial ethical claim.

That is the least pluralism does: the diversity argument shows how its prescriptive implications are much more substantial. The fact that fundamental values are plural and incommensurable shows not only that utility is not overriding but also that a range of other important goods must be regarded as no less important and possess, prima facie, no less weighty claims to promotion in practice. There are, in effect, both negative and positive aspects to the normative implications of pluralism. Negatively, pluralism rules out ethical prescriptions that advance single goods or narrow ethical formulas as overriding all other considerations in all circumstances. But it follows that, positively, pluralism provides support to more expansive approaches to ethics and politics which honor a greater range and diversity of important goods.

The limit to this is, of course, context. If ought implies can, then the basic pluralist thrust toward multiplicity of value must, as argued earlier, be tempered by attention to what is possible in the circumstances – personal, cultural, political, and historical. This, too, follows from the concept of pluralism itself. It is a basic pluralist insight that conflicts of fundamental values, although not rationally resolvable in the abstract, may be resolvable for decisive reason in context. If that is so, then the concept of pluralism itself directs us not only to the narrowly descriptive view identified by Talisse, but also to a richer notion of contextual judgment, aspects of which have been developed in the previous discussion in this chapter and earlier. The diversity argument is not a move from a thinly descriptive meta-ethical view to an abstract prescription, as Talisse supposes, but a complex amalgam of description and prescription, nature and content, universal and particular.

A further series of objections to the diversity argument has been advanced in a probing article by Patrick Neal. One of Neal's points is that the supposed link between pluralism and diversity depends on an 'equal value postulate' that is contradicted by the idea of incommensurability (Neal 2009: 872). If there is a prima facie imperative to maximize the range of basic goods that are possible for people in a particular society, that is because it is assumed that, as I have expressed it elsewhere, 'the pluralist must endorse all such goods equally, in the sense that they have an equal claim on us until we are presented with a particular context in which we must choose among them' (*LVP* 137). It is only if the goods are in some sense equally valuable that we have a presumptive obligation to pursue all of them, in practice as many as possible (subject to coherence), rather than just some arbitrary selection. But (the objection runs) we cannot say that basic goods are equally valuable, because if they are incommensurable that means that they cannot be subjected to common units of measurement that would show them to be equal. Under pluralism we cannot know that basic goods are equally valuable; therefore, we have no reason to treat them equally at any stage. 'Only if we knew that the values were metrically equal would it become plausible to entertain the idea that more is better' (Neal 2009: 873). Since we cannot know that, we should not accept the diversity argument.

The objection itself depends on a false assumption: that values can be equal in the sense required here only if they are 'metrically' equal – that is, they can be equal only if their equality is measurable. It is true that, on the pluralist view, basic human values are not measurably equal – they are not all worth four units of utility, for example. However, metrical equality can be contrasted with 'rough equality', or 'parity', an idea now familiar in the value-pluralist literature (Chang 1997: 5; Chang 2002). As James Griffin explains, two different ways of life may be incompatible and incommensurable – such that 'a choice between them can mean uncompensated loss of value' – yet still 'roughly equal' because both are 'of a high quality', making them both 'worthy of pursuit' (Griffin 1997: 38). The two are 'in the same league, as it were'. We cannot say that they are exactly equal because each has strengths and weaknesses different from those of the other, but neither can we say that either is superior overall. As Derek Parfit writes, 'Must it be true, of Proust and Keats, either that one was the greater writer, or that both were *exactly equally* as great?' (Parfit 1984: 431).

The point can be transferred from ways of life to their component values or goods. What places the two ways of life in the same league are their 'elements' or 'ingredients' – that is, the constituent goods, benefits, and virtues that provide their content (Griffin 1997: 38). Even if these goods are incommensurable – to exchange one for another is to suffer uncompensated loss – they, too, may be roughly equal in value. They will not be measurably equal, but equal in the sense that they are all of high quality and worthy of pursuit. Liberty is in the same league as equality, for example. They are equally the fundamental building blocks of alternative ways of life. This is what Berlin means when he refers to basic human values as 'equally ultimate': they occupy the same moral bedrock in the sense that none is intrinsically superior or inferior to any other (*L* 213). It is another way of putting the point, made earlier, that if values are incommensurable, there is no reason to rank one ahead of another unless or until a specific context gives us such a reason. In this way, again, basic values possess a prima facie or presumptively equal status. If so, the starting point of the diversity argument is sound.

Neal also finds fault with the way the principle of diversity combines elements of multiplicity and coherence. For Neal, to try to combine such diverse considerations is itself incoherent because it involves an attempt to add 'qualitative' matters to a 'quantitative' starting point. Although the coherence condition 'make[s] good sense' in itself, it 'may serve to *undermine* the quantitative criterion, not serve as a *supplement* to it' (Neal 2009: 876). The reason is that

> the conditions of coherence are sensible because they show us that it is not the range ... of values that matters, but rather the degree to which a given range ... has enough practicality and unity to lead to human flourishing to a greater degree than some alternative range.

But surely *both* range and content matter here. If range or multiplicity did not matter at all, then pluralists might be satisfied with a single-valued society, which would meet the coherence requirement splendidly. Range does matter, for the reasons given earlier in connection with multiplicity. That being the case, there is nothing wrong with combining considerations of range and coherence within the same principle. In a sports team or a business enterprise, it is usually an advantage to include people with different skills, knowledge sets, and personalities, but at the same time it is always an advantage if the various members can work together, achieving at least some acceptable level of cooperation. If the human good has several distinct components, then it is better (prima facie) that more of these be promoted rather than fewer. That presumption may be rebutted in cases where promoting X will interfere with Y and Z. But that is a qualification, not a contradiction of the basic presumption.

Is Liberalism the Best Political Vehicle for Diversity?

The second phase of the diversity argument is from diversity to liberalism: if pluralism recommends a diversity of values in a given society, then liberalism is the best political vehicle for promoting that diversity. Here too there have been objections.

One complaint is that if, as I have argued, pluralist diversity rules out lopsided political settlements that enforce a single, narrow conception of the good, then that stricture applies to liberalism itself. Are liberal politics, even in their ostensibly 'neutral' form, not ultimately based on a distinctively liberal conception of the good, one that emphasizes certain values, such as individual liberty, at the cost of others? Along these lines, John Gray argues that although the liberal framework accommodates a range of goods and good lives, it unavoidably does so in terms that place limits on that range. Some values and ways of life that are legitimate points on the pluralist spectrum are excluded or their opportunities diminished: 'liberal societies tend to drive out non-liberal forms of life, to ghettoize or marginalize them, or to trivialize them' (Gray 2013: 188).

Gray is correct that liberalism has costs in pluralist terms. Consequently, pluralists should not attempt to defend liberalism by appeal to absolute neutrality or even to a Rawlsian scheme according to which liberal principles can be accepted for 'political' purposes only, independently of 'comprehensive' liberal beliefs (Rawls 1993). Liberal pluralists should accept that any liberal framework rests ultimately on a combination of values that amounts itself to a comprehensive position, which necessarily carries costs in terms of values foregone or diminished.[14]

However, the same can be said of any political position. All viable societies need some political framework, and any such framework will reflect some conception of the good that excludes alternatives. The question is not whether we can identify a framework based on a conception of the good that will impose no costs and exclude nothing, since clearly there can be no such thing. The question is how well liberalism fares against its competitors in terms of its capacity to accommodate diversity as defined earlier. The basic answer has already been given. A liberal framework, although not limitlessly accommodating of diversity, is more accommodating than the alternatives because it meets the dual requirements of value multiplicity and coherence more satisfactorily than its rivals. It does so through its characteristically balanced approach in contrast with the lack of multiplicity typical of authoritarians, and the incoherence of postmodernism and radical multiculturalism.

To this, there may be a further response. Even if liberal societies do maximize value diversity within their own borders, would it not expand that diversity still more if the world contained societies that promoted non-liberal political forms in addition? As Gray writes,

> If liberal societies are to be commended on the pluralist ground that they harbour more genuine values than some illiberal societies, does it not follow that the human world will be still richer in value if it contains not only liberal societies but also illiberal regimes that shelter worthwhile forms of life that would otherwise perish?
>
> (Gray 2013: 186)

So, the optimally pluralist world is one in which there will be a multiplicity of political regimes, non-liberal as well as liberal.

This does not follow. Gray's argument confuses three kinds of plurality and diversity: (1) of values; (2) of cultures; (3) of political regimes. He assumes that they all cohere, but they do not.

To begin with, recall the distinction introduced in Chapter 1 (and reinforced in Chapter 3) between value pluralism and cultural pluralism, or the analytical and holistic senses of pluralism. While the former is about the plurality and incommensurability of values, such as liberty, equality, Nussbaum's capabilities, and so on, the latter is about the plurality of whole cultural systems of value. The point was made that if we are talking about value pluralism, then we are talking primarily about the plurality of values, not the plurality of whole cultures. Indeed, on the value-pluralist view whole cultures cannot be plural in just the same way as individual values – that is, incommensurable. Whole cultures overlap on the great goods, and so cannot be incommensurable. To treat whole cultures as incommensurable is to confuse value pluralism with cultural relativism.

When it comes to the norm of diversity, how does this apply to values and cultures respectively? This issue was touched on in Chapter 3 during my discussion of the relation between value pluralism and multiculturalism. If value plurality is the primary focus of value pluralism, then value diversity (incorporating considerations of multiplicity and coherence) is the primary norm of value pluralism, for the reasons already given. If values are plural and incommensurable, then we should maximize the value diversity that is possible in the circumstances.

Does the same notion of diversity apply to cultures? It does to some extent. If cultures are constellations of values, then to promote value diversity may to some degree involve promoting a diversity of cultures. Different cultures will constitute different combinations of values and so be instrumentally valuable in increasing value diversity overall. On the face of it, a multicultural world will be richer in values than a monocultural world.

However, the desirability of cultural diversity on value-pluralist grounds is subject to an important qualification. Cultural diversity is valuable on these grounds only so far as it serves the end of value diversity, and some cultures are less hospitable to value diversity than others. A society that regards women as inferior beings to be restricted within limited social roles is a society that seriously limits the diversity of values that its members may pursue. Such a restrictive attitude may extend to its view and treatment of other cultures. Conservative, authoritarian, and imperialist cultures are poor vehicles for value diversity.

Consequently, a world in which cultures like these are multiplied is unlikely to be the most desirable world from a value-pluralist perspective. Rather, value pluralism and its primary norm of value diversity point to a concern not simply with the multiplication of cultures but with the content of those cultures. Value pluralists will not promote cultures regardless of content but cultures that are themselves internally value-diverse. For the reasons already given, these are likely to be liberal cultures.

At this point, we have reason to distinguish value diversity and cultural diversity and to qualify the latter with a prior concern for the former. But Gray's assumption is that both value and cultural diversity are promoted by the third kind of diversity listed above, that of political regimes. Once again this is too facile. On this view, a world of liberal political societies will be made more pluralist if some liberal polities are replaced by fascist political regimes. Is that really true?

The addition of fascist regimes at the expense of liberal polities does, on the face of it, add to greater political diversity internationally – at least until the fascist regimes attempt to swallow up the remaining liberal ones, as is their usual ambition. However, such a move also reduces cultural and value diversity overall. It will add fascist cultures that were not present before, but each of these will reduce cultural diversity within its own sphere of power because it will enforce – and brutally so – a single conception of the good. Consequently, such a politics will reduce the range of individual values – the principal concern of value pluralists – that may be pursued by its subject peoples. When the liberal Weimar regime was replaced by Nazism, the result might be said to increase political diversity globally, but not value or cultural diversity. The reduction of individual liberties brought with it a closing off of different ways in which values might be expressed and developed.

Moreover, I have argued that the central normative implication of value pluralism is not value multiplicity alone but value diversity, which involves an element of coherence. Merely to argue for the multiplication of political perspectives is to ignore the issue of coherence that will clearly arise between liberal and non-liberal cultures. To take the Nazi example again, the rise of that form of politics meant the extinction of others, and with that the destruction of the cultures and values they cherished.

Consequently, the best pluralist world will not be, as Gray supposes, an ideologically indiscriminate series of political cultures. It will certainly contain and promote cultural variation, but this will be framed, politically, by liberal principles. To conclude otherwise would be to speak of a diversity of political types (or rather a multiplicity of such types, since coherence will be at a premium), but it will promote neither value nor cultural diversity.

Another complaint against liberalism as a vehicle for diversity is that its characteristic rights and liberties make space not only for genuine goods but also for evils. As Neal puts it, the 'liberal space might enable more flowers to bloom, but it might also enable more weeds to grow, some of which might prevent flowers from growing' (Neal 2009: 880).[15] How do we know that liberalism produces a better ratio of flowers to weeds than alternative political forms? We could settle this only by examining the substantial conception of the good for which liberalism stands and by comparing this with the good proposed by its rivals. That would require 'substantive knowledge of the good – knowledge about which values and ways of life purported to be good by various individuals and groups actually were objectively good' (Neal 2009: 880). The 'spatial' notion of diversity does not help us with this judgment one way or the other.

> If we desire a flourishing garden, we will have to do something other than look for the largest plot of land and grant permission for a hundred flowers to bloom. ... Size and quantity are not the appropriate tools of evaluation here.
>
> (Neal 2009: 881)

It is ironic to see liberalism criticized on the ground of 'evils' when one reflects on what *non*-liberal regimes are capable of. Liberal democracies are not perfect but, as argued earlier, their democratic element enables more voices to be heard in politics in contrast with reliance on the wisdom of an absolute monarch or dictator or oligarchy.[16] Further, liberal principles recognize the rights of individuals and minorities. These are protections against evils, and they are protections not possessed by non-liberal systems.

Neal's more specific complaint is that liberalism has no claim to superiority merely because of the space it offers people to pursue their own values. But if we want a hundred flowers to bloom, we will surely be better off with the space made available by liberalism rather than the straitened council allotments assigned to us by authoritarians. Of course, with more space for more blooms we do also run the risk of more weeds, but that is only to say that space is a necessary but not a sufficient condition for diversity. Neal is correct that once we have our space we need to do more than 'grant permission' for diverse blooms to emerge. Gardens also need cultivation. But that requirement is more of a problem for the laissez-faire stream of liberalism than for the egalitarian stream recommended here. Egalitarian liberals do not stand back and hope for the best; they are prepared to balance liberty with intervention for the purpose of promoting opportunity.

Neal argues that we cannot say that space is an advantage because what really matters is 'substantive knowledge of the good'. But how do we acquire this, and what does it mean to acquire this, in advance of experiencing the putative goods and evils in practice, which in turn requires social space for these different experiences?

The space offered by liberalism is likely to lead to the generation of genuine goods in two ways. First, the freedom to undertake what Mill called 'experiments of living' enables people to identify the good in the first place (Mill 1974 [1859]: 120).[17] The objection to liberalism as a net generator of evil over good assumes that we are already clear about where the line between good and evil is to be drawn. But this is sharper in some cases than in others; in many instances the distinction is disputed and it takes experience – at both the personal and social levels – to clarify our judgment and to reach agreement where that is possible. As Aristotle argued, practical wisdom tends to develop only with experience. Indeed, an important part of that experience, for most individuals and even whole societies, will be the making of mistakes. Liberalism does offer the freedom to make mistakes, but that is an important means of identifying the good.

Second, the examination and weighing of goods and evils, and of rival conceptions of the good, requires critical reflection, which in turn flourishes best in liberal spaces. Raw multiplicity of experience is one thing, the critical assessment of that experience is another. Critical reflection is not impossible under authoritarian regimes, but it tends to be driven underground or coded in non-political forms.[18] It is when critical reflection enters the public realm that it is more likely to make a practical difference to people's lives. For critical debate to become public, a society needs the kind of social space cleared by liberties and capacities of the kind traditionally championed by liberals.

One of the standard features of authoritarian political regimes and oppressive cultures is the promotion of a manipulated, sanitized, 'official' version of the society's historical experience. The very meaning of 'good' and 'evil' is at stake in these officially sanctioned myths and narratives. For such accounts to be challenged, and a better understanding achieved, the kind of space secured by liberal principles and institutions is invaluable if not essential.

Thus far, my defense of the spatial case for liberalism appeals to the limits of our ethical knowledge in advance of experience, but there is also an argument to be made based on the results of experience. According to Neal, we have no reason to suppose that greater individual liberty, in itself, will lead to a greater preponderance of good over evil.

But we do have a reason to believe this – namely, our historical experience of liberal societies in comparison with authoritarian ones. A society that enforces one particular set of values as that which should inform the personal lives of all its members had better be sure that it has made the right choice – both the right choice of values and value rankings to endorse, and of values and rankings to exclude. But the obvious danger, indeed likelihood demonstrated by history, is that the choice will be made by a dominant elite or dictator whose view is biased, erroneous, harmful, or at least disputable on reasonable grounds. If we are worried about mistakes and the promotion of evil, experience shows that the alternatives to liberalism are even more prone to the making of mistakes and the promotion of evil. We are likely to have fewer mistakes, fewer mistakes with major consequences for great numbers of people, and fewer mistakes that are hard to correct, if we leave people the freedom to decide for themselves how to live rather than authorizing others to decide for them.

The Shape of the Argument

Three final issues need to be considered, which bear on the shape of the diversity argument overall rather than the details of its component steps. The first is whether the argument proves too much. If pluralism implies a norm of diversity, which in turn is best fulfilled by liberalism, then that seems to indicate a logical link between pluralism and liberalism: a case for liberalism is implicit in the concept of pluralism. If so, does the argument show that the justification of liberalism is eternal? That would conflict with Williams's persuasive view, introduced in Chapter 4, that the justification of liberalism is not eternal but subject to historical context. The liberal understanding of political legitimacy, Williams argues, is valid only under the conditions of modernity.

One way of reconciling these claims might be to regard the starting point of the argument, the concept of value pluralism, as itself subject to historical context. The idea of pluralism, it might be argued, is also the product of modernity, so anything that follows from it is subject to the same contextual limitations. However, this is not convincing. It is true that value pluralism is not conceptualized explicitly before the work of Weber, Berlin, and other thinkers of the twentieth century, but intimations of the idea can be traced back to the ancient world (Apfel 2011). The *Antigone* of Sophocles, for example, expresses a strong sense of conflict among incommensurable values, in this case competing duties to city and family. What this suggests is that pluralism is no modern invention but a permanent feature of human ethical experience. It may be more or less prominent under different conditions, but its reality is indeed eternal.

The diversity argument is compatible with Williams's historical contextualism for a different reason. Pluralism itself is part of the permanent structure of human ethics, not just a function of modernity. Therefore, the norm of value diversity, which follows from pluralism, is part of that permanent structure too. However, diversity as presented here is not a simple idea but a combination of multiplicity and coherence. As explained earlier, both of these have contextual elements. The goal of multiplicity, as a practical imperative, requires attention to what is possible in the circumstances, which include historical and economic factors. Similarly, coherence is a matter to be judged in context, since its terms will change according to which values are in play and in which combination – again dependent on circumstances. In short, pluralism may be eternal but its implicit norm of diversity brings in contextual considerations. Those considerations will determine what diversity demands at any one time and place. These particular demands will in turn determine the extent to which liberalism is a valid response.

A second issue is whether I have tailored the notion of value pluralism to get the political result I want. Although I claim to be arguing from value pluralism to liberalism, is it not really a constrained form of value pluralism that enables me to reach that political end? Have I not smuggled into the concept of pluralism an idea that is already a liberal idea, namely the particular notion of coherence that I propose? It is the requirement of coherence among values that leads, in politics, to the principle of balance, hence to liberalism. So, the argument works, as far as it does, only by assuming the conclusion in its premises.

I do not think so. It is true that a key move in the argument is the introduction of the idea of coherence. However, I do not present coherence as part of the concept of value pluralism itself, so it is not true that I smuggle into the concept a value that is already friendly to liberalism. Rather, coherence enters the argument as a plausible assumption about what is required for the value-pluralist norm of multiplicity to be applied in practice. Recall that the most basic normative message of pluralism is that many values have a roughly equal claim on us. Prima facie we should promote all genuine values equally if we should promote any. But the circumstances in which we find ourselves always oblige us to be selective within the full range of conceivable values, giving us a reason to focus on some to the exclusion or diminution of others.

One such circumstance is the extent to which the values we pursue fit with one another or come into conflict. By and large, the package of values to which we are committed needs at least some degree of internal coherence. But under modern conditions, in which there is widespread disagreement about the nature of the good life, that coherence can only be minimal. At the political level, coherence is best reflected by a model of balancing competing values rather than trying to transcend that competition altogether or refusing to regulate it at all. The model of balance fits well with the classical liberal commitment to constitutional checks and balances. The project of political balance is taken a step further by the egalitarian-liberal approach that seeks equilibrium between liberty and social justice and between different senses of liberty. In general, this case proceeds not by deducing conclusions from the concept of pluralism alone but by adding to that concept plausible assumptions concerning its practical application.

A final question is the following. In the case I have outlined, what is the role of value pluralism? Is it not true that all the work is being done by the idea of coherence, which leads to balance, hence liberalism? If that is so, this is not really a distinctively pluralist case for liberalism at all. The same argument could start simply with the need for social coherence, omitting any reference to value pluralism. The pluralist component is redundant.

However, the work in the argument is done not by the idea of coherence alone but by the idea of diversity, which includes both coherence and multiplicity. It is the imperative to promote a multiplicity of values that gets the argument started; coherence then comes in to qualify that imperative in particular circumstances. The initial appeal to multiplicity generates a fundamental drive toward respect for and promotion of a range of values and conceptions of the good. Multiplicity, then, remains an important part of the argument, and multiplicity is a direct implication of value pluralism. So, the argument is distinctively pluralist in its foundation. If pluralism is true, the diversity argument makes a distinctive contribution to the defense of liberalism.

I do not say that the case I construct is the only way to argue for liberalism. It may, for example, be possible to begin with the idea of social coherence alone and proceed to interpret this in light of modern conditions in the manner of Rawls. Such a non-pluralist procedure would be especially attractive if we were sure that basic values were not in fact plural and incommensurable in the way pluralists believe they are.

However, just as there is no argument that demonstrates conclusively that value pluralism is correct, neither is there any argument that shows conclusively that it is false. Indeed, value pluralism is a plausible and cogent hypothesis about the nature of human values and human well-being. If that is so, then it is worth considering what, if pluralism were true, its social and political implications would be. This is what the diversity argument attempts to do.

Conclusion

Bearing in mind the limitations of contextualism, we have reason to look for another approach to the problem of value pluralism. One such approach is 'conceptual', deriving norms from reflection on the concept itself. For example, pluralism implies a 'diversity argument': the concept entails the desirability of value 'diversity', which in turn recommends the politics of liberalism. Diversity should be understood as combining elements of multiplicity and coherence, and these ideas involve different requirements at different levels of experience: individual, social, and political. At the political level, diversity is best satisfied by a balancing of values that is distinctive of liberal principles and institutions.

The diversity argument can be defended against a series of objections. In particular, the link between pluralism and diversity has been said to breach Hume's law against deriving values from facts. But pluralism is in part an evaluative concept, so the argument moves from value to value rather than from fact to value. Another objection sees liberalism as itself a monist position, which excludes significant goods and ways of life that ought to be respected by a pluralist. In reply, liberal pluralists can argue that no political view can include the entire range of human values and combinations of value. The best that can be achieved is a political structure that is more accommodating than its rivals, and that is what is provided by liberalism.

Another key issue is whether the diversity argument is compatible with the attention to historical context demanded by Williams. If pluralism is a permanent feature of human ethics, then is it not the case that an argument that links pluralism and liberalism conceptually shows liberalism to be eternally valid – which would contradict Williams's persuasive view that a liberal ranking of values is appropriate only under modern conditions? However, both the multiplicity and coherence components of diversity have contextual dimensions that place historical limits on the case for liberalism. The diversity argument endorses the promotion of multiple values, and of their coherence, only to the extent and in the form in which this is possible in the relevant historical circumstances.

Notes

1 Compare those views where survival is said to be the paramount consideration under all circumstances: see Jonathan Riley, discussed in Chapter 2, and the realist aspect of Bernard Williams, examined in Chapter 4.
2 See, similarly, Nagel's account of contingent and noncontingent conflict, discussed in Chapter 1, and Nussbaum's picture of conflict among capabilities, examined in Chapter 2.
3 By 'radical' multiculturalism, I mean the form that rejects the limits of liberalism, and that amounts to a species of cultural relativism, in contrast with the liberal multiculturalism that I argued in Chapter 3 can be endorsed from a pluralist point of view.
4 This point was made in connection with the reliance placed on leadership by Weber and Schmitt: see Chapter 3.
5 See also *LVP* 173–4.
6 Links between pluralism and liberal-democratic institutions are further developed in Chapter 8.
7 See, e.g., Francis Fukuyama, who argues that the balance between liberty and equality may legitimately be struck in different ways by different liberal democracies: Fukuyama 1992: 293–4. I agree in general, but question whether 'the individualism of Reagan's America or Thatcher's Britain' is as defensible, on the ground

of balance, as some of the alternatives. See my later discussion of classical vs egalitarian liberalism.
8 Waldron is highly critical of Berlin for his neglect of institutional matters, but the following will suggest that Waldron's institutional values are consistent with Berlin's basic position and even enhance it by showing how liberal constitutionalism is a sensible modern response to pluralist conflict at the political level. I pursue this theme in Chapter 8.
9 For more detailed responses to this question, see my *LVP* ch. 9; Crowder 2007, 2009, 2013b, ch. 9.
10 The same point can be made in relation to the idea of 'human well-being'. If the plural and incommensurable values are conceived as components of human well-being, as they are by Nussbaum, then 'well-being' is not advanced as a discrete value in its own right but only as the human context for the whole range of basic values and their various interpretations.
11 A similar objection is put forward by Polanowska-Sygulska in *UD* 295–6.
12 See also Talisse 2012: 63, 72.
13 Curiously, Talisse seems to think that there is something odd about presenting more than one argument for the same conclusion: Talisse 2012: 68. For other responses to Talisse, see Galston 2004; Spicer 2015; de Graaf 2015.
14 For more detailed argument defending Berlinian liberal pluralism against Rawlsian political liberalism, see my *LVP* Chapter 7 and Galston's *LP* Chapter 4.
15 See also Kekes 1997; Zakaras 2013a: 76.
16 I return to the link between pluralism and democracy in Chapter 7.
17 The relation between Berlin's value pluralism and Mill's fallibilism is discussed by Zakaras 2013a. Zakaras's article is followed by an exchange with Galston and myself: Galston 2013; Crowder 2013a; Zakaras 2013b.
18 See Berlin on the 'superfluous men' of Tsarist Russia, including Alexander Herzen and Ivan Turgenev (Berlin 2008: 213–4, 303–4).

References

In-text abbreviations are noted in brackets.

Apfel, Lauren J. (2011), *The Advent of Pluralism: Diversity and Conflict in the Age of Sophocles* (Oxford: Oxford University Press).
Berlin, Isaiah (2002), *Liberty*, ed. Henry Hardy (Oxford: Oxford University Press). [*L*]
Berlin, Isaiah (2008), *Russian Thinkers*, ed. Henry Hardy and Aileen Kelly (London: Penguin).
Berlin, Isaiah (2013), *The Crooked Timber of Humanity: Chapters in the History of Ideas*, ed. Henry Hardy, 2nd edn (Princeton: Princeton University Press). [*CTH*]
Berlin, Isaiah and Beata Polanowska-Sygulska (2006), *Unfinished Dialogue* (Amherst, NY: Prometheus Press). [*UD*]
Chang, Ruth, ed. (1997), *Incommensurability, Incomparability, and Practical Reasoning* (Cambridge: Cambridge University Press).
Chang, Ruth (2002), 'The Possibility of Parity', *Ethics* 112 (4): 659–88.
Crowder, George (2002), *Liberalism and Value Pluralism* (London: Continuum). [*LVP*]
Crowder, George (2007), 'Two Concepts of Liberal Pluralism', *Political Theory* 35: 121–46.
Crowder, George (2009), 'Pluralism, Liberalism and Distributive Justice', *San Diego Law Review* 46 (4), 773–802.
Crowder, George (2013a), 'Justification and Psychology in Liberal Pluralism: A Reply to Zakaras', *Review of Politics* 75 (1): 103–10.

Crowder, George (2013b), *Theories of Multiculturalism: An Introduction* (Cambridge: Polity).

de Graaf, Gjalt (2015), 'The Bright Future of Value Pluralism in Public Administration', *Administration and Society* 47 (9): 1094–102.

Dworkin, Ronald (1984), 'Rights as Trumps', in Jeremey Waldron, ed., *Theories of Rights* (Oxford: Oxford University Press).

Fukuyama, Francis (1992), *The End of History and the Last Man* (London: Penguin).

Galston, William (2002), *Liberal Pluralism: The Implications of Value Pluralism for Political Theory and Practice* (Cambridge: Cambridge University Press). [*LP*]

Galston, Williams (2004), 'Liberal Pluralism: A Reply to Talisse', *Contemporary Political Theory* 3 (2): 140–7.

Galston, William (2013), 'Between Logic and Psychology: The Links between Value Pluralism and Liberal Theory', *Review of Politics* 75 (1): 97–101.

Gray, John (1995), *Enlightenment's Wake: Politics and Culture at the Close of the Modern Age* (London: Routledge).

Gray, John (2013), *Isaiah Berlin: An Interpretation of His Thought*, new edition (Princeton: Princeton University Press).

Green, Thomas Hill (1991 [1881]), 'Liberal Legislation and Freedom of Contract', in David Miller, ed., *Liberty* (Oxford: Oxford University Press).

Griffin, James (1997), 'Incommensurability: What's the Problem?', in Ruth Chang, ed., *Incommensurability, Incomparability, and Practical Reasoning* (Cambridge: Cambridge University Press).

Hampshire, Stuart (1989), *Innocence and Experience* (Cambridge, MA: Harvard University Press). [*IE*]

Kekes, John (1993), *The Morality of Pluralism* (Princeton: Princeton University Press). [*MP*]

Kekes, John (1997), *Against Liberalism* (Ithaca, NY: Cornell University Press).

Mill, John Stuart (1958 [1861]), *Considerations on Representative Government*, ed. Currin V. Shields (Indianapolis: Bobbs-Merrill).

Mill, John Stuart (1974 [1859]), *On Liberty*, ed. Gertrude Himmelfarb (Harmondsworth: Penguin).

Montesquieu, Charles de Secondat, baron de (1949 [1748]), *The Spirit of the Laws*, trans. Thomas Nugent (New York: Hafner).

Moore, Matthew (2009), 'Pluralism, Relativism and Liberalism', *Political Research Quarterly* 62 (2): 244–56.

Neal, Patrick (2009), 'The Path between Value Pluralism and Liberal Political Order: Questioning the Connection', *San Diego Law Review* 46 (4): 859–82.

Nozick, Robert (1974), *Anarchy, State and Utopia* (New York: Basic Books).

Parfit, Derek (1984), *Reasons and Persons* (Oxford: Clarendon Press).

Rawls, John (1971), *A Theory of Justice* (Oxford: Oxford University Press).

Rawls, John (1993), *Political Liberalism* (New York: Columbia University Press).

Spicer, Michael (2015), 'On Value Pluralism, Its Implications, and the Nature of Philosophy', *Administration and Society* 47 (9): 1077–86.

Stokes, Geoffrey, ed. (1997), *The Politics of Identity in Australia* (Cambridge: Cambridge University Press).

Talisse, Robert (2012), *Pluralism and Liberal Politics* (New York: Routledge).

Talisse, Robert (2015), 'Value Pluralism: A Philosophical Clarification', *Administration & Society* 47 (9): 1064–76.

Turnbull, Colin (1973), *The Mountain People* (London: Jonathan Cape).

Waldron, Jeremy (2016), *Political Political Theory: Essays on Institutions* (Cambridge, MA: Harvard University Press). [*PPT*]

Walzer, Michael (1983), *Spheres of Justice: A Defence of Pluralism and Equality* (Oxford: Blackwell).

Williams, Bernard (2013), 'Introduction' to Isaiah Berlin, *Concepts and Categories*, ed. Henry Hardy, 2nd edn (Princeton: Princeton University Press).

Zakaras, Alex (2013a), 'A Liberal Pluralism: Isaiah Berlin and John Stuart Mill', *Review of Politics* 75 (1): 69–96.

Zakaras, Alex (2013b), 'Reply to Galston and Crowder', *Review of Politics* 75 (1): 111–4.

6 Toleration and Autonomy

In the previous chapter, I argued that the problem of value pluralism may be approached 'conceptually' by reflecting on the idea of value pluralism itself. At the level of a society, this implied a commitment to the promotion of the maximum 'diversity' of values, a goal combining considerations of multiplicity and coherence. Diversity in turn implied a case for liberalism as the political vehicle most likely, at least under modern conditions, to maximize the desirable diversity of values.

The current chapter has two aims. First, I want to pursue the practical implications of diversity further. Pluralist diversity implies a case for liberalism, at least under modern conditions, but can we say whether any particular form of liberalism meets the requirements of pluralism more completely than any other? In connection with economic distribution, I have already argued briefly in favor of egalitarian or redistributive forms of liberalism against classical or laissez-faire versions. I have also suggested, even more briefly, that a pluralist liberalism will be multiculturalist, meaning that it will celebrate the coexistence of more than one culture within its jurisdiction and that it will use public policy to support that coexistence.

I want now to look more closely at the multiculturalist side of liberal pluralism. My first question is: to what extent does pluralist diversity (primarily of values and secondarily of cultures) offer liberals guidance in formulating an appropriate attitude to culture, in particular to minority cultures, and more especially still to non-liberal minority cultures. This issue has very significant implications for public policy, raising questions about the proper treatment of religious and other strongly traditional groups in the United States and elsewhere.

One axis of debate in this matter pits those who see liberalism as standing primarily for the autonomy of the individual person against those who believe liberalism should be primarily identified with maximal toleration of the beliefs and practices of different social groups.[1] On the pro-autonomy side, traditional groups are often seen as placing serious restrictions on the autonomy of their members, and for this reason seen as open to criticism and perhaps intervention by the liberal state. On the pro-toleration side, the ideal of individual autonomy is typically viewed as too demanding a principle for liberal politics, since many non-liberal groups do not value that kind of personal freedom. To use the state to intervene in such groups in order to promote individual autonomy, or even to criticize them for their resistance to that ideal, is to fail in liberalism's principal duty of group toleration.

I approach this issue through the work of William Galston, who has emerged as a leading pluralist voice in recent years. Against the background of Berlinian pluralism, Galston argues in favor of what he calls the 'Reformation' view favoring group toleration against the 'Enlightenment' position that emphasizes personal autonomy. He does so by linking pluralism with a goal of diversity, much in the manner of the argument in the previous chapter, and then connecting diversity with group toleration. I argue that, while pluralism does indeed imply diversity, pluralist diversity does not support the kind of group toleration Galston upholds. Galston's argument here depends on running the idea of value pluralism together with that of cultural pluralism, a mistake I have touched on before and will tackle here at greater length. Indeed, Galston's diversity-based argument leads, on inspection, not to group toleration but to personal autonomy.

Personal autonomy can also be linked with value pluralism more directly. This is the second purpose of the chapter: to show how the concept of pluralism generates, in itself, another line of argument to set beside the diversity thesis. Roughly, I show that to take the plurality of values seriously is to acknowledge the reality of hard choices that are best made by those capable of personal autonomy. The best pluralist society will be one in which people are enabled to be autonomous – a liberal society on the Enlightenment model.

I begin by setting out Galston's position as an attempt to combine value-pluralist foundations with an insistence on toleration of illiberal group practices. In the next two sections, I argue that the logic of pluralism tends away from pro-toleration conclusions and toward the pro-autonomy view I advocate. This is true in two respects in particular. First, Galston's argument follows the typical pro-toleration route of relying on a right of exit to protect the members of illiberal groups. Here I argue that such a right, to be effective, presupposes a capacity for personal autonomy. Second, Galston's more distinctively pluralist argument is that pluralism implies a commitment to cultural diversity, hence toleration of a range of non-liberal cultural practices. On this point, I show that what is required here is a diversity not merely *among* cultural groups but *within* them as well, which again brings with it a case for personal autonomy as a moral and political ideal. I then reinforce my case for individual autonomy with a further argument based on value pluralism, emphasizing the link between the kind of choices that pluralism involves and the capacities necessary to make those choices well. A final section responds to a series of objections.

Berlin and Galston on Group Toleration

Galston's support for group toleration builds on that of Berlin but goes further. For Berlin, the reality has to be accepted that most political societies are formed around a dominant national culture, but such societies should be tolerant of minority groups (national, migrant, religious, and so on) in their midst. To be tolerant of a minority group is usually to refrain from interfering with its internal affairs, its beliefs, values, and institutions. It is not, however, to provide state support to the group or even positive evaluation – Berlin is not a multiculturalist. 'I believe that the common culture which all societies deeply need can only be disrupted by more than a moderate degree of self-assertion on the part of ethnic or other minorities conscious of a common identity' (Gardels 1991: 21).

Berlin's view to some extent reflects his preference for negative liberty over positive liberty as an ideal in politics.[2] Berlinian toleration might be described as essentially negative liberty applied to the situation of minorities: they are neither helped nor hindered, simply left alone. However, what happens when the negative liberty of a minority group as a whole comes into conflict with the negative liberty of individual members of the group? For example, a group may deny individual freedom of religion to its members. Should the state step in to ensure individual liberty or should it avoid interfering? At this point, Berlin would probably favor the negative liberty of the individual. Galston would give a different answer.

Galston opposes state interference, in the name of individual liberty, and especially in the name of personal autonomy, in the internal affairs of minorities. In a well-known article, the rival values of toleration and personal autonomy are linked by Galston with the historical emergence of 'two concepts of liberalism' (Galston 1995).[3] 'Reformation' liberalism, looking back to the Lockean response to the European wars of religion, takes as its central value the toleration of religious and cultural diversity. By contrast, 'Enlightenment' liberalism, including in its pantheon the key figures of Kant and John Stuart Mill, sees the distinctive task of liberalism as the promotion of a specific vision of the human good, namely that of the autonomous or rationally self-directing individual.

Most of Galston's readers took his original article to be championing the Reformation view, arguing for the priority of toleration over individual autonomy in the liberal schedule of values. More recently he has distanced himself somewhat from that impression, writing that his intention was not to reject the Enlightenment view but rather to identify a 'balance' between autonomy and toleration (*PLP* 183). Nevertheless, it is fair to say that Galston's emphasis has always been rather more on the toleration side of this issue. He describes his goal as the 'maximum feasible accommodation' of diverse ways of life within a liberal order and strongly objects to the 'civic totalism' that would seek to enforce liberal public values within all groups (*LP* 20; *PLP* 24).

In particular, Galston remains opposed to the promotion of a 'Socratic/Millian' concept of personal autonomy as an ideal for liberal policy (*PLP* 182; see also *LP* 21). Personal autonomy is the kind of strong self-direction that comes from critical reflection on one's own norms. The model is that of Socratic self-questioning or the 'individuality' that Mill discusses and celebrates in *On*

Liberty, where the individual obeys no customary injunction without being prepared to examine its justification. As Mill writes, 'it is the privilege and proper condition of a human being, arrived at the maturity of his faculties, to use and interpret experience in his own way' (Mill 1974 [1859]: 122). For Galston, this ideal lies at the heart of the Enlightenment 'commitment to sustained rational examination of self, others, and social practices' (*LP* 21).

The trouble with personal autonomy, according to Galston, is that it is too demanding. The Enlightenment outlook presupposes a particular, rationalist and individualist understanding of the human good that is too exclusive of the legitimate cultural diversity to be found in a modern society. If liberals insist on promoting the ideal of individual autonomy in all spheres of society, they risk alienating 'many citizens of goodwill' and creating opponents in place of allies (*LP* 26).

The Reformation ideal, by contrast, is recommended by its realistic acknowledgment of the wide diversity of belief and practice within modern societies. The central, guiding ideal of Galston's liberal state is a presumption in favor of the 'expressive liberty' of all citizens, meaning the absence of obstacles to 'individuals and groups leading their lives as they see fit, within a broad range of legitimate variation, in accordance with their own understanding of what gives life meaning and value' (*LP* 3).

Two points need highlighting. The first is the opposition between Galston's expressive liberty and Mill's personal autonomy. Galston's phrase 'own understanding' may seem no different from Mill's 'own way', but there is a crucial distinction. Expressive liberty does not require reflection. The understanding it expresses may be acquired unreflectively from unexamined tradition – and it may be deeply mistaken. All that matters for the Reformation ideal is that people be left alone to believe and live as they wish, irrespective of what it is that they believe and wish.[4]

Second, does that mean that Galston's expressive liberty is equivalent to Berlin's negative liberty? Here Galston's phrase 'individuals and groups' contains a crucial ambiguity. If expressive liberty refers to the freedom of individuals to live as they please, that would seem no different from Berlinian negative liberty, and it would be attractive to liberals. However, Galston also refers to the expressive liberty of groups, and that is a different matter. The expressive liberty of groups is a distinctly collective form of negative liberty, with consequences that are much more questionable from a liberal – and pluralist – point of view, as we shall see.

Given the group-oriented aspect of expressive liberty, Galston's liberal polity will be wary of imposing its public principles on the internal arrangements of groups within civil society, even where these maintain practices that are explicitly illiberal in character – such as arranged marriages, sexual discrimination, or indoctrinating forms of education. For example, Galston supports the right of the Old Order Amish to forbid, on the ground of religious belief, access by Amish children to public upper-year high school education. 'Expressive liberty', he insists, 'protects the ability of individuals and groups to live in ways that others would regard as unfree' (*LP* 29). Liberal standards would continue to apply in the public realm but need not be mirrored within civil associations. Not all ways of life are protected by the principle of expressive liberty, but the range of legitimate variation will be very wide.

Value pluralism enters the picture at the level of fundamental justification. Galston's starting point is Berlin's notion of the irreducible plurality and incommensurability of human goods, which opposes the idea of moral monism (*LP* 4–6; *PLP* ch. 2). Against monism, pluralists see moral values as 'qualitatively heterogeneous' (i.e., incommensurable) and consequently not subject to any 'common measure' or 'summum bonum' or 'comprehensive lexical orderings' (*LP* 5). Consequently pluralism, in contrast with monism, contemplates the likelihood of many cases where moral decision making will be highly problematic, since there will be no absolute or universal ordering, such as that of utilitarianism, to which we can appeal for a solution.

Nevertheless, Galston follows Berlin (and Hampshire, Kekes, Nussbaum, and Williams) in holding that reasoned moral decision making under pluralism, although often hard and sometimes impossible, is not *necessarily* impossible. 'Value pluralism', Galston writes, 'does not rule out the possibility of compelling (if nonalgorithmic) arguments for right answers in specific situations' (*LP* 35). Indeed, Galston, recalling his experience of wrestling with clashes among plural considerations while he was working as an official in the Clinton administration, finds it 'remarkable how often we could reach deliberative closure in the face of this heterogeneity' (*LP* 7).

According to Galston, the form of politics that fits best with a value-pluralist outlook is Reformation liberalism. Against anti-liberal pluralists like John Gray and John Kekes, Galston argues that liberalism is maximally capable of accommodating the expressive liberty of the many ways of life that are worthy of respect according to a pluralist view. He presents several arguments for this claim, but the strongest is based on a link between pluralism and diversity:

> if moral pluralism is the most nearly adequate depiction of the moral universe we inhabit, then the range of choiceworthy human lives is very wide. While some ways of life can be ruled out as violating minimum standards of humanity, most cannot. If so, then the zone of human agency protected by the norm of expressive liberty is capacious indeed.
>
> (*LP* 37)

If values are plural and incommensurable, then many different general rankings will be valid as long as they pass a threshold of minimum decency. Such a wide range of legitimate ways of life is best accommodated by Reformation liberalism, with its stress on expressive liberty.

Further, these many ways of life will include some, like the Amish way of life, that are based on explicitly non-liberal beliefs hostile to individual autonomy. Value pluralism thus supports, according to Galston, a form of liberalism that is closer to Reformation-style toleration of diversity rather than to an autonomy-based Enlightenment liberalism.

Expressive Liberty and Personal Autonomy

The obvious concern with Galston's position from a pluralist point of view is with his emphasis on expressive liberty in preference to other important goods. Galston presents expressive liberty and value pluralism as distinct sources for his overall position, which might suggest that his emphasis on expressive liberty is valid independently of pluralism. But once the pluralist genie is out of the bottle any normative claim can be assessed by pluralist standards.

Consequently, even though Galston does not make expressive liberty overriding, he does speak of a presumption in its favor, and that claim has to be examined from a pluralist perspective. Given the combined arguments of Williams and Welzel in Chapter 4, we might accept that a priority of this kind may reasonably be accorded to some conception of individual liberty under modern conditions. But why should this take the form of expressive liberty? In particular, why should modern pluralists privilege expressive liberty in preference to personal autonomy?

Two problems with Galston's position stand out immediately. First, recall that, in Galston's formulation, people possess expressive liberty as long as they live according to whatever understandings give their lives 'meaning and value', which requires none of the critical reflection that is central to personal autonomy. But surely people have an interest not only in living as they wish, but in living in accordance with values and rules that actually make sense and are justified. As Will Kymlicka writes,

> Since we can be wrong about the worth or value of what we are currently doing, and since no one wants to lead a life based on false beliefs about its worth, it is of fundamental importance that we be able rationally to assess our conceptions of the good in the light of new information or experiences, and to revise them if they are not worthy of our continued allegiance.
> (Kymlicka 1995: 81)

If so, critical reflection and consequently personal autonomy are essential to the best kind of life, and expressive liberty is insufficient.

The second problem with privileging expressive liberty is that, in effect, it allows non-liberal groups to oppress their own members. Expressive liberty is, at least in part, the liberty of the group as a whole to live as it pleases – this is the aspect of the idea stressed by Galston. But some groups are hostile to liberal values, including freedom of speech and religion, gender equality, personal autonomy, and even expressive liberty as it applies to the individual (i.e., negative individual liberty). When this collective kind of expressive liberty is promoted or condoned by the state, the result may be less like a 'liberal archipelago', as Chandran Kukathas puts it, and more like a 'mosaic of tyrannies', in Leslie Green's words.⁵ For example, Susan Okin notes that traditional, non-liberal cultures are typically patriarchal and that consequently women and children in such societies are especially vulnerable to norms that distort or circumscribe their free development (Okin 1999).

The standard defense against this objection appeals to a right of exit: individuals are sufficiently protected against intra-group oppression if they are free to leave the group. Thus, Galston argues that a liberal state may legitimately leave groups alone as long as it guarantees 'enforceable rights of exit' (*LP* 104). But what does it mean to be free to exit a group?

One answer, advanced by Kukathas, is that people are always free to leave their groups as long as they are not prevented from doing so by force (Kukathas 2003: 103–14). This is a strict negative liberty standard: all that counts is the absence of coercion; whatever other obstacles there may be to action, they are irrelevant to 'freedom'. Kukathas gives the hypothetical example of Fatima, the Muslim wife of a Malay fisherman. She has no desire to leave her village community, since her identity is closely defined by her roles as wife, mother, and Muslim. Although Kukathas does not quite say so, it probably does not occur to Fatima even to imagine how her life might be otherwise than it is. Nevertheless, Kukathas insists, she is free to exit. The fact that she stays shows that she has 'acquiesced' in her life. But whether or not she can be said to have chosen her fate, what matters for Kukathas is that she possesses the negative liberty to leave if she wished – no one is forcing her to stay.

Most liberals will, rightly, be deeply dissatisfied with this view. The fact that no one is forcing Fatima to stay is consistent with her having no realistic prospect of leaving because of obstacles other than simple coercion.⁶ These include the costs that are often attached to exit, including economic and psychological costs, the risks of failure in the society into which one is exiting, lack of economic resources with which to make exit possible if one has decided in that direction, and (perhaps most significant for the present discussion) the kind of social conditioning that makes exit unimaginable in the first place.

Okin, for example, emphasizes the range of ways in which women and girls in particular can be prevented from leaving groups defined by allegiance to traditional patriarchal cultures. Women's choices in these contexts are severely limited by lack of education, since girls are frequently thought less worth educating than boys, and by damaging education designed to train girls to accept confining gender roles. Traditions of early or arranged or even forced marriage further restrict women's choices in these groups, as do patterns of general socialization that undermine women's self-esteem while imposing on them the expectation that they will be the principal transmitters and perpetuators of the culture. The upshot is that, for many women in traditional cultures, the prospect of exit can be literally 'unthinkable' (Okin 2002: 222). On this view, Fatima is free to exit only in the narrowest, most formal sense, on a level with the legendary freedom of the poor to dine at the Ritz.

Galston agrees that genuine freedom to exit must be 'more than formal'; it must mean that individuals have real choices when it comes to staying or going

(*LP* 104). A group cannot legitimately claim that its members have a right of exit merely because the group refrains from coercion while effectively 'disempowering' people from living outside the group. Groups may not legitimately keep their members within 'a kind of mental and moral prison' (*LP* 105). But if that is so, that must mean that in order to count as genuinely free to exit, one must be 'empowered' to do so – that is, one must have the positive capacity to overcome the various obstacles to exit listed above: informational, economic, and psychological. Crucially, it would seem, real freedom of exit would seem to involve the capacity to stand back from the group's norms and to assess them critically – that is, the capacity for autonomous judgment. And if that is so, then Galston's position relies on a commitment to personal autonomy after all.

Galston comes close to conceding this conclusion in some places. In one passage, he allows that a precondition for a genuine right of exit is that those who might claim this must not be 'servile' in the face of their parents', or the group's, authority. He cites approvingly Eamonn Callan's view that 'as a parent, I cannot rightly mold my child's character in a way that effectively preempts "serious thought at any future date about the alternatives to my judgement"' (*LP* 105, citing Callan 1997: 154).

This is surely right. A person cannot be said to have a genuine right of exit if she is incapable of independent thought as a result of her upbringing. But then, it is hard to see how this kind of conditioning can be prevented short of encouraging the development in children of a form of character in which 'serious thought' along these lines is possible and valued. And once again, it is hard to see how this can be anything less than a case for the facilitation of individual autonomy. Indeed, in the earlier article Galston goes so far as to allow that protecting the capacity to exit against conditioning of this kind 'brings us back some distance toward policies more typically associated with autonomy concerns' (Galston 1995: 534).

At this point, however, Galston argues that although a realistic right of exit does imply a capacity for autonomy, this need only be 'a more modest conception of autonomy as freedom of choice' in contrast with 'a Socratic/Millian ideal of autonomy, understood as rational reflection and self-creation' (*PLP* 182). This distinction is not developed by Galston, but a similar preference for a weaker rather than stronger form of autonomy can be found in several liberal thinkers.

David Johnston, for example, distinguishes between 'moral' and 'personal' autonomy (Johnston 1994: 71–7). Moral autonomy consists of a capacity to form and act on projects and values, together with a sense of justice, taking into account the interests of others. Personal autonomy is self-definition in a stronger sense, involving the ability to subject one's own projects, values, and sense of justice to critical reflection. Johnston argues that only moral autonomy is an essential ideal for good society; personal autonomy, although desirable from a comprehensively liberal point of view, is too demanding to be a necessary goal of public policy because such a policy would assume that 'a life of personal autonomy is intrinsically superior to relatively nonautonomous ways of life' (Johnston 1994: 98).

Similarly, Anthony Appiah distinguishes the 'strong' autonomy of critical reflection from a more moderate 'core' autonomy that involves 'an availability of options, an endowment with minimum rationality, an absence of coercion', declaring the latter to be an adequate ideal for liberal purposes while the former is 'outlandishly exigent' (Appiah 2005: 40, 38).

How can the defender of strong autonomy respond? First, what reply can be made to Johnston's claim that a policy commitment to strong autonomy assumes the superiority of 'a life of personal autonomy'? One possibility might be to distinguish between strong autonomy as a substantial end that is characteristic of a whole way of life and strong autonomy as a procedural entry-point into a way of life that may itself not regard autonomy as especially valuable.[7] As an example of substantial autonomy, one may take J. S. Mill's celebration of 'individuality' as the life of energetic and restless self-creation. An example of procedural autonomy is provided by those educated women who embrace Islamic traditions, such as the wearing of head scarves, as a result of conscious and considered reflection on their own identity (Benhabib 2002: 94–100). Procedural autonomy seems consistent with the equal valuation of lives that are not substantially autonomous, and it might be argued that this kind of autonomy is all that autonomy-based liberalism need insist on.

I do not wish to rely on this argument, however. For one thing, the procedural-substantial distinction is a little too neat. Certainly, someone can decide autonomously to enter a heteronomous way of life: the armed forces or religious orders, say. But for that decision to be made autonomously usually requires, in the first place, a social environment in which autonomy is at least minimally supported. Procedural autonomy usually needs substantial autonomy. A stronger response to Johnston's objection is that the substantially autonomous way of life is indeed superior, but I shall come to this later.

Second, is the ideal of personal autonomy really so outlandishly exigent? Appiah supposes that to support strong autonomy is to 'assign us all to undertake a comprehensive assessment of norms and values' and that this confuses 'the job description of the citizen with that of the moral theorist' (Appiah 2005: 51). But to reflect critically on one's options, or even on one's life as a whole, is not necessarily to question everything at once. It is more likely to take the form of a piecemeal inquiry into how well a proposed course of action is likely to cohere with other aspects of one's life, provisionally taken as given (Richardson 1994: 152–8).

Of course, one's goals in life may come to be revised in the light of a proposed course of action, but that still need not amount to a Nietzschean project of total revaluation of all values. In this connection, Johnston concedes 'the need for the members of any good society to possess some capacity to reexamine their own projects and values critically' (Johnston 1994: 98). Without such a capacity, as Kymlicka points out, people cannot be said to be living their lives 'from the inside' – that is, to be living lives that they really affirm as their own (Kymlicka

1995: 81). Galston, with his emphasis on 'expressive liberty', should also accept this point.

Third, even if a capacity for personal autonomy were not essential to a good life or to a good liberal society, it might still be essential to a realistic freedom of exit. It is precisely at the point when a person is contemplating transferring her cultural allegiances, one might argue, that she most needs to be able to step back from her current identifications (at least some of them) in order to either re-affirm or revise them. In the absence of evidence that Fatima, for example, can do this, she cannot be said to possess real freedom to exit.

Ironically, then, one might argue that it is those theorists who rely most heavily on exit rights who thereby rely most heavily (despite their claims to the contrary) on the capacity for personal autonomy. Conversely, part of the reason why writers like Appiah and Johnston place less emphasis on strong autonomy is that they place less emphasis on the need for freedom to exit.

But then, need for a right of exit is not the only reason why we should support personal autonomy as an ethical and political ideal. Okin, for example, argues that a realistic right of exit is only a necessary, not a sufficient condition for genuine freedom. 'Rights of exit provide no help to women or members of other oppressed groups who are deeply attached to their cultures but not to their oppressive aspects' (Okin 2002: 226–7). For the claim to be plausible that the members of such groups – or any groups – are genuinely living in accordance with 'their own understanding' of what gives life meaning, there must be more options open to them than either exit or uncritical conformity. There must, in addition, be room for dissent. In the terms introduced by Albert Hirschman (1970), there must be the possibility not only of exit but also of 'voice'. This point connects with the value of diversity, which I examine next.

Diversity of What?

Up to this point, I have argued that a commitment to personal autonomy emerges out of Galston's own case for expressive liberty. Expressive liberty looks like an adequate liberal ideal only if it is backed up by a right of exit, but a right of exit is genuine only if backed by personal autonomy. But what about Galston's argument from value pluralism? How far does pluralism support his pro-toleration conclusion? Recall that Gaston's basic claim here is that if value pluralism is true, then values may legitimately be ranked in many different ways – that is, pluralism implies a commitment to respect for a wide diversity of ways of life. Further, that kind of diversity is best accommodated by liberalism, in particular by toleration-based liberalism.

Galston is broadly correct to link value pluralism with diversity, and diversity with liberalism, but his arguments here need reinforcement and adjustment. When the reinforcements have been added and the adjustments made, it turns out, once again, that the kind of liberalism that fits best with pluralist diversity is autonomy – rather than toleration-based. The logic of Galston's pluralist reasoning again leads in a pro-autonomy direction.

First, consider Galston's argument from value pluralism to the valuing of cultural diversity within a single political society. There is a serious problem here, which can be brought out by recalling the similar argument from Gray, discussed in Chapter 5. Gray accepts that pluralism implies the valuing of cultural diversity, but denies that this is best promoted within a liberal state. Liberal states inevitably promote liberal ways of life within their borders, at best marginalizing, at worst undermining, non-liberal ways of life. Rather, the cultural diversity indicated by pluralism is best served, Gray believes, by a diversity of political communities, some of which are liberal, some not. Liberalism is merely one valid political form among others, appropriate for those cultures that privilege distinctively liberal goods but inappropriate for others. However, Gray's argument is flawed. Liberal pluralists can concede that liberalism has its costs in terms of goods and ways of life forgone, but still rightly insist that it imposes fewer such costs than the alternatives. Modern liberal democracies are not accommodating of all forms of life equally, but they do better in this respect than North Korea.

Galston is therefore on strong ground when he argues that the pluralist concern for moral diversity is best satisfied (under modern conditions) by liberal democracies. But will this be a toleration-based liberalism? Galston's reason for supporting this interpretation is that 'from a value-pluralist standpoint, there are many valuable ways of life, individual and collective, that are not autonomous in the sense that they are not the product of conscious reflection and choice but, rather, of habit, tradition, authority, or unswerving faith' (*LP* 49). The range of lives that count as legitimate and valuable under pluralism includes many in which individual autonomy is not valued.

Two main replies are possible. First, Galston's argument here cuts both ways. It is true that some ways of life do not value individual autonomy, but these same ways of life generally have little time for the negative liberty or 'freedom of choice' that tends to be favored by the advocates of toleration-based liberty either. From the perspective of her culture, Fatima is not free but obligated to live as she does.

Second, and more importantly for the current discussion, a case for personal autonomy is also implicit in Galston's commitment to diversity itself. His reply to Gray is, in effect, that pluralists must care about diversity not only *among* political communities but *within* them as well. The diversity celebrated by value pluralists suggests the desirability not so much of multiple types of political regime, as advocated by Gray, since many such regimes will be inhospitable to cultural difference. Rather, pluralism points to those political regimes that are capable of accommodating multiple ways of life. Consequently, pluralist diversity is not best promoted through the serial political chauvinism celebrated by Gray; rather, it is optimally expressed by political societies that are prepared to embrace a form of liberal multiculturalism.

But here we should take Galston's own logic a step further, returning to a theme that has developed through a series of earlier discussions.[8] If pluralism implies the valuing of diversity *among* cultures within political societies, then it implies the valuing of diversity *within* cultures too. Pluralist diversity should be a diversity not merely of states (Gray), nor merely of cultures within states (Galston), but of internally diverse cultures. Internally diverse cultures will tend to be liberal cultures. Further, they will tend to be liberal cultures based on personal autonomy. The kind of liberalism that, on the logic of Galston's own view, most adequately promotes diversity will be Enlightenment liberalism.

Why and in what sense must the cultures within a pluralist polity be internally diverse? I have made this point already in previous chapters, but it is worth reinforcing because it remains widely under-appreciated in the pluralist literature. It is certainly not adequately acknowledged by either Gray or Galston. The notion of value pluralism is primarily a notion of the plurality and incommensurability of individual *values*, not of ways of life. This must be so, because if it were primarily cultures that were incommensurable there would be nothing to distinguish value pluralism from cultural relativism. Pluralism, as a distinctive position, points to a deep plurality of value that cuts across cultural difference; conflicts among incommensurable goods can occur as easily within cultures as among them. Indeed, on the distinctively pluralist view, cultures, unlike goods, *cannot* be wholly incommensurable because they all overlap within the admittedly wide but nevertheless finite horizon of the great goods.

This does not mean that pluralists should deny the fact or the value of cultural diversity altogether; on the contrary, pluralists should value cultural diversity. But they should do so only to the extent that this follows from, and is subordinate to, their primary concern, which is respect for the diversity of human goods. What makes cultures valuable on this view is that people will interpret and pursue the same basic goods in different ways in different contexts, giving rise to a diversity of value patterns that should, prima facie, be respected. But a natural limit to the value of cultures from a value-pluralist perspective is set by the extent to which they fail to promote value diversity internally.

A political society is culturally diverse when its members are genuinely able to pursue a multiplicity of ways of life, assuming that these are at least minimally coherent. Similarly, a culture is internally diverse when its members are genuinely able to pursue a multiplicity of minimally coherent goods and personal projects, either interpreting the culture in new or different ways, or transforming it.

Diversity of values connects with another dimension of diversity internal to cultures, which Galston calls 'the diversity of human types' (*LP* 59). This refers to the natural diversity of individual talents and potentialities. Here there is an obvious link with value diversity, since different kinds of individuals will pursue different kinds of values, and different values will help to produce variant personality types. Galston is rightly concerned that such individual potentialities are under threat in 'narrow-valued societies', since these 'will allow only a small fraction of their inhabitants to live their lives in a manner consistent with their flourishing and satisfaction. The rest will be pinched and stunted to some degree, and some ways of life will be ruled out altogether (no Socrates in Sparta)' (*LP* 60).

This worry about the fate of the individual in the narrow-valued society is justified but it ought to be taken further. If this is a legitimate concern within societies, then it should also be a legitimate concern within the cultures that animate societies whether these belong to majority or minority groups. Galston's own definition of 'diversity' refers to 'legitimate differences among individuals and groups' (*LP* 21), but his focus on groups tends to obscure the worry about individuals.

One can take this line of argument further still: legitimate and valuable diversity may apply not only among individuals but within them as well. As Michael Sandel argues, we may think of a single human being as containing 'a plurality of selves' in the sense of competing identities corresponding to the different talents and potentialities that people usually possess (Sandel 1982: 63). 'True diversity', writes Emily Gill, 'requires, then, the imagination necessary to make use of the range of available options. These must be available within the culture in the objective sense. But they must also be available within the individual, as it were, in the sense of becoming real possibilities that we can imagine as defining our identities' (Gill 2001: 37).

A diverse culture, in these terms, is one that makes room for, and empowers, a range of personal projects and character types, but also one that enables its members to explore some range of these as real options within a single life. Plato acknowledged individual differences, but insisted on matching each person with a single correct social slot. Liberal pluralists who wish to maximize diversity within a single polity should support individuals who want to experiment with multiple lines of self-development.

There is a link here with personal autonomy. A diverse culture, one that does justice to the variety of human goods, personalities, and options within a single life, must be one in which individual liberty has a prominent place. But individual liberty in what sense? Similar considerations apply here to those already canvassed in connection with realistic rights of exit. To be genuinely able to strike out on one's own path requires freedom from coercion (negative liberty) and access to any necessary material resources (effective freedom), but also, and crucially, the capacity for critical reflection on the conventions of one's own culture. It requires personal autonomy. Pluralist diversity is optimally satisfied by a society that accommodates and enables multiple ways of life, each of which allows its individual members to pursue and develop a variety of goods, virtues, and personal projects. In such a society, different people will be brought up in different ways of life, but they will be genuinely free to interpret those ways of life in their own way. For such an ideal to be realized, a capacity for personal autonomy is an essential prerequisite.

This amounts to taking seriously the value-pluralist injunction to maximize the range of goods that people can pursue within a single society. It also satisfies, but goes further than, Galston's ideal of expressive liberty, the freedom to live in accordance with '*one's own* understanding of what gives life meaning' (my emphasis). The autonomy view takes this more seriously than does Galston's group-toleration view, which allows 'one's own understanding' to be equated with that of a group, or (more likely) a group's dominant voices.

I now have an answer to the question, raised earlier, of how far Galston's emphasis on expressive liberty can be reconciled with his value pluralism. The answer is that there is indeed a problem if the argument sticks with the idea of expressive liberty as Galston conceives it. From the perspective of pluralism, expressive liberty is only one value among others. If living in accordance with one's own understanding is compatible with the uncritical following of group custom, then that may conflict with important values of truth and justice. However, the problem begins to dissolve if it is accepted that we ought to be talking about personal autonomy, since personal autonomy has a special connection with value pluralism that expressive liberty lacks. Pluralism implies a commitment to value diversity, which in turn suggests a particularly important role for critical reflection. I expand on this in a moment.

To sum up: value pluralism does suggest a principle of maximum diversity, but at what level? Gray's diversity of political societies is rightly superseded by Galston's insistence on cultural diversity within political societies. But cultural diversity, in turn, is subordinate to a diversity of goods, which brings with it an intra-cultural concern for a multiplicity of individual projects, talents, and characters, and even of potentialities within the individual. The pluralist requirement that political societies be culturally diverse points to liberalism, as Galston shows. The further requirement that the constituent cultures themselves be internally diverse points once again to autonomy-based liberalism.

Hard Choices and Personal Autonomy

So far I have argued that a case for autonomy-based liberalism can be made by following Galston's own arguments to their logical conclusions. His case for expressive liberty folds into a case for personal autonomy, as does his argument for diversity. I want now to map a more direct route from pluralism to autonomy that does not pass through Galston. This can be roughly summarized as follows. Pluralism imposes hard choices on us where incommensurable values conflict, and to cope well with those choices we need to be capable of reasoned critical reflection – that is, personal autonomy.[9]

Why should we respond autonomously to the choices pluralism imposes on us? In the face of conflicting incommensurables should we not just as well decide arbitrarily, or randomly, or in accordance with a rule or tradition that is not itself questioned? To answer this, we need to look more closely at the distinctive kind of choice involved where the conflicting goods are incommensurable. Two features are especially important.

First, such a choice calls for a reasoned rather than arbitrary response. To cope well with a choice among deeply plural goods is to choose for good reason. But again, why should we be committed to reason here? Why not say that from a pluralist point of view rational choice is itself merely one value among others and that one may equally cope with pluralist choice by plumping arbitrarily among the alternatives?

The answer refers again to the argument for value diversity. If value pluralism is true, then many goods make a genuine contribution to human well-being and we must take all of these seriously. In particular cases, some of these goods will conflict and we shall have to choose among them. But even when we choose against a good, we should, on the pluralist view, recognize that the good we forgo is still valuable. Its loss is a real one, even though we have made the best possible decision in the circumstances – this aspect of the pluralist outlook accounts for the element of tragedy in some moral choices, where the good forgone is important.

It follows that, at least in cases where the values at stake are significant, pluralist choice should not be merely arbitrary or casual. If these are genuine human goods, we must not be indifferent to them even when we have to choose against them. To respect those goods we choose against is to choose against them only for good reason. Consequently, choices among such goods call for a reasoned response in which we should try to think about what particular package of goods is desirable and coherent in the particular case before us. To take plural values seriously is to be committed to practical reasoning.[10]

Granted the need for practical reasoning, the next question is: why should this involve the critical reflection that is essential to personal autonomy? Why should we not rest content with thinking about the best means of pursuing ends that are uncritically received from conventional rules or traditions?

The requirement for critical reflection is the second feature of pluralist choice that I want to emphasize. Conflicts among incommensurable values cannot be decided for good reason merely by the mechanical application of conventional rules, because these tend to rest on monist assumptions. Utilitarianism, for example, elevates 'utility' (however defined) to the status of supervalue, overriding or commensurating all other goods. But under pluralism, this can be no more than one proposal among others. The rational pluralist cannot rely on utilitarianism or any other ready-made monist procedure to resolve deep moral conflicts, but must go behind such perspectives to assess for herself the values they embody.

Nor, contrary to the conservative view of Kekes, can pluralists answer such questions merely by appealing to the authority of local tradition.[11] Traditionalism is really another name for cultural relativism, which was distinguished from value pluralism in Chapter 1. Further, under modern conditions traditions are contested, multiple, and conflicting, as noted in Chapter 3. For pluralists, reasonable disagreement concerning the good life is a permanent possibility in all human societies because of the deep structure of human value. Traditional and other conceptions of the good life are essentially generalized rankings of incommensurable values. Pluralists should not accept that all such conceptions are automatically on a moral par, since some promote the great goods and value diversity more satisfactorily than others. Nevertheless, the wide range of genuine human goods implies a wide range of legitimate permutations of those goods – that is, of reasonable rankings. Concerning these there is consequently room for people to disagree on reasonable grounds.

An argument for personal autonomy follows. Pluralists cannot resolve the deepest value conflicts simply by citing a local or personal conception of the good, because under pluralism these are subject to reasonable, therefore permanent, disagreement. Where the nature of the good life is subject to reasonable disagreement, conceptions of the good cannot be permanent bases for decision but must be subject to revision themselves and to balancing with other such conceptions. That kind of decision is possible only through the exercise of personal autonomy.

The foregoing amounts to a distinctive line of argument from value pluralism to the recognition of individual autonomy as a human good of especial importance. Pluralism is a thesis about the deep structure of values in human experience at large, across all cultures and periods. If pluralism is true, the moral experience of all human beings will include choices among incommensurable values. These are difficult choices that call for autonomous judgment if they are to be made well – that is, they call for critically reflective judgment in accordance with norms of practical rationality implicit in the concept of pluralism itself. The capacity for personal autonomy therefore contributes, on a pluralist view, to the good life for any human being (at least under modern conditions). Human lives are likely to go better to the extent that those living them are able to choose critically and wisely when they are confronted by choices among conflicting goods.

To say that on a pluralist view personal autonomy is a human good 'of especial importance' is not to make the monist claim that autonomy is overriding. To begin with, the argument for personal autonomy is subject to the historical context explained in Chapter 4. Personal autonomy is one of the emancipatory values that are rendered more useful by modern conditions. It is only in modernity, with the waning of survival needs and the waxing of material ambitions, that individual self-direction becomes the desirable good that it now is.

Moreover, even within the framework of modernity my view does not demand that individual autonomy be accepted as a trump in every case. I do not deny the possibility of cases where autonomy appropriately yields to rival considerations, such as urgency or security or the demands of personal relationships. But, as I have noted before, pluralists can recognize rules or principles that apply not absolutely but generally. Berlin, for example, allows that even in liberal politics there may sometimes be a good reason to subordinate liberty to other values, such as 'equality, or justice, or happiness, or security, or public order' (*L* 214).

Galston offers useful guidance in this regard when he argues that pluralism is compatible with 'powerful but rebuttable presumptions' – rules that apply across a wide range of cases, but that can be overridden in particular circumstances. 'Rights', for example, 'have great moral weight, but they do not function as trumps in every shuffle of the deck' (*LP* 77). Galston, of course, makes this claim for expressive liberty, but I have argued that it suits autonomy better.

What about the role of the state? If personal autonomy is an element of the best human lives (at any rate in modernity), it would appear that, at a minimum, the state ought not to prevent or discourage its citizens from being autonomous. But this is only a minimum; there is good reason to expect more of the state than this. This point parallels my earlier discussion of exit rights, where I argued that realistic exit rights require, in addition to negative liberty, effective freedom and personal autonomy.

Mere non-interference with the processes by which personal autonomy emerges amounts, in effect, to shutting many people out of the possibility of autonomy, since individual autonomy is effectively discouraged by the conformist environments created by illiberal groups. Nor is the mere presence of a liberal society outside the walls of an illiberal group sufficient to make autonomy a real possibility for many of the group's members, since such groups typically have effective means of insulating themselves from outside influences. Galston allows this point implicitly when he defends Amish resistance to public education and then qualifies that defense with the right of exit. If the methods of the Amish were not effective at insulating their members from the liberal world outside, there would be no point either in defending those methods or in insisting on realistic rights of exit.

The capacity for autonomous judgment does not emerge in people automatically; rather, it requires certain conditions, including access to resources and education in how to reflect critically on available options. These conditions will not be met by illiberal groups themselves, and they will be distributed only very unevenly by the free market. Consequently, their likeliest guarantor will be the state. The pluralist case for personal autonomy as a central human good flows into a case for a liberal state that is entitled to promote that capacity in its citizens.[12]

Dilemmas, Heteronomy, Truth, and Intervention

This position is bound to attract objections. I consider four presented by Galston. First, it might be argued that value pluralism is not always encouraging to practical reasoning. Some conflicts among incommensurables cannot be resolved rationally, in which case reasoned critical reflection is irrelevant (*PLP* 190).

To the extent that this is true, it is as much of a problem for the pro-toleration view as for mine. Such a view depends as much as mine on the possibility that pluralism does not rule out reason giving entirely, since only then can a reasoned defense of any political position be offered. Galston, as we have seen, takes the sensible line that while pluralism may lead to rationally insoluble dilemmas in some cases, it is compatible with reasoned resolutions in others. But then, in those cases where reasoning is possible, it may be more or less critically reflective. I have argued that it ought generally to be more critically reflective rather than less. Further, even in those cases where a rational resolution is not possible, autonomy may have a role, since we shall still have to think for ourselves in order to identify *which* cases fall under that description. Overall, I do not claim that personal autonomy solves all problems, only that it is a necessary tool in coping well with those problems that can be solved.

Second, it may be objected that my view is unduly dismissive of heteronomous ways of life. As Galston puts it, pluralism 'does not insist that all valid ways of life must reflect choice', but allows that 'many lives based on habit, tradition, or faith fall within the wide range of legitimacy' (*PLP* 190).

A preliminary issue is whether such ways of life really exclude the capacity for personal autonomy altogether. Critical reflection need not be wholly absent from military or monastic lives, for example. But even to the extent that such lives are genuinely non-autonomous, I do not claim that they are not 'valid'. I claim only that they are lacking in a human value of especial importance and that where whole societies are structured in this way, such societies are less likely to be successful or satisfying overall.

In this connection, Galston writes that 'value pluralism distinguishes between permitted and forbidden ways of life' – that is, between those above and those below a threshold of minimal respect for universal values (*PLP* 190). But recognition of the great goods is not the only ethical message of pluralism. The ethical implications of pluralism include the basic principle of respect for the full range of human values, from which follow the case for value diversity (partly accepted by Galston) and the case for personal autonomy. Diversity and autonomy then become criteria for comparing and judging alternative ways of life.

Galston himself explains, as we saw, how more diverse societies do better than more restrictive societies at releasing the natural 'diversity of human types'. Similarly, a way of life in which personal autonomy is encouraged is better from a pluralist point of view than one in which personal autonomy is stifled or neglected. The autonomy-friendly way of life releases more of a society's potential for diversity and makes its members better prepared for the hard choices that inevitably confront them.

None of this means that the non-autonomous way of life is simply 'invalid'. All human societies above the threshold of minimal morality will have something valuable to offer (Taylor 1994: 66). A society that does not value autonomy may be rich in other goods, and from a pluralist point of view these must be respected. My point is that, on a pluralist view, such a society lacks a value of exceptional (although not overriding) significance, one that is essential to the making of good choices when incommensurable goods conflict – that is, choices that give the full range of human values their due. Indeed, a society that is lacking in this respect is likely, as a consequence, to be less satisfactory overall. That is because it is less likely to get the most out of the options available to it and out of its own human resources. It is less likely, that is, to maximize its internal value diversity and to encourage its members to develop their potential.

A third objection to my position concerns the truth of value pluralism. According to Galston, I am insisting that all individuals live their lives as consciously aware and committed value pluralists ... It is one thing to say that X is true, another to say that truth is good, yet another to say that truth is the highest good, or some sort of deontological side-constraint on legitimate ways of life.

(*PLP* 190)

In reply, I certainly do not claim that truth is 'the highest good', since pluralism does not recognize an overriding good. I do, however, claim that truth, like practical reason, is an especially important good under pluralism, on Galston's own model of a value that attracts a strong rebuttable presumption in its favor.

Galston speculates that this claim assumes that only if people accept pluralism do they have a reason to be tolerant, and he responds that this concern is misplaced because 'there are many roads to tolerance' (*PLP* 190). I agree that pluralism is not the only route to that desirable destination. Powerful cases for toleration can be found in the work of some monist thinkers, such as Mill, whose liberal-utilitarian monism is complex in content and qualified by a healthy scepticism.

My reason for valuing truth as an especially weighty good under pluralism is that truth and practical reasoning are intimately linked and that both connect with the idea of respect for value plurality. To take seriously the full range of human values is to appreciate and acknowledge those things that are truly valuable to human well-being. As Bernard Williams writes, 'one who properly recognises the plurality of values is one who understands the deep and creative role that these various values can play in human life' (Williams 2013: xxxviii). It is only to the extent that we are aware of the truth of pluralism – that is, of the content and the deep plurality of human goods – that we are in a position to think effectively about what combination of goods we should pursue in a particular case. Again, a way of life that does not acknowledge that truth will no doubt exhibit other goods. It will, though, as in the case of personal autonomy, be lacking in an especially valuable good, one that is essential to good practical reasoning under pluralism, and therefore an important contributor to human well-being.

Finally, it may be objected that a commitment to encouraging individual autonomy as a public policy ideal will cause the state to intrude too much into the internal affairs of groups whose norms are not liberal. In this connection, Galston cites with approval Kukathas's complaint against Kymlicka, whose insistence that group rights be circumscribed by a concern for civil liberties and individual autonomy is said to lead to the society's being 'drawn down the path of interfering with groups that do not accept these values' (*LP* 21).

My answer is, first, that a consistently liberal-pluralist state must be prepared to defend the values of diversity and personal autonomy against the norms of its minority illiberal groups if necessary, for the reasons I have already given. Value pluralism is not relativism; on the contrary, it implies principles that can be used to criticize the practices of cultural and other groups.

Second, however, this critical potential in the liberal-pluralist outlook need not translate into policies that are excessively intrusive. For one thing, I am not proposing that the state promote liberal values within groups whose membership is plainly voluntary, like sports clubs or organizations with limited and specific purposes. In these cases, freedom of exit is sufficient and usually readily available. Rather, I am concerned with those groups, including cultural and religious groups, whose norms tend to pervade a person's whole life, making exit (and voice) more problematic. Moreover, as Kymlicka points out, heavy-handed prohibitions are unlikely to be the most prudent means of promoting personal autonomy and indeed will often be counter-productive (Kymlicka 1995: 170–2). More positive and subtle approaches, such as the provision of attractive alternatives or incentives, are more in keeping with the spirit of liberal pluralism and may well be more effective in any case.

Conclusion

I have argued that a case for autonomy-based liberalism can be constructed along two lines: first, by following to its logical conclusion the typical pro-toleration reliance on a right of exit; second, by tracing the implications of value pluralism. It might be thought that, on a value-pluralist view, the conflict between the two liberalisms comes down in the end to a conflict between two basic values that are incommensurable with one another: toleration of group diversity on the one hand, and promotion of individual autonomy on the other. In that case, is it not a mistake to argue, as I have, that in this conflict individual autonomy ought to have a general (even if not absolute or overriding) priority? Galston perhaps has this thought in mind when he floats the idea that, rather than deciding for one kind of liberalism over the other, we ought to be trying to strike a balance between them.

In principle the idea of striking a balance between group toleration and individual autonomy is reasonable, but of course it begs the question of what that balance should be. The balance struck by the group-toleration case exemplified by thinkers like Galston and Kukathas is too skewed in favor of the group against the individual. In its concern to respect claims made in the name of some minority groups within liberal democracies, it has lost sight of the traditional liberal concern for the ultimate human minority, the individual person. My interpretation of liberal pluralism recovers the claims of the individual against the group, but still leaves room for people to live in accordance with non-liberal norms if that is what they really want for themselves. The key requirement that the person be capable of autonomous judgment serves as both a protection for the individual and a conduit for the survival of groups whose members genuinely see the group's norms as reflecting *their own* deepest convictions. In this way, I believe my conclusion is actually more faithful than Galston's to his own principle of expressive liberty.

I do not deny that my solution has costs. The introduction of even a relatively moderate form of personal autonomy into some groups may lead to substantial changes. But change is not necessarily destruction. Moreover, for the value pluralist, no system is without costs. Pluralists must accept that any political framework will be informed by *some* general ranking of values and that any such ranking will tend to emphasize some goods at the expense of others. The only question is how far a proposed ranking answers to fundamental pluralist concerns. These concerns include group diversity, but this must be a diversity of groups that are themselves internally diverse. Further, to live in a group that is itself internally diverse is inevitably to be faced with choices among incommensurable values, choices that are best made by those who are capable of the critical reflection characteristic of strong personal autonomy.

Notes

1 To some extent this echoes Berlin's dichotomy between negative liberty (toleration) and positive liberty (autonomy). However, there is a question of what kind of negative liberty is implied by the group toleration examined in this chapter. I pick up this theme shortly.
2 See 'Two Concepts of Liberty' in *L*. But note also Berlin's qualifications to this view: see Chapter 1.
3 A revised version appears in *LP* ch. 2.
4 See, similarly, the account of 'conscience' in Kukathas 2003: 47–9.
5 Compare Kukathas 2003 and Green 1995: 270.
6 For a leading account of obstacles to exit beyond simple coercion, see Barry 2001: 150–1.
7 Versions of this distinction can be found in Dworkin 1988: 18, 104–8; Brighouse 2000: 80–2; Reich 2002: 95, 102.
8 See Chapters 1, 3, and 5.
9 My argument for personal autonomy here is not the same as the empirical case rejected in Chapter 2. The argument here is a normative case based on the concept of value pluralism. Nor is the current argument the same as that of Joseph Raz, which moves in the opposite direction: if we assume the value of personal autonomy, then there must be 'a variety of [desirable] options to choose from', hence a plurality of goods: Raz 1986: 398. In contrast with Raz's argument from autonomy to pluralism, I argue from pluralism to autonomy. For a critical discussion of Raz's argument on this point, see *LVP* 202–5.
10 Thus, we have seen Kekes make the point that in the absence of practical reasoning our choices among incommensurable goods would be arbitrary and 'too scattered' to do justice to the values in question: *MP* 97–8. Similarly, Nussbaum argues that practical reasoning occupies a place 'of special importance' among the plural human capabilities she identifies, since it serves to 'organize and suffuse all the others, making their pursuit truly human': *WHD* 82. See, further, the discussion of coherence in Chapter 5.
11 See Kekes *MP*, 1997, 1998, discussed in Chapter 3.
12 I leave open the question of whether the liberal state is entitled to promote not only personal autonomy but also a range of 'civic' or 'democratic' virtues, as advocated, for example, by Macedo 2000 and Gutmann 1995. For an account of distinctively 'value-pluralist virtues', see my *LVP* ch. 8.

References

In-text abbreviations are noted in brackets.

Appiah, Kwame Anthony (2005), *The Ethics of Identity* (Princeton: Princeton University Press).

Barry, Brian (2001), *Culture and Equality* (Cambridge: Polity).
Benhabib, Seyla (2002), *The Claims of Culture: Equality and Diversity in the Global Era* (Princeton: Princeton University Press).
Berlin, Isaiah (2002), *Liberty*, ed. Henry Hardy (Oxford: Oxford University Press). [*L*]
Brighouse, Harry (2000), *School Choice and Social Justice* (Oxford: Oxford University Press).
Callan, Eamonn (1997), *Creating Citizens: Political Education and Liberal Democracy* (Oxford: Oxford University Press).
Crowder, George (2002), *Liberalism and Value Pluralism* (London: Continuum). [*LVP*]
Dworkin, Gerald (1988), *The Theory and Practice of Autonomy* (Cambridge: Cambridge University Press.
Galston, William (1995), 'Two Concepts of Liberalism', *Ethics* 105: 516–34.
Galston, William (2002), *Liberal Pluralism: The Implications of Value Pluralism for Political Theory and Practice* (Cambridge: Cambridge University Press). [*LP*]
Galston, William (2005), *The Practice of Liberal Pluralism* (Cambridge: Cambridge University Press). [*PLP*]
Gardels, Nathan (1991), 'Two Concepts of Nationalism: An Interview with Isaiah Berlin', *New York Review of Books*, 21 November: 19–23.
Gill, Emily (2001), *Becoming Free: Autonomy and Diversity in the Liberal Polity* (Lawrence: University of Kansas Press).
Green, Leslie (1995), 'Internal Minorities and Their Rights', in Will Kymlicka, ed., *The Rights of Minority Cultures* (Oxford: Oxford University Press).
Gutmann, Amy (1995), 'Civic Education and Social Diversity', *Ethics* 105 (3): 557–79.
Hirschman, Albert O. (1970), *Exit, Voice and Loyalty: Responses to Decline in Firms, Organizations and States* (Cambridge, MA: Harvard University Press).
Johnston, David (1994), *The Idea of a Liberal Theory: A Critique and Reconstruction* (Princeton: Princeton University Press).
Kekes, John (1993), *The Morality of Pluralism* (Princeton: Princeton University Press). [*MP*]
Kekes, John (1997), *Against Liberalism* (Ithaca, NY: Cornell University Press).
Kekes, John (1998), *A Case for Conservatism* (Ithaca, NY: Cornell University Press).
Kukathas, Chandran (2003), *The Liberal Archipelago* (Oxford: Oxford University Press).
Kymlicka, Will (1995), *Multicultural Citizenship: A Liberal Theory of Minority Rights* (Oxford: Oxford University Press).
Macedo, Stephen (2000), *Diversity and Distrust: Civic Education in a Multicultural Society* (Cambridge, MA: Harvard University Press).
Mill, J. S. (1974), *On Liberty [1859]*, ed. Gertrud Himmelfarb (Harmondsworth: Penguin).
Nussbaum, Martha (2000), *Women and Human Development: The Capabilities Approach* (Cambridge: Cambridge University Press). [*WHD*]
Okin, Susan (1999), *Is Multiculturalism Bad for Women?*, ed. Joshua Cohen, Matthew Howard, and Martha Nussbaum (Princeton: Princeton University Press).
Okin, Susan (2002), '"Mistresses of Their Own Destiny": Group Rights Gender, and Realistic Rights of Exit', *Ethics* 112 (2): 205–30.
Raz, Joseph (1986), *The Morality of Freedom* (Oxford: Clarendon Press).
Reich, Rob (2002), *Bridging Liberalism and Multiculturalism in American Education* (Chicago: University of Chicago).

Richardson, Henry S. (1994), *Practical Reasoning about Final Ends* (Cambridge: Cambridge University Press).

Sandel, Michael (1982) *Liberalism and the Limits of Justice* (Cambridge: Cambridge University Press).

Taylor, Charles (1994), 'The Politics of Recognition', in Amy Gutmann, ed., *Multiculturalism: Examining the Politics of Recognition* (Princeton: Princeton University Press).

Williams, Bernard (2013), '"Introduction" to Isaiah Berlin', *Concepts and Categories*, ed. Henry Hardy, 2nd edn (Princeton: Princeton University Press).

7 Democracy and Compromise

In the previous two chapters, I have examined conceptual links between value pluralism and liberalism on the grounds of diversity (primarily value diversity, secondarily cultural diversity) and personal autonomy. In this chapter, I consider another set of conceptual connections, between pluralism, democracy, and compromise.

Both democracy and compromise can be readily connected to pluralism. Democracy is commended by pluralist diversity, since it involves the political recognition of many voices or points of view, hence many values. Compromise is linked to pluralism in two ways: first, because it is involved in the process of negotiation that is typically part of democracy; second, more directly, if values are plural and incommensurable, then responding to conflicts between them will usually take the form not of a rigid, either/or system of ranking, but rather of compromise in the form of balancing or trade-off.

However, although democracy and compromise undoubtedly play a central role in pluralist politics, they also raise critical questions. The key issue is one of limits. Pluralists cannot agree that all forms of democracy are equally acceptable, since some are less inclusive than others, ignoring or suppressing legitimate interests and genuine values. What, then, are the limits of democracy and compromise from a pluralist point of view? I shall argue that although we get some guidance from the great goods and context (especially historical), the best answer is provided by the diversity and autonomy criteria.

The chapter proceeds in six main sections. I first look at the relation between democracy and pluralism, distinguishing between majoritarian and liberal forms of democracy and arguing that standard liberal restraints on majority rule are endorsed by pluralism. In the second section I examine another democratic form, deliberation. Here my view is that deliberation should be seen as a supplement to liberal democracy rather than a substitute for it. Third, I set out the basic concept of compromise and the role this plays in pluralist thought, before, fourth, turning to some of the key types of compromise, following the analysis pioneered by Richard Bellamy. Again, these types of compromise all have strengths and weaknesses from a pluralist perspective. Fifth, I consider another form of compromise that has been prominent in the literature, namely 'modus vivendi', associated in particular with the work of John Gray. This highlights the question of the limits of compromise, which I consider in a final section. Here I argue that Avishai Margalit's notion of 'rotten compromises' is not an adequate constraint on compromise from a pluralist point of view and that we should return for this purpose to diversity, autonomy, and democracy.

Pluralism and Democracy

Compared with his commitment to liberalism, Berlin's attitude to democracy is at best one of lukewarm support. Indeed, Jeremy Waldron argues that Berlin is either indifferent or hostile to democracy. According to Waldron, Berlin is at best 'not particularly concerned with political participation'; at worst his 'general hostility to democracy and participatory liberty ... is a matter of record' (*PPT* 285, 286). It is true that Berlin does not have as much to say about democracy as he does about liberty. It is also true that when he does touch on democracy it is often to stress that liberty and democracy are distinct ideas and that they may come into conflict (*L* 208–12).[1]

However, although it is fair to say that Berlin is less enthusiastic about democracy than about liberty, it is too simple to conclude that his attitude to democracy is merely one of 'hostility'. To point out, as Berlin does, that liberty and democracy may conflict is not necessarily to favor liberty in that conflict. As noted before, Berlin makes it clear that liberty is not always overriding when it collides with other values (*L* 172–3). Negative liberty, for example, may in some circumstances have to give way to national self-determination, which is closely associated with democracy (*L* 200–8).[2]

Irrespective of Berlin's own views, the logic of his value pluralism supports democracy on the basis of value diversity. Berlin was not interested in making this connection – he had other things to do. But the connection is there to be made. The essence of democracy is the notion of allowing or enabling a range of different voices to have a say in the process of governance. If, as seems likely, those different voices are bearers of a range of different values, then democracy begins to recommend itself as a political expression of value pluralism.

To put this relation round the other way, value pluralism implies a commitment to a diversity of values within a particular society, and that diversity is in turn promoted by democracy. As I argued in Chapter 5, to take value pluralism seriously is to acknowledge the full range of human values and to be willing to promote as great a range of those values as possible within the relevant social and historical circumstances. In Chapter 5 my concern was to connect pluralist diversity with liberalism, but a similar point could be made on behalf of democracy. To promote the value diversity commended by pluralism is to turn away from hegemonic politics toward the inclusion in the political process of many different voices. While liberalism enables people to pursue their own values, democracy makes it possible for those values to be voiced publicly and be made part of the process of collective self-government.

Richard Bellamy expresses the link between pluralism and democracy as follows:

> By allowing preferences, interests and values to be voiced, rather than excluding them from debate ... democratic politics enables the attitudes of hegemonic groups to be challenged, forces minority or hitherto marginalized positions to be addressed, and so is sensitive to difference and avoids domination.
>
> (Bellamy 2000: 194)

Democracy thus opposes the domination of both people and their values. 'Such domination involves not just the oppression of human beings but of a diversity of ways of life, values, interests and allegiances. In other words, it is linked to the denial of pluralism' (Bellamy in *LAP* 122).

However, democracy promotes diversity, including a diversity of values, in different ways and to different degrees depending on what kind of democracy we are talking about. For my purposes, it is important to distinguish between three species of democracy: majoritarian, liberal, and deliberative.

Majority rule has always been the standard device for translating the democratic idea into practice, but majoritarianism can, of course, be abused. J. S. Mill's problem of the tyranny of the majority arises when the majority uses its power not simply to defeat minorities in debate but to oppress them, treating them without respect and violating their basic liberties (Mill 1974 [1859]: ch. 1). In pluralist terms this exclusive and bullying kind of democracy is likely to reduce the range of options available to people and perhaps reduce the extent to which their views can be heard in the first place. Consequently, pluralism suggests a commitment not to mere majoritarianism but to democracy at its most inclusive.

How is democracy made more inclusive? The orthodox approach is that of liberal democracy: the balancing of the majoritarian imperative by the recognition of individual and minority rights. In Berlin's words, 'Democracy is not *ipso facto* pluralistic. I believe in a specifically pluralist democracy, which demands consultation and compromise, which recognizes the claims – rights – of groups and individuals' (*CIB* 144). Pluralism, then, implies a case for liberal rather than illiberal democracy – that is, for democracy constrained by respect for the basic rights and liberties of individuals and minorities. (Note that Berlin recognizes in this passage that pluralism also implies a case for compromise, which I come to later in the chapter.)

But liberal democracy is far from unproblematic. What rights are we talking about, and how should they be prioritized when they conflict? The content of rights rests on conceptions of the good that imply selections and rankings of values, and when rights collide we need to decide which should take priority. At the levels of both rights and their background values, we are faced with the problem of value pluralism. In the case of conflicting rights, for example, 'rights to privacy can collide with freedom of speech, confronting us with a choice between incommensurable values' (*LAP* 119). How are conflicts among rights to be resolved if in both cases we are dealing with plural and incommensurable values?

One answer is to negotiate. However, this so often takes the form of bargaining in which the outcome simply reflects the interests of the stronger party. In pluralist terms, such a process scarcely guarantees attention to the full range of political voices and their values that was the promise of democracy. Is there a form of negotiation that is more satisfactory from a pluralist perspective?

Deliberation

Bellamy claims to have identified just such a form. This is not negotiation as ordinarily understood, nor is the democracy he has in mind the standard model of liberal democracy. Rather, Bellamy advocates a qualified or enhanced 'reciprocal' form of negotiation in which the parties work toward a mutually satisfactory settlement instead of pursuing a competitive and exclusive self-interest. This becomes the animating feature of a 'democratic liberalism' in which political engagement returns to center-stage instead of a liberal reliance on rights insulated from the political process. These are positions that Bellamy insists are more in keeping with value pluralism than are orthodox negotiation and liberal democracy.

They are also positions identical with what is usually called 'deliberative democracy'. This is a democratic form in which not only representatives and officials but also ordinary citizens are called upon to justify their views in conversation with one another. A central principle is 'reciprocity', which requires the parties to support their position with a set of arguments and evidence that is accessible to others and to listen respectfully to what others have to say in return. As defined by Amy Gutmann and Dennis Thompson, deliberative democracy is

> a form of government in which free and equal citizens (and their representatives), justify decisions in a process in which they give one another reasons that are mutually acceptable and generally accessible, with the aim of reaching conclusions that are binding in the present on all citizens but open to challenge in the future.
>
> (Gutmann and Thompson 2004: 7)

Bellamy arrives at a similar view, which might be interpreted in either of two ways. In a weaker version, he could be seen as proposing that his deliberative principles supplement those of liberal democracy. In a stronger version, his view is that liberal democracy should be wholly or largely replaced by deliberative principles and mechanisms. If he intends the weaker version, then his position is less controversial but also less challenging. I shall assume that Bellamy's claim is probably the stronger claim.

One reason why Bellamy is more likely to be making the stronger claim is that he arrives at his position after a vigorous critique of liberal democracy on pluralist grounds. Liberal democrats, he argues, are fundamentally concerned with placing limits on the power of the state. Such limits standardly take the form of individual rights, in which certain claims are protected from political revision by constitutional devices such as bills of rights. The problem with this approach, Bellamy argues, is that it depends on the existence of a consensus regarding the content and inter-relationship of the rights in question. Such a consensus is questionable from a pluralist perspective in two respects. The content of the rights is open to question because it rests on conceptions of the good that imply selections and hierarchies of value and even if the content can be agreed upon disagreement is likely to resurface over how to prioritize the values when they conflict with one another.

Bellamy's solution is his democratic liberalism, in which the securing of rights is replaced by the enabling of politics. Rather than 'shying away from politics' (*LAP* 12) by trying to place rights beyond dispute, we should make rights themselves subject to democratic debate. Thus, Bellamy's position is democratic liberalism rather than liberal democracy.

But not any politics will do. We should not rely on the politics of interest-group competition, or of rights, or of 'separating warring parties' (*LAP* 101–2). These forms of politics correspond to the three forms of compromise that Bellamy calls 'trading', 'trimming', and 'segregation', which I discuss later. Still less should we be content with the non-rational quest for hegemony characteristic of agonism (*LAP* 12).[3]

Instead, the model should be one of negotiation. For Bellamy, this does not mean bargaining for one's own advantage. Rather, the basic idea is that the parties to a political dispute should deliberate with one another: they should enter into a genuine conversation in which each side offers accessible justifications to the other and listens to the other's justifications in turn. The object is not to outmaneuver the other side but to achieve a 'compromise through the search for mutually acceptable solutions' (*LAP* 106).

As it is for Gutmann and Thompson, the key norm in Bellamy's deliberative democracy is reciprocity. The justifications offered by each party must be accessible to the other – that is, they must be justifications the other party is capable of understanding and might accept. This excludes 'totally self-regarding claims and arguments that rely on implausible premises or evidence not susceptible to public assessment, or which require the wholesale adoption of the views of the proposer' (*LAP* 106). So, for example, reciprocity excludes reliance on religious beliefs that others cannot be reasonably expected to share. It includes acceptance of the same principle of 'hearing the other side' (*audi alteram partem*) as that advanced by Hampshire (see Chapter 2). For Bellamy, reciprocity 'implies respecting that people can be reasonably led to incommensurable and incompatible understandings of values and interests, and seeing the need to engage with them in terms they can accept' (*LAP* 121).

Negotiation involves close attention to context, since to address abstract principles alone is to invite paralysis in decision making.

> It cannot be settled a priori how far any individual's or group's interests and values need to be set aside or moderated, the level at which shareable norms and concerns have to be invoked, or the nature appeals to common ground will take. All depend on the demand or policy under discussion and the complexion of the community deciding the matter, since these factors largely determine the type of compromise to be negotiated.
>
> (*LAP* 106)

The compromise appropriate to a particular case will emerge out of the negotiation of that case by the parties in context. In this respect, Bellamy's view connects strongly with the contextual approaches discussed in Chapter 3.

To attend to context is to engage with all the complexity of a concrete situation, but Bellamy sees this as an advantage rather than an obstacle to compromise. 'Compromise finds the complexity of particular ties and sources of plurality an aid rather than a hindrance, since it allows incommensurable demands to be brought together' (*LAP* 12). For example, the presence of multiple issues within a dispute may allow a party to yield on one issue in order to gain concessions on another.

How convincing is Bellamy's view? First, his pluralist critique of liberal democracy is overstated. The key claim was that a regime of rights depends on a consensus that is impossible to sustain in the face of conflicting plural values. But liberal democrats could reply that they are well aware of the contestability of the nature, content, and ordering of rights, yet this does not prevent rights fulfilling an important function. The general notion of human rights is widely respected even though there is much disagreement about exactly which rights should have this status and how conflicts among such rights should be dealt with when they arise. Bellamy makes the same mistake as the agonists, especially Schmitt and Mouffe, in attributing to liberal democracy a demand for a level of consensus that it does not make or need to make.

Moreover, liberal democrats might point out that under liberal democracy there is already political negotiation and that to some extent this extends even to the recognition of rights. The US Supreme Court, for example, is the ultimate arbiter of the shape, content, and priority of rights in the United States, but there is clearly a political element in the process by which it arrives at these decisions and in the process by which it is appointed.

Bellamy would no doubt reply that the negotiation involved here is of the wrong kind: self-interested or partisan horse-trading rather than the reciprocal deliberation he is recommending. But the negotiation that exists already under liberal democracy does include the work of genuinely deliberative institutions and practices – for example, the citizens' juries, constitutional conventions, deliberative polls, and other arrangements that have been developed in many places.[4] So, Bellamy's argument must be one of degree: that although there may be pockets of deliberation at present, these are too few, and that it is deliberation – rather than bargaining, appeal to rights, and so on – that ought to be the norm.

How far this is true depends on the positive phase of Bellamy's argument: the pluralist case in favor of deliberation and democratic liberalism. Here, too, his claim goes too far. The idea that there ought to be more occasions for deliberation in politics, and more deliberative mechanisms, may be readily accepted. There is warrant for this in pluralism, because deliberation may to some extent enable different voices to be heard, hence diverse values to be respected, that would be pushed to one side in a wholly majoritarian or interest-group system. But Bellamy's argument goes much further than this, to the demand that reciprocal deliberation should be elevated into the central model of politics. This is asking too much.

First, there are problems of practicability. These include the obvious political, institutional, and cultural difficulties in the way of replacing existing representative systems with arrangements that enable all or most decisions to be made by the deliberation not only of representatives and officials but also of ordinary citizens. Perhaps this could be achieved incrementally, although it would take some effort of imagination to envision this happening given current realities.

More awkward for Bellamy's own argument is the thought that a deliberative system is no less dependent than liberal rights on consensus. A commitment to deliberation is a commitment to a substantial set of values: the values of rationality, justification, and reciprocity. These are, of course, important considerations, but they are not the only important human goods. They reflect, to a degree, an approach to politics, and perhaps to life more generally, that is more characteristic of some conceptions of the good than others. To what extent, then, will they support the kind of consensus necessary to maintain a political system in which deliberation is dominant?

This question leads to a second: to what extent is deliberation a *desirable* approach to politics in pluralist terms? An obvious concern is with the protection of rights under a deliberative scheme. Bellamy makes it clear that liberal rights will not be sacrosanct but subject to democratic negotiation. Will that not place the interests and values of individuals and minorities in jeopardy? Bellamy might reply, in line with what I said above, that there is no absolute separation of rights from politics even under current forms of liberal democracy. But that response goes only so far, since Bellamy is advocating a radically transformed system in which rights have no special protection from democratic negotiation at all.

Bellamy's deeper defense on this point must be that the fate of rights will be a concern only on orthodox understandings of what negotiation means – that is, self-interested and partisan trading. This is not the kind of negotiation contemplated by Bellamy's argument. For Bellamy, negotiation is constrained by reciprocity and motivated by a principled desire on the part of all parties to achieve mutual benefit.

The trouble with this reformed negotiation is threefold. First, there are the practical difficulties already mentioned. Second, the reforming of negotiation would seem to involve the use of forms of compromise that Bellamy argues against. For example, complexity is said to be an advantage because it enables concessions on one issue to be exchanged for gains on another, but that looks a lot like self-interested bargaining.[5]

Perhaps, though, Bellamy would allow that bargaining and rights still have their uses and should not be rejected altogether. The point is to deny their elevation to dominant models of politics. That is compatible with their acceptance as all having a partial contribution to make to a reformed politics.

But then, the same point may be made about deliberation. A third and more serious problem with Bellamy's picture of deliberative negotiation as framing rather than merely contributing to politics is the classic pluralist point that it emphasizes too narrow a selection of values. Iris Young, for example, argues that the emphasis in standard models of deliberation on reasoned argument is 'culturally specific', favoring 'dispassionate and disembodied' styles of communication over 'more excited and embodied' styles (Young 2000: 37–40).

Similarly, Michael Walzer suggests that deliberation, while it can contribute significantly to politics, is not all there is to politics and indeed is not of its essence. 'Politics has other values in addition to, and often in tension with, reason: passion, commitment, solidarity, courage, and competitiveness (all of which require qualification)' (Walzer 1999: 59). Walzer proceeds to find these other values in 'a wide range of [political] activities' quite unlike Bellamy's reciprocal negotiation. His list includes political education, organization, mobilization, demonstration, debate, bargaining, lobbying, and so on. This is not to say that there is no place for deliberation in politics; on the contrary, 'we make room for it, and should do that' (Walzer 1999: 68). But for Walzer, deliberation is more like an optional extra than an essential focus for politics. 'There is no setting in the political world quite like the jury room, in which we don't want people to do anything *except* deliberate' (Walzer 1999: 67).

It is not necessary to go as far as Young and Walzer to see in their comments significant pluralist rebuttals to Bellamy. Reasoned argument is unlikely to harm any genuine cause, and it is open to question whether politics has the essence Walzer attributes to it – or any essence. Moreover, reasoned and reciprocal deliberation embodies values that have an important place in inter-cultural relations and in politics more generally. But there are in these fields, as Walzer says, 'other values' that are no less important. Pluralists have to acknowledge this. Deliberation should have an honored place in politics, but the case for its having a dominant status and function is unconvincing.

Pluralism and Compromise

I turn now to the notion of compromise. What is the relation between pluralism and compromise? How far does this vary with particular types of compromise?

In particular, what is the role of compromise in responding to the problem of value pluralism?

I begin with some working definitions, although I shall revise these. 'Basically', writes Fabian Wendt, 'compromises are agreements between two or more parties in which the parties accept some arrangement that they regard as a mere second-best' (Wendt 2016: 8). Similarly, Avishai Margalit describes a compromise as an agreement reached between two or more parties as a result of a negotiation that has the following features. First, the agreement must involve 'mutual concessions' (*OC* 20). The parties achieve consensus but at the price of conceding some of what they want. In some cases this can amount to 'giving up on a dream', where ideal 'dream points' are abandoned in favor of achieving agreement on more realistic goals (*OC* 44). Second, the agreement must not be the result of coercion. Third, the agreement implies the mutual recognition of the parties. Each recognizes that the claims and interests of the other are to some degree legitimate. Hence, the difficulty of even commencing negotiations when one party regards the other as, for example, a terrorist with whom one does not negotiate.

Compromise is pervasively important in pluralist thinking. Recall (from Chapter 1) that Berlin recognizes compromise as a routine response when incommensurables conflict. When the great goods collide, 'the collisions, even if they cannot be avoided, can be softened. Claims can be balanced, compromises can be reached' (*CTH* 19). When fundamental values conflict, Berlin seems to be saying, there is still the possibility of compromise among them.

How far is this true? Might there not be situations where we respond, or should respond, to value conflict in more absolute terms? One possibility is simply to choose one value option and reject the other completely; another to adopt a principle of ranking on the model of Rawls's 'lexical' ordering, where the top option has to be wholly satisfied before the next comes into play, and so on (Rawls 1971: 42–4).

One reason why pluralists may be unhappy with these more absolute, either/or solutions to value conflict is that, in the political realm at any rate, pluralists have reason to aspire to inclusive democracy, as we have seen. If different political actors are bearers of different values, then an outlook that commends the promotion of value diversity has reason to be democratic. Moreover, pluralist democracy will not be straightforwardly majoritarian but inclusive, aiming at the recognition of as wide a range of views as possible. This will require negotiation, since such a goal can be reached only by discussion rather than force.

Compromise is also important to pluralists in another sense. In most cases we do indeed resolve value conflicts in the way Berlin describes, with some degree of compromise – 'so much liberty and so much equality', for example (*CTH* 19). This is especially plausible from a pluralist perspective, which insists that the claims of competing values (if they represent incommensurables) possess unique normative force. A pluralist is likely to respect each claim as much as possible and decide against it only to the extent necessary. Consequently, an element of compromise would seem natural. Even where some form of ranking of values or options is essential, this will probably be qualified: 80% liberty, 20% equality, maybe.[6] Although, as Berlin puts it, 'priorities must be established' (*CTH* 19), these are unlikely to be absolute.

If this is correct, then my working definitions of compromise need some adjustment. First, both Wendt and Margalit define compromise as an arrangement between two or more parties, but on the pluralist view a compromise may occur within the mind of a single person. That is because the practical reasoning of a single person may, and probably will, represent a compromise between contending values. I can be torn between justice and mercy, and eventually compromise between the two. My considered view is a compromise.

Of course, this is not to say that pluralists cannot also recognize compromises between multiple parties, and it is fair to say that such inter-personal or inter-group compromises are more immediately important in politics. The pluralist outlook allows multiple levels of compromise: intra-personal, inter-personal, and inter-group. But it is worth noting that multiparty compromises are likely to be, in terms of the values involved, compound compromises – compromises between positions (of groups or individuals) that are themselves intra-personal compromises among competing considerations.

This last observation bears on a second point at which the working definitions of compromise need adjusting. Wendt, in particular, stresses the idea that a compromise must be a 'second-best' arrangement. This makes sense so far as we are talking about a compromise between two or more parties. But if the position of a single party is also a compromise between conflicting values, then each party's 'best' solution is also a compromise. For a pluralist, it would be odd to say that the optimal solution to a conflict of liberty and equality must be the complete triumph of one over the other. Both are genuine values that deserve due consideration, and due consideration is highly likely to yield some degree of compromise. In such a case, it makes little sense to say that the solution is second-best; rather, it is the best possible solution in the circumstances. A single person's favored position will probably be a compromise. So, once again, a compromise between parties is probably a compound compromise in terms of the values or norms involved.[7]

Consequently, it may be reasonable to formulate a pluralist understanding of compromise as something like the following. A compromise is a ranking or balancing of competing values whereby each value makes some concession to the other in the circumstances. No single value is overriding. Such a ranking or balancing of values may take place within the practical reasoning of a single person or within arrangements made by multiple parties. To say this is to reinforce the ubiquity of compromise from a pluralist point of view.

Trading, Trimming, and Segregation

There are, of course, different kinds of compromise. The literature on compromise has expanded considerably in recent years, leading to several significant proposals for how the broad notion might be analyzed.[8] However, for my purposes, which center on the post-Berlinian literature of value pluralism, the most pertinent and substantial account is that of Bellamy, who explicitly links the need for compromise with the problem of value pluralism.[9] Indeed, Bellamy sees the plurality and incommensurability of values as providing 'the greatest challenge' to the dominant liberal and communitarian political theories of our time (*LAP* 2). Such theories have in common an aspiration 'to restrict politics within a putative consensus on constitutional or communal values. Pluralism challenges such consensual agreement, however, and creates clashes of principles, values and interests that can be defused only through political compromise' (*LAP* 93).

What form should political compromise take? Bellamy's preferred model, 'democratic negotiation', has already been discussed. But what about the three principal forms he opposes: trading, trimming, and segregation?[10]

The basic idea of trading is that a compromise among conflicting values is reached by self-interested exchange through the market. Traders 'bring something to a market and take something away, after exchanging freely with others to mutual advantage' (*LAP* 96). 'Mutual advantage' here means the outcome, whatever it may be, of traders pursuing their rational self-interest. Competing interests represent competing values. 'We treat different views and values as subjective preferences. We can then reach agreement by trading the resources needed to satisfy them' (*LAP* 10). So, justice and compassion, for example, are balanced in accordance with the capacities of those who favor these values to bargain in the marketplace for resources that will promote them. In essence, interested parties bid for the values they want to see advanced.

One theorist who thinks in these terms is Friedrich Hayek. In *The Road to Serfdom* (1944), Hayek acknowledges the plurality and incommensurability of values and consequently the problem of value pluralism. The problem is resolved, he argues, through the mechanism of the market. Since under pluralism there is no single correct ranking of competing values, the ranking of values should be left to individual choice. The most natural institution through which individual choice is expressed is the free market, where values are pursued through the medium of voluntary exchange.[11]

Bellamy points out a serious problem with this from a pluralist perspective. Trading is all about exchange, and exchange needs a medium. Usually, the medium of trade is money, but even bartering assumes a common medium in the strength of interest the parties have in the exchange. However, the bedrock pluralist idea is that of incommensurable values, which includes the notion that among fundamental values there is no common medium. The notion of a common medium is part of what pluralism rejects.

Pluralists have further problems with trading that Bellamy does not mention. One is that Hayek's argument contains a logical gap. It is true that, under pluralism, there is (in the abstract) no uniquely correct ranking of rival incommensurable values. It does not follow that the only or best response is to leave value rankings up to individuals. That solution, in effect, ranks individual choice above other values, which is what the pluralist premise denies (*LVP* 227–8). Another difficulty is that, even if we accepted individual choice as an important value, it does not follow that the market is the best means to promote it, at any rate without qualification. The extent to which people can get what they want in the market is obviously constrained by their bargaining power, which varies greatly according to 'accidents of natural endowment and the contingencies of social circumstance' (Rawls 1971: 15).

The second kind of compromise considered by Bellamy is 'trimming'. 'Value differences allegedly make politics impossible', he writes. 'So we must trim them away when debating in public, reserving their expression to private discussion' (*LAP* 11). Controversial issues are bracketed so that progress can be made toward agreement in more tractable matters. This counts as compromise in the sense that opposing parties refrain from public expression of their strongest ideals for the sake of agreement. It also amounts to compromise in terms of a give and take among different values: disputed combinations of values are removed from the agenda so that other formulas, with better prospects of agreement, can be brought more clearly into focus.

As Bellamy notes, the most prominent political theorist associated with this approach is John Rawls. In *A Theory of Justice* (1971), Rawls employs the 'veil of ignorance' to get us to set aside matters that would bias our thinking about justice. Crucially, these include our conception of the good life – for example, our religious affiliations, if any. Rawls's position is thus an instance of the broader school of liberal 'neutrality' among conceptions of the good, and liberal neutrality as a whole is one version of trimming. In the Rawlsian terminology, controversial issues of the good are trimmed out of public discourse, which is focused on principles of 'the right' that all citizens have reason to accept as the essential terms of social cooperation.

Later, in *Political Liberalism* (1993), Rawls trims further because of a concern for 'stability' (Rawls 1993: xv–xvi, 140–4). He worries that the framework of right identified in *A Theory of Justice* will not be stable because it may depend on a comprehensively liberal view of the good – one that applies to people's personal lives as well as their public roles – after all. Acceptance of the 'original position' that contains the veil of ignorance may itself presuppose such a comprehensive view because it models an acceptance of personal autonomy, a distinctively liberal value. A comprehensively liberal starting point does not take sufficiently seriously the extent of reasonable disagreement about the truth of comprehensive moral doctrines, including those supporting liberalism, in modern societies. The 'fact of reasonable pluralism' under modern conditions must be taken as axiomatic.[12] Liberal states must justify their constitutional principles to their citizens, but those citizens include people who do not subscribe to a comprehensive liberal conception of the good.

Consequently, Rawls argues that the justification of a liberal constitution must avoid reliance on any comprehensive conception of the good and appeal only to 'public reason', which is based on an 'overlapping consensus' among streams within a shared public political culture (Rawls 1999).

Comprehensive views may still be debated freely in personal or family or associational settings or in the media, but there is an overriding public interest, rooted in the respect for citizens that is a fundamental commitment for modern democracies, to keep these matters out of the public arena where constitutional essentials are concerned.

From a pluralist perspective there are two problems with this approach, as Bellamy acknowledges. First, Rawls's emphasis on stability is questionable, since stability is only one value among others. Although stability is certainly an important consideration in politics, issues arise when it comes into conflict with other values, such as justice.[13] Should the status quo be maintained if it is unjust? The answer will depend on the particular case, but the immediate point is that stability cannot, from a pluralist perspective, be automatically overriding. In Rawls's argument, the value of stability is the prime motivation for excluding comprehensive doctrines from public debate. Once it is appreciated that stability, although important, has to be balanced against other considerations, Rawls's case for a trimmed public reason is correspondingly weakened.

Second, a pluralist will expect that the disagreement that pervades the realm of the good will extend into that of public reason or the right as well.[14] A given conception of the good represents a particular combination of incommensurable values, the components of which are interpreted and weighted in a certain way. The merits of that configuration of values are open to dispute. But the same can be said of the right. For pluralists, the right is also a particular configuration of values that, on the face of things, might reasonably be criticized. Rawls's two principles of justice, for example, have been subjected to various criticisms along these lines.[15]

Bellamy's third model of compromise is 'segregation'. The basic idea is that 'good fences make good neighbors' (*LAP* 100). Conflict is controlled by keeping potential belligerents apart and more broadly 'by preserving the integrity of each value, culture or interest within its own domain'. Warring cultural groups can be given their own nation-states or spheres of self-determination. Clashing values can be separated into different institutions – for example, the separation of powers identifies different institutions for the legislative, executive, and judicial functions of government, each of which can be said to emphasize a different set of values.[16] Alternatively, values can be kept apart by rules forbidding the application to one sphere of values more appropriate to another.[17]

Bellamy seems uncertain whether segregation is a true form of compromise or rather the avoidance of compromise. Having included segregation among his 'three models of democratic compromise', he later describes it as 'avoiding all compromise' (*LAP* 95, 100). The former is his better view. What segregation does avoid is negotiation, but to equate all compromise with negotiation is to prejudge the matter in favor of Bellamy's own preferred version of compromise.[18]

The leading proponent of the segregation approach in the pluralist literature is Michael Walzer, in *Spheres of Justice* (1983). Walzer presents his view of justice as 'pluralist' in two senses. First, there are multiple legitimate accounts of justice in accordance with the multiple ways justice is understood by different societies or cultural traditions. This is essentially a culturally relativist position. However, Walzer's second sense of pluralism is in essence a value-pluralist view. In this part of his theory he identifies distinct 'spheres' of value, each dominated by a particular good – examples include 'membership', 'security and welfare', and 'money and commodities'. Each of these goods has unique authority in its own sphere – this is Walzer's version of incommensurability.

Consequently, 'justice' should be understood as each sphere minding its own business.[19] A 'complex equality' obtains when that happens; the different spheres and their goods are then in balance. This has implications for individuals, whose capacities tend to vary across the different spheres. Injustice occurs when the good appropriate to one sphere invades and dominates another, enabling one kind of person to control everyone else. The key example in modern times is the danger of the sphere of money and commodities becoming dominant, thus handing omnipotence to capitalists. To prevent this happening, all societies have rules (enforced in varying degrees) placing limits on what can be bought and sold – for example, human beings, political office, and so on. These 'blocked exchanges' are especially important under contemporary conditions and amount to borders that require vigilant policing.

'The theoretical flaw in this strategy', writes Bellamy, 'lies in assuming these borders are not themselves contested' (*LAP* 100). How should the spheres or goods be defined that should be kept separate? Where should the borders be located that must be policed? American election campaign finance is an example. A traditional blocked exchange is the purchase of political office. But the US Supreme Court has consistently upheld questionable forms of campaign finance on the ground of free speech. In Walzer's terms, is this an invasion of the sphere of office by money, or is it the defense of that sphere, assuming that political office in a democracy is inseparable from free speech and that campaign finance is a form of free speech? The issue is contestable, and Bellamy would argue that it can be settled only by a further level of compromise. 'Setting the boundaries [required for segregation] itself requires compromise and the participation of those affected both within and outside them' (*LAP* 100–1). Segregation presupposes the existence of agreed boundaries, but these turn out themselves to be controversial.

Perhaps a deeper flaw of segregation lies in supposing that it can wholly circumvent the fundamental pluralist problem of conflict. Bellamy does not spell this out, but it could be why he is so doubtful that segregation counts as a strategy of compromise at all. There may, it is true, be cases where conflict among values can be managed by separating them out, but there will be many other cases where segregation is inapplicable. A divorce settlement that involves dividing the family cat is a case in point.

Even in cases where segregation is applicable in principle, there are limits to the extent to which it can be applied in practice. For example, there are no jurisdictions where the separation of powers is complete – Berlin notes that

Montesquieu was mistaken when he described the English Constitution in these terms (Berlin 2013a: 165). Moreover, even when values are segregated that may not prevent conflict arising at another level. In the US, where there is a strong separation of powers, conflict among the branches of government cannot be avoided altogether – indeed, it is routine.

Bellamy, then, is highly critical of trading, trimming, and segregation as models of compromise, and his general tendency is to reject these in favor of his preferred model of democratic negotiation. But how fatal are Bellamy's objections to the three models he opposes? From a pluralist perspective these certainly have problems, but do those problems require that trading, trimming, and segregation be rejected wholesale?

Trading, for example, may be too focused on a particular kind of value, namely the satisfaction of interests or preferences, to be the only or invariably best answer. However, this is not to say that pluralists must see trading as altogether impermissible. For one thing, bargaining is one way in which politics proceeds in reality, and one way that compromise is arrived at more generally. It would be impracticable to condemn it completely. Further, it is a legitimate approach to those kinds of conflict which really can be adequately translated into the terms of a common medium, such as money – for example, bargaining over a price. In more complex conflicts, trading needs to be balanced by other approaches that better represent other considerations. But that is not to say that trading is wholly irrelevant or un-pluralist; only that it is no more than part of a more complete pluralist account.

Similarly, although trimming has serious drawbacks, it should not be concluded that all trimming should be taken off the table. The objections noted amount to saying that we should beware of assuming that stability is overriding and that there will be disputes on pluralist grounds about the content of the right. They do not mean that stability is not a very important political value or that there is no need for any conception of the right. Both the good and the right are subject to pluralist dispute, but it may still be that there is less dispute about the latter than about the former and that consequently some notion of trimming remains a useful focus for politics.[20]

To say that segregation has limits is not to say that it is wholly impossible or undesirable or that its contribution to the repertoire of compromise is negligible. The blocked exchanges emphasized by Walzer play an important role in all political systems, and the constitutional doctrine of separation of powers has pluralist resonance, as I shall argue in Chapter 8.

To conclude here, we should take note of Bellamy's critical analysis of trading, trimming, and segregation as indicating different means of compromise and recognize that they have serious limitations and deficiencies, especially from a pluralist point of view. But it does not follow that we should jettison them entirely. It is possible that, while none of these methods is adequate on its own, each captures an aspect of a more satisfactory picture. Indeed, they all enter into Bellamy's own theory of democratic negotiation.

Modus Vivendi

Another influential account of compromise among plural and incommensurable values is the 'modus vivendi' championed by John Gray and others. Gray is well known for his use of value pluralism to attack liberalism, to which I responded in Chapters 4 and 5. In this chapter, I am concerned with the alternative he offers.

Gray's views in this area are various and not easy to reconcile. Sometimes he adopts an agonist position, asserting that pluralism imposes on us 'radical' rather than rational choices among incommensurables: 'choice without criteria, grounds, or principles' (Gray 2013: 97).[21] At other times he takes a contextualist view that emphasizes the authority of local tradition: 'Judgements of the relative importance of [competing incommensurable] goods appeal to their role in a specific way of life' (Gray 2000c: 98). Then again, he sometimes concedes that under modern conditions traditions are themselves conflicting (Gray 2000b: 53–4).[22]

If any view is now dominant in Gray's thinking, it is his attraction to the idea of modus vivendi.[23] When traditions collide, Gray now believes, such conflicts should be 'settled by achieving a modus vivendi' among the parties, in which they 'find interests and values they have in common and reach compromises regarding those in which they diverge' (Gray 2000c: 99). The goal of modus vivendi is peaceful coexistence.

> The aim of modus vivendi cannot be to still the conflict of values. It is to reconcile individuals and ways of life honouring conflicting values to a life in common. We do not need common values in order to live together in peace. We need common institutions in which many forms of life can coexist.
>
> (Gray 2000b: 5–6)

Modus vivendi yields an approach to politics that diverges from both traditional conservatism and liberalism. Instead of the loyalty to tradition that Gray sometimes favors, modus vivendi yields a loose kind of pragmatism, a case-by-case response unconstrained by any principles other than a general concern for peaceful accommodation rather than conflict. Liberalism is not wholly discredited, but its claims are radically qualified: 'liberal institutions are merely one variety of modus vivendi, not always the most legitimate' (Gray 2000c: 101; also 2000a: 332). The only limits to legitimate modus vivendi are set by an ultra-thin notion of 'minimal standards of decency and legitimacy', explicitly consistent with non-liberal solutions (Gray 2000b: 109).

Gray's account of pluralist modus vivendi is unclear in some important respects. One question concerns the relation of modus vivendi to traditionalism. Does Gray intend modus vivendi to displace tradition altogether or merely to complement it in cases where traditions are divided or multiple? At first sight it might seem that the two ideas are intended to be complementary, that the role of modus vivendi is only to fill in the gaps when traditions fail or collide. But on reflection it appears that tradition must always fail as a guide for pluralist choice, since, as Gray observes, traditions are always contested. This reflection fits with the emphatic tone in which Gray declares the end of conservatism as a coherent social philosophy (Gray 1995: ch. 7; 2000b: 53–4). Yet in some of his later writing about pluralism, he continues to say that a single 'way of life' can serve as a criterion for resolving conflicts among incommensurable goods within that way of life and that modus vivendi comes in only when ways of life conflict (Gray 2000c: 87).

There is another ambiguity: what does 'modus vivendi' mean exactly? Rawls, for example, distinguishes two kinds of political settlement: a balance of power based on self-interest and a moral settlement based on a principled commitment to peaceful coexistence (Rawls 1993: 146–9). Only the first kind of settlement is associated by Rawls with the term 'modus vivendi'. Gray makes no such distinction, and his use of the term seems to straddle both meanings. Either way, he is faced with a problem. If by modus vivendi he means a balance of power, then he is exposed to Rawls's objection that such a settlement is inherently unstable because it depends wholly on the shifting interests of the parties. On the other hand, if Gray's modus vivendi is a principled commitment to peaceful coexistence, what prevents it from amounting to a form of monism?

Indeed, the accusation of monism may seem to be a problem for Gray on either interpretation of his notion of modus vivendi. In each case, there appears to be an overriding value: either self-interest or peace. How is Gray's position any different from the liberal universalism he condemns, other than in the content he gives to his privileged values? While Gray accuses the liberals of privileging their values of individual liberty, toleration, and so on, liberals could retort that Gray merely substitutes for liberal concerns a doctrine of self-interest or of peace at any price. Presumably, the Munich Agreement of 1938 would count as a legitimate modus vivendi according to Gray's definition. But a settlement that won a temporary peace by delivering the Czechs into the hands of the Nazis is a dubious expression of the spirit of value pluralism.

Gray might respond that he does not intend to present modus vivendi as an overriding norm. In one place, for example, he describes modus vivendi as only 'a contingent good' – contingent on 'human interests', which may change (Gray 2000b: 135). But then, what are the interests in question, when do they call for modus vivendi and when do they not? What happens when modus vivendi does not apply: do we then return to traditionalism? If so, we would seem to be back with the problem of divided and competing traditions. Gray does not consider these questions.

Indeed, the general tendency of what he says suggests that he does regard modus vivendi as a universal principle. 'Because they are practised by human beings', he writes, 'all ways of life have some interests in common', and these 'give us reason to pursue coexistence' (Gray 2000b: 136). But again, Gray does not tell us what the common interests are apart from observing that they are 'many and varied'. Nor does he explain how the common interests give us reason to pursue coexistence. In fact, he admits, 'it is frequently those interests that divide us' (Gray 2000b: 136).

But perhaps the accusation of monism can be avoided. John Horton makes two suggestions. First, the goal of modus vivendi need not be conceived as overriding: 'the special place of the goods of peace and security in the political process does not mean that for everyone these will be always and everywhere the supreme good, necessarily overriding all other goods' (Horton 2010: 438). Berlin, it will be recalled, says something similar about individual liberty: it can be emphasized without becoming paramount.

Moreover, the idea of peace having a special place connects with Berlin's view, touched on in Chapter 5, about the risks of violence. The use of force on a large scale is always a hazardous undertaking because it carries huge costs and leads to unforeseeable consequences (*CTH* 18). From a pluralist point of view, which insists that all human goods must be taken seriously, it will be hard to be confident that the gains from large-scale violence will outweigh the losses. If so, peace will usually be the better option. However, that is not always so. Perhaps if Britain and France had opposed the Nazis earlier, they might have avoided the even worse violence to come.

One way of capturing this notion of the 'special place' of peace is through Galston's idea of a rebuttable presumption. Pluralists can endorse something like a presumption in favor of peace, but a presumption that can be rebutted in appropriate circumstances (*LP* 69–78). This is also the view of Margalit, who writes that peace stands as a presumptive goal but one that can be overcome in sufficiently exigent cases. 'In rare cases, the moral presumption is reversed in favour of war, and the burden of proof is on those who do not advocate war' (*OC* 79). These are cases in which 'the very idea of morality is challenged, as in the case of Hitlerism' (*OC* 79–80). So, the Munich Agreement can be rejected as a valid modus vivendi because it purchases peace at too high a price.

However, if modus vivendi allows peace to be traded off against other goods, the question arises of when and how this should occur. As Horton concedes,

> there are at least two broad questions here: the first concerns the indeterminacy of the level of peace and security that constitutes a basic minimum, while the second is about trying to specify more precisely how peace and security relate to other values, although with respect to the latter we should certainly not expect the result to be some algorithm or fixed hierarchy of values.
>
> (Horton 2010: 444)

So, the precise balance to be struck between peace and other values will depend on the detailed circumstances of the case. As Horton remarks, 'what is found acceptable is always a contingent and circumstantial matter and something that has to be settled by those involved' (Horton 2010: 439). This is fair, but it does not answer the question of whether there is 'a basic minimum' of peace to be sought in any situation. I shall come back to this shortly, when I discuss the limits to compromise.

Horton's second suggestion for separating modus vivendi from monism is that peace may be seen as 'an essential precondition for the achievement of almost any other goods' (Horton 2010: 438). On this view the special place of peace is owed not to its being more valuable than other goods, even presumptively, but simply to its having to be achieved first, as a practical matter, before other goods can be enjoyed. The priority of peace would be sequential rather than normative.

This echoes the similar move sometimes made by defenders of political realism, the difficulties of which were discussed in Chapter 4. There, social order was reframed as a precondition for justice and other goods, thus enabling those realists who accept such a move to avoid any hint of monism. But the consequence was that realists then become indistinguishable from the moralists they are supposed to be opposing. Moralists, too, can accept that social order is a precondition for their ideals.

Similarly, defenders of modus vivendi can avoid the charge of monism by presenting peace not as a super-value or even a rebuttable presumption but as a precondition for the enjoyment of other goods. But by doing so they raise the question of what really separates them from those they claim to oppose. In the case of Gray, these include liberal universalists and cultural traditionalists. Both liberal universalists and cultural traditionalists can agree that peace is by and large necessary for the other values they advocate – individual rights and liberties in the case of liberal universalists, the goods embodied in particular customary ways of life in the case of cultural traditionalists. Peace must usually 'come first' in a sequential sense but not in a normative sense. If liberals and traditionalists can accept this, then advocates of modus vivendi are not saying anything new.

Horton's attempt to formulate modus vivendi in a moderate and balanced way is reasonable, but it also shows how hard it is to distinguish this view from equally moderate versions of the 'idealist' theories it is meant to supplant. Horton makes it clear that modus vivendi should not be understood as equivalent to the 'balance of power' approach rejected by Rawls, which addresses only self-interest. Rather, it reflects 'a variety of factors', including not only self-interest but also 'more general prudential considerations and whatever moral principles and other values can be effectively mobilized in support of a particular political settlement' (Horton 2010: 440). Again,

> ideals in the form of goals or political aspirations, and moral principles and conventions that set limits to what we are willing to do in pursuit of our interests, play an important part in political life, and not just as a smokescreen for baser motivations (although, naturally, they can sometimes be that).
>
> (Horton 2010: 441)

All of this sounds fair, but it leaves us with the question of what the notion of modus vivendi is telling us that is distinctive. What is the difference between a modus vivendi that recognizes the importance of ideals and an idealist position that acknowledges the limitations of political and other realities? Horton raises this question himself when he asks whether modus vivendi or, more broadly, the realism with which it is associated amounts to no more than a way of 'reforming or revising liberal moralism' or whether it constitutes an independent position (Horton 2010: 445). If the goal is the latter, he candidly concludes that 'we are still some way from having a clear understanding of what that would amount to' (Horton 2010: 446).

The Limits of Compromise

A final problem with modus vivendi, foreshadowed above, is also a problem for compromise more generally: what are its limits? When does the price that must be paid for peace become unacceptable? It is clear that there are cases when the value of peace is overridden by other values – for example, the Munich Agreement. Margalit lists other leading candidates, including the Connecticut or 'Great' Compromise, in which the Framers of the US Constitution obtained the consent of the Southern states by not banning slavery, and the Yalta agreement of 1945 in which Churchill and Roosevelt agreed with Stalin to the forced repatriation of thousands of Soviet citizens and (implicitly) accepted the Stalinist domination of central and eastern Europe after the War.[24] The more specific question here is: what are the limits of modus vivendi, and of compromise more generally, from a pluralist perspective?

One answer can be ruled out immediately, the idea that certain values or causes are 'sacred'. In this connection, Margalit refers to 'religious' models of politics which make certain goals holy or overriding all other values in all circumstances (*OC* 24). Peace, for example, can be such a sacred goal in the hands of pacifists. But, of course, this kind of view is the antithesis of value pluralism, which denies that any good is overriding.[25]

A second answer is that the limits of compromise are set by the minimal norms implicit in universal values. In this way, Gray argues that the Munich Agreement was not a legitimate modus vivendi because it was imposed by the Nazis, whose norms fall short of 'mimimal standards of decency and legitimacy that apply to all contemporary regimes' (Gray 2000b: 109). These minimal standards are demanding enough to exclude regimes like those of the Nazis but also relaxed enough to admit many non-liberal outlooks. 'In contemporary circumstances', they include the rule of law, a capacity to maintain peace, effective representative institutions, popular accountability, satisfaction of basic needs, protection of minorities from disadvantage, and institutions that reflect a common way of life (Gray 2000b: 106–7).

As usual, Gray leaves us with unanswered questions. One might wonder what regimes meet these minimal standards other than liberal regimes. Further, one might ask why, under pluralism, these values should be privileged rather than others – the same question that Gray asks the liberals. Again, he provides no answers apart from his references to 'contemporary circumstances' and 'human interests', neither defined. Why should we believe that Gray's minimal standards are anything more than his own personal preferences, or indeed the assumptions of a liberal order that he claims is valid only locally? Gray does not tell us.

A more systematic version of Gray's position could be constructed by grounding the minimal standards to which he refers in some more substantial account of 'the great goods', such as those discussed in Chapter 2. Nussbaum's central human capabilities, for example, may provide such an account. However, as we saw, there are two major problems with relying on such a move. First, the content of the great goods is disputed. Second, even where that content is agreed upon, the problem of value pluralism arises when the great goods come into conflict. The idea of the universal minimum gets us so far and no further, circling back to the familiar problem of how to resolve conflicts of fundamental and incommensurable values.

A third way of defining the limits of modus vivendi, and of compromise more broadly, is advanced by Margalit with his notion of 'rotten compromises'. These must never be agreed to, whatever the circumstances. The rotten compromise is like 'a cockroach in the soup' (*OC* 61). No matter what merits the soup may have, the cockroach makes it inedible. So, rottenness is a limit on modus vivendi: 'rotten compromises are not allowed, even for the sake of peace' (*OC* 1). The same thought applies to any compromise: 'rotten compromise must be avoided, come what may' (*OC* 3).

What is a rotten compromise? Margalit offers this basic definition: 'I see a rotten compromise as an agreement to establish or maintain an inhuman regime, a regime of cruelty and humiliation, that is, a regime that does not treat humans as humans' (*OC* 2). Any compromise that brings aid and comfort to an inhuman regime is rotten. The definitive inhuman or rotten regime is that of Nazi Germany, and the definitive rotten compromise is the Munich Agreement.

The test for a regime's inhumanity appears to be fundamentally Kantian: to fail to treat humans as humans is to use people merely as means to an end, as instruments without the capacity for forming legitimate purposes of their own (*OC* 59–60). Inhumanity will also, of course, include treating people as subhuman or animals or mere obstacles to desirable ends. Such conduct includes 'crimes against humanity', which consist of offences that go beyond 'the mild form of institutional humiliation' that marks a merely 'indecent' society and cross into a region of 'grave cruelty and humiliation' that 'undermine the notion of shared humanity' (*OC* 62).[26]

Moreover, inhuman regimes act in ways that violate not only particular moral rules but also the whole concept of morality itself. 'Attacking the idea of shared humanity … is attacking a constitutive element of morality as the domain that should regulate all human relations' (*OC* 64). The constitutive element in question is the inclusion of all human beings in the category of the human and therefore the recognition of all human beings as bearers of equal moral worth. When Hitler withholds that respect from some groups, he rejects morality itself. So, the Munich Agreement is the definitive rotten compromise because it is a compromise with the definitive rotten regime, that of a leader who preaches the denial of morality's essence. Margalit condemns this kind of compromise as 'radical evil' (*OC* 22).

Has Margalit identified the limits of compromise? First, a compromise that involves the rejection of morality is objectionable by definition, but is Margalit right to equate a failure to respect persons (in Kant's sense) with a rejection of morality? In effect his view identifies morality with liberal morality, which in the fullness of history is only one human ethic among others. Aristotle, for example, does make respect for persons a requirement of ethics, since on his account there is no equality of moral worth between free citizens on the one hand, who must be male, and slaves or women on the other. However, let us assume that respect for persons is a requirement of morality under modern conditions on the basis of the argument for liberal norms set out in Chapters 4–6. Inhuman regimes, defined by their failure to respect persons, deny morality itself, at least in modern terms.

Still, does it follow that any compromise with an inhuman regime must be rotten and therefore renounced? Wendt makes the point that some compromises of this kind may be justified because the consequences of renouncing them may be even worse than the consequences of accepting them (Wendt 2016: 64). Indeed, Margalit seems to agree when he writes, 'Compromises should never be allowed in cases of crimes against humanity, except to save the lives of the people threatened by such regimes' (*OC* 63). To compromise with the Nazis is odious but not to do so may in some circumstances be more terrible still. The more general point here is that decisions about whether to compromise need to have regard not only to the nature of the regime or party one is compromising with, but also to the consequences both of compromising and refusing to compromise.

Liberal pluralists will regard Margalit's test for rottenness – whether the regime one is dealing with is inhuman as measured by whether it respects persons – with some ambivalence. On the one hand, the idea of there being compromises that should never be made suggests an absolute formula that must be applied to every case – a monist approach. On the other hand, liberals will be wary of any compromising of the principle of respect for persons. Countervailing considerations would have to be exceptionally strong to justify any trading off of such a fundamental value.

Nevertheless, respect for persons cannot be an absolute value on the pluralist view, because there are no absolute values on that view. It may help to note that Kantian respect for persons is not a mystical notion to be worshipped for its own sake but a principle that rests on the reasoned claim that human beings are uniquely valuable. Uniquely valuable in what way? Various answers have been attempted: rationality, autonomy, and so forth. But whatever these unique values might be, pluralists will ask why they should be ranked above other values.

A reasonable conclusion is that while a very strong presumption in favor of respect for persons is consistent with pluralism, that presumption can be rebutted in sufficiently exigent circumstances – for example, where action has to be taken to avoid or end a devastating global war. The presumption is not rebutted in the case of the Munich Agreement, which treated thousands of people as pawns in exchange for no credible benefit, – since Hitler could not be trusted to keep his side of the bargain. By contrast, President Truman's decision to use nuclear weapons to end the Second World War may be more defensible, since at least it was more likely to achieve its purpose.

Even if respect for persons were thought to be a necessary limit to compromise in all cases, it would not be a sufficient limit. Margalit's test excludes only the very worst compromises, those that involve crimes against humanity. What about more routine cases? There could be a compromise which did not involve inhuman treatment or complicity with an inhuman regime but which was still undesirable. For example, necessary legislation might be watered down to placate a wealthy interest group.

My claim is that limits applicable to these more prosaic political cases are implicit in the conceptual approach developed in the current chapter and the two preceding. That discussion has identified three principles that are both broad enough to do justice to value plurality and specific enough to indicate a useful framework for a desirable politics: first, the promotion of value diversity (and secondarily, cultural diversity), which excludes authoritarian politics and points to egalitarian or redistributive liberalism (Chapter 5); second, support for personal autonomy and consequently for an Enlightenment form of liberal multiculturalism (Chapter 6); third, an inclusive or liberal form of democracy, supplemented but not replaced by deliberative practices (see earlier in this chapter). Given modern conditions, these principles place limits on the forms of politics that are acceptable on pluralist terms. Consequently, they place limits on the forms of compromise consistent with those politics. The Munich Agreement, for example, would not be an acceptable compromise according to any of the three principles.

Conclusion

Value pluralism has close conceptual ties with both democracy and compromise. Democracy, along with liberalism, is a political expression of the pluralist norm of value diversity. A system that enables many voices to be heard is a system that enables many values to be channeled into politics. This result is at its strongest, however, not simply when the majority rules but when democracy is at its most inclusive. Liberal forms of democracy, which respect the rights of individuals and minorities, are consequently closer to realizing pluralist diversity than is mere majoritarianism. This is not to say that liberal democracy is perfect, since for one thing there will still be a problem of what to do when rights conflict. Deliberative practices make an important contribution in this and other ways, as Bellamy points out, but they supplement liberal democracy rather than replacing it.

Compromise is connected with pluralism in two ways. First, compromise is closely associated with negotiation, hence with democracy. Second, conflicts among incommensurable values are more usually resolved by compromise than by more rigid forms of ranking. Different kinds of compromise should be acknowledged, including trading, trimming, and segregation, each of which has both weaknesses and strengths from a pluralist perspective. Another notable form of compromise, especially prominent in the work of Gray, is modus vivendi, or compromise for the sake of peaceful coexistence. However, Gray's account throws up unanswered questions of the meaning and limits of modus vivendi. Margalit's idea of 'rottenness' is an attempt to define the limits of compromise, but there are significant difficulties with this from a pluralist point of view. The limits of compromise are best captured by the principles of value diversity, personal autonomy, and inclusive democracy.

Notes

1 Waldron, in *PPT*, also chastises Berlin for ignoring the importance of democratic institutions, in particular constitutional mechanisms. For a defence of Berlin on this count, see Chapter 8 and Crowder 2019.
2 For a more detailed account and defense of Berlin on the relation between liberty and democracy, see Crowder 2013. See also Ella Myers (2013), who argues that Berlin's thought contains both anti-democratic and pro-democratic elements.
3 Bellamy has affiliations with the agonists in his criticism of liberal democracy as evading politics and relying too much on consensus, but his deliberative solution contrasts with theirs. Although his concern for democracy makes him closer to Mouffe than to Weber or Schmitt, the deliberative form of democracy is rejected by Mouffe (2000).
4 A range of deliberative devices currently in use is discussed in Fishkin 2018.
5 In addition, reciprocity requires people to abstain from 'inaccessible' arguments, which is surely an instance of the 'trimming' or even 'segregation' he rejects. These forms of compromise are discussed later.
6 These percentages are, of course, metaphorical and random examples.
7 Compare Wendt 2016: 3.
8 Distinctions are proposed between, e.g., moral and non-moral compromises and between pragmatic and principled compromises. See Weinstock 2013; Wendt 2016; Rostbøll and Scavenius 2018.
9 Bellamy's argument is critically examined in Overeem 2018.
10 There is some ambiguity as to whether Bellamy sees these as unsatisfactory models of compromise, or as models of consensual politics, or as 'meta-political' concepts (*LAP* 3) that do not amount to forms of compromise at all. I treat them as models of compromise because they all fit my definition, above.
11 This leads Hayek to oppose 'democracy' so far as it involves the imposition of planning and control on the market: see Hayek 1944: ch. 5.
12 But note that the fact of reasonable disagreement is explained by the 'burdens of judgement', which in turn include an element of value pluralism: see my *LVP* 165–71 and Galston's *LP* 46.

13 These issues are akin to those raised by political realism, which emphasizes the value of order and legitimacy: see Chapter 4.
14 See Kekes in *MP* 203–11; Kekes 1997: 172–5; Gray 1995: 109–10; Gray 2013: 181–3.
15 See, e.g., Hart 1973 on the priority of liberty.
16 See Chapter 8.
17 See Walzer 1983, discussed below.
18 Also, the equation of all compromise with negotiation fits awkwardly with the possibility of intra-personal compromise raised earlier.
19 This is not unlike the position of Plato in the *Republic*, where he defines justice in both the city and the individual as each part fulfilling its own function and not interfering with others. 'So, perhaps justice is, in a certain sense, just this minding one's own business' (Plato 1955 [n.d.]: 181).
20 Trimming also plays a significant role in deliberative democracy. Reciprocity is an obvious example, and this figures prominently in Bellamy's own theory of democratic negotiation. See also the idea of 'economy of moral disagreement', where deliberators 'try to find justifications that minimize their differences with their opponents' (Gutmann and Thompson 2004: 7).
21 See also Gray 1993: 288, 291; 1995: 105; 2013: 44, 105.
22 See Chapter 3.
23 Other advocates of modus vivendi theory include Horton 2010; McCabe 2010; Horton, Westphal, and Willems 2019.
24 *OC* 54–61, 95–113. He also mentions the Missouri Compromise of 1820: 2010: 57.
25 See Sinnott-Armstrong (2013) for an argument that 'absolutist' religions (those claiming superiority over rival beliefs) are incompatible with the more demanding kinds of compromise. But this leaves open the thought that not all religions are absolutist. Even monotheist beliefs need not be held in an absolutist way, and to that extent monotheism may be compatible with compromise and with pluralism: see Crowder 2014.
26 For Margalit's notion of 'decency', see Margalit 1996.

References

In-text abbreviations are noted in brackets.

Bellamy, Richard (1999), *Liberalism and Pluralism: Towards a Politics of Compromise* (London: Routledge). [*LAP*]
Bellamy, Richard (2000), 'Liberalism and the Challenge of Pluralism', in Richard Bellamy, ed., *Rethinking Liberalism* (London: Pinter).
Berlin, Isaiah (2002), *Liberty*, ed. Henry Hardy (Oxford: Oxford University Press). [*L*]
Berlin, Isaiah (2013a), *Against the Current: Essays in the History of Ideas*, ed. Henry Hardy, 2nd edn (Princeton: Princeton University Press).
Berlin, Isaiah (2013b), *The Crooked Timber of Humanity: Chapters in the History of Ideas*, ed. Henry Hardy, 2nd edn (Princeton: Princeton University Press). [*CTH*]
Crowder, George (2002), *Liberalism and Value Pluralism* (London: Continuum). [*LVP*]
Crowder, George (2013), 'In Defense of Berlin: A Reply to James Tully', in Bruce Baum and Robert Nichols, eds, *Isaiah Berlin and the Politics of Freedom: 'Two Concepts of Liberty' 50 Years Later* (New York: Routledge).
Crowder, George (2014), 'Value Pluralism and Monotheism', *Politics and Religion* 7 (4): 818–40.
Crowder, George (2019), 'Value Pluralism, Constitutionalism and Democracy: Waldron and Berlin in Debate', *Review of Politics* 81 (1): 101–27.

Fishkin, James S. (2018), *Democracy When the People Are Thinking: Revitalizing Our Politics Through Public Deliberation* (Oxford: Oxford University Press).
Galston, William (2002), *Liberal Pluralism: The Implications of Value Pluralism for Political Theory and Practice* (Cambridge: Cambridge University Press). [*LP*]
Gray, John (1993), *Post-Liberalism: Studies in Political Thought* (London: Routledge).
Gray, John (1995), *Enlightenment's Wake: Politics and Culture at the Close of the Modern Age* (London: Routledge).
Gray, John (2000a), 'Pluralism and Toleration in Contemporary Political Philosophy', *Political Studies* 48: 323–33.
Gray, John (2000b), *Two Faces of Liberalism* (Cambridge: Polity).
Gray, John (2000c), 'Where Pluralists and Liberals Part Company', in Maria Baghramian and Attracta Ingram, eds, *Pluralism: The Philosophy and Politics of Diversity* (London: Routledge).
Gray, John (2013), *Isaiah Berlin: An Interpretation of His Thought*, new edition (Princeton: Princeton University Press).
Gutmann, Amy and Dennis Thompson (2004), *Why Deliberative Democracy?* (Princeton: Princeton University Press).
Hart, H. L. A. (1973), 'The Priority of Liberty', *University of Chicago Law Review* 40: 534–55.
Hayek, Friedrich (1944), *The Road to Serfdom* (London: Routledge).
Horton, John (2010), 'Realism, Liberal Moralism and a Political Theory of Modus Vivendi', *European Journal of Political Theory* 9 (2): 431–48.
Horton, John, Manon Westphal, and Ulrich Willems, eds (2019), *The Political Theory of Modus Vivendi* (Cham: Springer).
Jahanbegloo, Ramin (1992), *Conversations with Isaiah Berlin* (London: Peter Halban). [*CIB*]
Kekes, John (1993), *The Morality of Pluralism* (Princeton: Princeton University Press). [*MP*]
Kekes, John (1997), *Against Liberalism* (Ithaca, NY: Cornell University Press).
Margalit, Avishai (1996), *The Decent Society*, trans. Naomi Goldblum (Cambridge, MA: Harvard University Press).
Margalit, Avishai (2010), *On Compromise and Rotten Compromises* (Princeton: Princeton University Press). [*ON*]
McCabe, David (2010), *Modus Vivendi Liberalism: Theory and Practice* (Cambridge: Cambridge University Press).
Mill, John Stuart (1974 [1859]), *On Liberty*, ed. Gertrude Himmelfarb (Harmondsworth: Penguin).
Mouffe, Chantal (2000), *On the Democratic Paradox* (London: Verso).
Myers, Ella (2013), 'Berlin and Democracy', in Bruce Baum and Robert Nichols, eds, *Isaiah Berlin and the Politics of Freedom: "Two Concepts of Liberty" 50 Years Later* (New York: Routledge).
Overeem, Patrick (2018), 'Compromise, Value Pluralism, and Democratic Liberalism', in Christian F. Rostbøll and Theresa Scavenius, eds, *Compromise and Disagreement in Contemporary Political Theory* (London: Routledge).
Plato (1955 [n.d.]), *The Republic*, trans. H. D. P. Lee (Harmondsworth: Penguin).
Rawls, John (1971), *A Theory of Justice* (Oxford: Oxford University Press).
Rawls, John (1993), *Political Liberalism* (New York: Columbia University Press).
Rawls, John (1999), 'The Idea of Public Reason Revisited', in *The Law of Peoples* (Cambridge, MA: Harvard University Press).

Rostbøll, Christian F. and Theresa Scavenius, eds (2018), *Compromise and Disagreement in Contemporary Political Theory* (London: Routledge).

Sinnott-Armstrong, Walter (2013), 'How Religion Undermines Compromise', in Steve Clarke, Russell Powell, and Julian Savulescu, eds, *Religion, Intolerance, and Conflict: A Scientific and Conceptual Investigation* (Oxford: Oxford University Press).

Waldron, Jeremy (2016), *Political Political Theory: Essays on Institutions* (Cambridge, MA: Harvard University Press). [*PPT*]

Walzer, Michael (1983), *Spheres of Justice: A Defence of Pluralism and Equality* (Oxford: Blackwell).

Walzer, Michael (1999), 'Deliberation, and What Else?', in Stephen Macedo, ed., *Deliberative Politics: Essays on Democracy and Agreement* (New York: Oxford University Press).

Weinstock, Daniel (2013), 'On the Possibility of Principled Moral Compromise', *Critical Review of International Social and Political Philosophy* 16 (4): 537–56.

Wendt, Fabian (2016), *Compromise, Peace and Public Justification: Political Morality Beyond Justice* (New York: Palgrave Macmillan).

Young, Iris (2000), *Inclusion and Democracy* (Oxford: Oxford University Press).

8 Constitutionalism and Public Policy

Reflection on the concept of value pluralism points to norms of value diversity, personal autonomy, democracy, and compromise as especially important in the realm of politics. Respect for value plurality implies a commitment to the promotion of as wide a range of values as possible at the level of social (as opposed to individual) life. This goal of value diversity (and, secondarily, of cultural diversity) indicates the desirability of both liberalism and democracy – liberalism in its egalitarian or redistributive form and democracy if it is inclusive rather than merely majoritarian. Further, the need to choose among competing incommensurable values points toward the values of personal autonomy and compromise. In short, the concept of pluralism pushes us, at any rate in the historical context of modernity, toward a form of liberal democracy that values fundamental rights and liberties, redistribution, multiculturalism qualified by a concern for personal autonomy, and democratic negotiation shaped by the foregoing principles.

With all this in place, I want now to consider two final lines of argument grounded in the concept of value pluralism. The first addresses political institutions. Might the logic of pluralism, subject to contextual considerations as before, not suggest, in addition to the broad principles already outlined, certain kinds of institution that will best implement those principles?

Here I respond to a recent argument by Jeremy Waldron that Berlin is guilty of neglecting institutions in general and constitutionalism in particular. Indeed, Waldron believes that Berlin is positively hostile to the constitutionalism of the Enlightenment because he is hostile to the Enlightenment as a whole. In reply, I argue that although Berlin makes little mention of constitutional institutions in his work, he is not hostile to them. He rejects only certain aspects of the Enlightenment, and constitutionalism is not one of them.

However, I am more interested in taking a step beyond Berlin: whatever his own views may have been, the logic of his political thought supports liberal constitutionalism. That is because there are strong conceptual links between pluralism and the standard constitutional devices of liberal democracy: separation of powers, checks and balances, and judicial review.

In making this case, I disagree with Waldron's claim that judicial review should be rejected. Waldron's position is based on democracy: judicial review is, according to him, undemocratic. I have already argued (Chapter 7) that Berlinian pluralism fits with democracy as long as this is inclusive in its outcomes, respecting the rights of individuals and minorities. Only in this way are all relevant voices properly respected, hence all relevant values. But contemporary democracy cannot be relied upon to be sufficiently inclusive. In part this is an effect of current political phenomena such as the war on terror and the populism that has become so influential. But underlying these developments is a permanent tendency in human societies toward hostility to minorities – a point conceded by Waldron himself. Under these conditions, it is unwise for pluralists to dispense with judicial review.

The second theme of the chapter is that conceptual connections can also be drawn between pluralism and routine practices used by public administrators in constructing and advising on public policy. The use of 'cycling', 'firewalls', and 'casuistry' enables administrators to settle conflicts among plural and conflicting values at the level of policy formation and advice and to do so within the political framework already indicated. The work of David Thacher and Martin Rein is central to this argument.

I begin the chapter by defending Berlin against Waldron's attack, before going beyond Berlin to argue that his value pluralism can be used to provide positive support for constitutionalism in general, and more specifically for the standard devices of separation of powers and checks and balances. A third section examines Waldron's case against judicial review on both general and pluralist grounds, arguing that it depends on an unrealistic assumption about attitudes to individual rights in contemporary democracy and in politics more generally. I then set out a series of pluralist arguments in favor of judicial review, which I proceed to defend against objections. In the final section, I look at distinctively pluralist approaches to public policy and administration.

Berlin and Constitutionalism

A frequent theme in recent political studies is that contemporary political theory pays too much attention to philosophical justification and not enough to institutional design. Jeremy Waldron makes this the central thesis of his aptly titled *Political Political Theory* (2016). According to Waldron, the tendency everywhere is to treat political theory as a branch of moral philosophy, focusing on normative values, principles, and arguments, and to neglect issues of how those norms are expressed in or contained by political structures such as legislatures, executives, and judiciaries. Much of this trend follows in the wake of Rawls's focus on justice as the paramount value in politics. Although Waldron does not deny the importance of justice, he objects that 'precious little attention is paid in the justice industry to questions about political process, political institutions, and political structures' (*PPT* 4, 3).

The most prominent target of Waldron's wrath is Isaiah Berlin. For Berlin, in Waldron's account, political theory is 'moral philosophy applied to social situations' (*PPT* 4, quoting *CIB* 46).

> To read almost any of Berlin's work is to read essays that are resolutely uninterested in the political institutions of liberal society. Beyond airy talk of freedom and openness, Berlin was simply unconcerned with the ways in which liberal or democratic political institutions might accommodate the pluralism he thought so important in human life.
>
> *(PPT* 4–5*)*

In particular, according to Waldron, Berlin seriously and culpably neglected an institutional area with which he ought to have been centrally concerned, namely constitutionalism.[1] Berlin's neglect begins with his failure to take an interest in the constitutionalism of the Enlightenment. The institutional designs proposed by thinkers such as Montesquieu, Voltaire, Madison, and Hume amount to a body of work that 'is massively important', having 'transformed our political thinking out of all recognition', and leaving as its legacy the American and French Revolutions, their constitutions, and their rejection of monarchical and aristocratic political forms (*PPT* 274). Yet

> Berlin, supposedly one of our greatest interpreters of Enlightenment thinking, had very little to say about this heritage of thought and constitutional achievement. I have ransacked his work and I mean it: there is almost nothing on Enlightenment constitutionalism in his writings – some few rags and paltry blurred shreds of paper here and there, but nothing of any significance.
>
> *(PPT* 274*)*

Why was this? Waldron suggests various possibilities. The most obvious is that Berlin 'was just uninterested in this aspect of the Enlightenment' (*PPT* 287), indeed that 'he just wasn't interested in law, constitutions, or institutional politics generally' (*PPT* 275). Waldron judges this to be 'probably the best explanation' (*PPT* 287). Nevertheless, a further possibility, Waldron thinks, is that Berlin deliberately avoided discussing Enlightenment constitutionalism because it was an inconvenient truth. 'This was not a blind spot at all but deliberate avoidance of an aspect of the Enlightenment heritage that would have falsified Berlin's central proposition that Enlightenment social design was a matter of monistic and bullying perfectionism' (*PPT* 287).

As noted in Chapter 1, Berlin traced the Soviet form of totalitarianism to the scientific and therefore monistic stream of thought that he found in the Enlightenment.[2] Waldron sees Berlin as equating all Enlightenment institutional design with that tendency. 'He proceeded in his work as though all attempts at social and political design were on a par, and as though everything invested in the eighteenth-century constitutionalist enterprise was beneath contempt' (*PPT* 275). 'According to Berlin, Enlightenment social design was arrogant and monistic, seeking a fatuous reconciliation of all values and a comprehensive solution of all conflicts in a glittering work of reason' (*PPT* 283). But Berlin found that the constitutionalist strand of Enlightenment thought did not fit this pattern, so he deliberately ignored it in order to preserve the overall narrative. At least, this is a possibility. But it is such 'a frightful thing to say about a public intellectual' that we should put it aside and return to 'maybe the more charitable explanation' that Berlin simply was not interested in Enlightenment constitutionalism (*PPT* 275). So charitable is Waldron that he repeats the charge of deliberate suppression later (*PPT* 287).

Waldron's thesis is striking, but how accurate is it? First, his contention that Berlin wrote very little about institutions in general and Enlightenment constitutionalism in particular is broadly correct. The contention becomes less convincing when Waldron extends it to Berlin's followers, since many people influenced by Berlin have used his work to write about institutions of various kinds.[3] Still, it is true that although Berlin himself wrote 'in the abstract about processes and mechanisms for conflict and balancing, it was the Enlightenment constitutionalists who sought to actually specify these processes in institutional terms' (*PPT* 284). This is fair enough, but an obvious reply is a simple appeal to division of labor. No one can write about everything that is important. Waldron has focused on institutions, Berlin on other matters. Should Waldron be taken to task for not spending more time on what interested Berlin?

What did interest Berlin? There is an important reason for Berlin's scholarly priorities that Waldron does not mention. Berlin has a reputation as a leading liberal thinker, yet it has sometimes been noticed that he writes relatively little about the foundations of liberalism and a great deal about the foundations and the political psychology of anti-liberal views.[4] His fascination with the writers of the Counter-enlightenment – Vico, Herder, Hamann, Maistre – is a case in point (Lilla 2001). He explains that these are the thinkers who present the strongest challenges to his own liberal and Enlightenment views:

> If you believe in liberal principles and rational analysis, as I do, then you must take account of what the objections are, and where the cracks in your structures are, where your side went wrong: hostile criticism, even bigoted opposition, can reveal truth.
>
> (*CIB* 70–1)

Berlin defends liberalism and the Enlightenment indirectly by looking at the alternatives.

But how can that be right given Waldron's stronger claim (or speculation) that Berlin is not merely neglectful of Enlightenment constitutionalism but actually hostile to it? The answer is that Waldron's stronger claim is mistaken. Berlin does not need Waldron's charity because there is nothing to excuse. He is not hostile, as Waldron supposes, to everything about the Enlightenment. Admittedly Berlin is often careless in his treatment of the Enlightenment, making it seem as though he thinks the Enlightenment was all of a piece and that the piece in question was false and dangerous. But this is far too simple a picture of Berlin's position. He clearly accepts the Enlightenment values of individual liberty, equality, and the authority of human reason, broadly understood.

'Fundamentally, I am a liberal rationalist. The values of the Enlightenment, what people like Voltaire, Helvetius, Holbach, Condorcet, preached are deeply sympathetic to me' (*CIB* 70).[5]

What Berlin opposes is a particular stream of Enlightenment methodology: namely, scientism and the monism that scientism encourages.[6] Consequently, he rejects the kind of utopian social engineering that results from applying such an outlook to social reform. That is, Berlin takes aim at the kind of institutional design that, in Waldron's apt words, seeks 'a fatuous reconciliation of all values and a comprehensive solution of all conflicts' – the design of communist utopianism, for example. However, that does not mean that Berlin rejects a more accommodating institutional design that leaves room for – is designed around – liberty and pluralism: to wit, Enlightenment constitutionalism. There is no evidence that Berlin opposes that kind of constitutional design. He may say little about constitutionalism but he is not hostile to it.

From Pluralism to Constitutionalism

I want to take a further step: irrespective of Berlin's own views, the logic of his political thought supports constitutionalism on the ground of value pluralism. Berlin was not interested in making this connection – he had other things to do. But the connection is there to be made.

The starting point is the pluralist commitment to diversity of values outlined in Chapter 5. To take value pluralism seriously is to acknowledge the full range of human values and to be willing to promote as extensive a selection of those values as possible within the relevant social and historical circumstances.

How does pluralist diversity connect with constitutionalism? A cogent argument is provided by William Galston, who appeals to the idea that under pluralism the goods of social peace and stability, although not overriding, have a special place as preconditions for other goods.[7] 'While pluralists cannot regard social peace and stability as dominant goods in all circumstances, they recognize that these goods typically help create the framework within which the attainment of other goods becomes possible' (Galston 2011: 236). For pluralists, values of social order cannot be absolutely overriding, since no single value is absolutely overriding. But in most cases these values are especially important for the purpose of social organization, since they create the conditions necessary to enable other goods to flourish.

Consequently, Galston argues, pluralists should accept a set of 'minimum conditions of social order', which include 'clear and stable property relations, the rule of law, a public authority with the capacity to enforce the law', and so forth (Galston 2011: 236). In other words, the achievement and maintenance of social order and stability require institutions embodying established and continuing laws, customs, and practices.

Further, each society will organize its social order and institutions in its own way, and its 'constitution' is precisely the general pattern of public organization that is peculiar to that society: 'every political community assumes a distinctive form and identity through its constitution' (Galston 2011: 238). A given constitution emphasizes those public values that are most important, or most fundamental, to the society in question. Because these differ from case to case, constitutions differ; no single version is appropriate universally or superior to all others. So, a constitution need not (until we know more about the particular social context) be written, or democratic, or liberal, or derived from popular sovereignty.

However, a constitution must perform certain functions, Galston believes. It must 'rest on, and often declare, a principle of authorizing legitimacy', create and define 'a political community's governing powers', direct public affairs 'toward distinctive ensembles of public purposes', and set out a level of '"higher" than ordinary law' which can be used to 'validate ordinary law' (Galston 2011: 229–30).

The role of a constitution as 'higher law' deserves emphasis because it seems to raise a problem for pluralists. Galston observes that a constitution

> represents an authoritative partial ordering of public values. It selects a subset of worthy values, brings them to the foreground, and subordinates other values to them. These preferred values then become the benchmarks for assessing legislation, public policy and even the condition of public culture.
> (Galston 2011: 238)

For pluralists, in other words, the 'higher law' aspect of constitutionalism implies a ranking of values. In any such case, a pluralist would have to ask why those specific values should be selected and held up as benchmarks rather than others.

The answer lies in Galston's careful phrase, 'partial ordering'. While value pluralism is defined by its rejection of absolute ordering, or formulas for ranking basic values that apply in every case, pluralists can (as noted before) endorse partial ordering, or rankings that apply only in specific circumstances or contexts. Thus, Galston notes that the privileging of constitutional principles may not apply in exigent circumstances where they conflict with public order or in a personal context where an individual's core identifying values are at stake. Moreover, the emphasis on constitutional values as against others in the public sphere does not preclude the possibility of conflict among constitutional values, such as basic rights, themselves.

Recall, too, that on Galston's account a given constitution is not a universal prescription but the specific choice of a particular society. This, too, links with the notion of a contextual rather than absolute ranking, since it suggests that a given constitution will reflect a given cultural tradition. The US Constitution, for example, expresses a political culture that is not the same as that of the UK or Australia, whose constitutions will correspondingly differ.

So, from a value-pluralist perspective there is good reason to regard political institutions as important and to want these to be characterized by constitutionalism. What will such institutions look like? Here we should return to Waldron, who gives his position the promising label of 'democratic constitutionalism'. How does Waldron bring constitutionalism and democracy together? Two prominent features of his view are his defense of the separation of powers, and his claim that, with some qualification, legislation should not be subject to judicial review. Waldron's support for separation of powers is very much in line with Berlinian value pluralism, but his rejection of judicial review is open to question on the same ground.

Waldron defines separation of powers as 'a qualitative separation of the different functions of government – for example, legislation, adjudication, and executive administration' (*PPT* 45). This is a different idea from the 'dispersal' of power, which prevents power from concentrating in any one set of hands, since that is possible without separating functions; and from checks and balances, in which one exercise of power is reviewed by another – again, this does not necessarily involve the separation of functions (*PPT* 49–53). Waldron's question is: what, if anything, justifies the doctrine of the separation of powers as such, independently of the cognate notions of dispersal and checks and balances?

He finds that 'the canonical literature' gives no clear answer. Montesquieu, for example, speaks vaguely of the separation of powers being essential to 'liberty', or the avoidance of tyranny. But he does not explain why.[8] The object lesson is that of 'Turkish justice', in which the Sultan possesses all the powers of government and uses them arbitrarily (*PPT* 58). But why should an adequate remedy for Turkish justice not be dispersal of power into multiple hands? What is added by separation of powers into multiple functions?

Waldron's answer is that separation of powers is needed to reflect the idea of 'articulated governance' (*PPT* 62). Political power is not a simple whole but a complex series of components – legislative, executive, judicial – each with its own distinctive character. The components are 'articulated' in a process in which each plays a distinctive role, contributing to the overall purpose of governing. Consequently, the 'integrity' of each link in the process should be maintained: each 'should do its own work' and not contaminate or be contaminated by the others (*PPT* 65).

The value-pluralist resonance of this view is readily apparent. Democratic governance is a pluralist rather than monist conception, containing multiple elements that can be distinguished from one another and assigned different functions and ends.[9] True, every link in the chain of democratic governance answers to 'concerns about liberty, dignity, and respect' that animate the process as a whole (*PPT* 64). But each link also embodies its own particular, distinct values: in the case of legislation the values of democratic recognition and deliberation; for the executive decisiveness and impartiality in application of the laws; for the judiciary the virtues of impartial interpretation. The different tasks of governance express different norms. Indeed, the principal values embodied in articulated governance are incommensurable; the better understanding of democratic governance is pluralist rather than monist.

Value pluralism also suggests a point not stressed by Waldron: that separation of powers needs to be supplemented by the further idea of checks and balances. The message of pluralism is not only that institutional norms are distinct from one another but also that there is no absolute hierarchy among them. Consequently, there is no absolute hierarchy among the institutions that express those norms. 'It is probably a mistake', writes Waldron, 'for any branch of government to assume the mantle of popular sovereign' (*PPT* 43). There may be (at least according to the traditional public policy model) a sequential order that begins with an initiative of the elected executive, and proceeds to legislation, which is then implemented by administration and interpreted or reviewed by the courts. But this does not indicate that any one phase is more important or valuable than any other in absolute terms – all make a distinctive contribution to the articulated whole. The institutional expression of this view is the checking and balancing of each institution by the others. Decisions 'ought to be as sensitive as possible to the views of all elements in the polity' (*PPT* 43). As Michael Spicer writes, constitutional checks and balances 'provide multiple veto points' that 'make it less likely that important values will be overlooked in shaping public policy decisions' (Spicer 2001: 522).

Waldron on Judicial Review

The notion of checks and balances leads to the second of my themes from Waldron's democratic constitutionalism, that of judicial review of legislation. Waldron formulates the issue as follows: 'Should judges have the authority to strike down legislation when they are convinced that it violates individual rights?' (*PPT* 195). Note that this question concerns only judicial review of legislation, not of executive action, which Waldron believes raises other issues, and to which he is more sympathetic. In addition, although Waldron identifies various forms of judicial review, he is concerned only with the 'strong' family of versions, which include a court's striking down a piece of legislation (*PPT* 199–200). Waldron's question is whether judicial review is justified in these strong terms.

His basic answer is no, subject to a qualification I come to in a moment. The fundamental problem is the undemocratic nature of judicial review, which empowers unelected officials to override decisions made by elected representatives.[10] Given the link between value pluralism and democracy, this looks like a concern for pluralists too.[11] Most of Waldron's discussion is directed to the context of the United States. But his deeper point is that judicial review is illegitimate wherever it occurs because of the conflict with democracy that is inherent in it. That is an issue for all liberal democracies.

At least, Waldron claims to show that judicial review is illegitimate in these terms if he is granted a series of assumptions – this is the qualification mentioned above. These assumptions are required for what Waldron calls his 'core' case against judicial review. If they do not hold, then the situation becomes 'non-core' and he concedes that he will be forced away from his favored line of argument toward some other line he does not specify (*PPT* 239–41). The most important of these assumptions for my purposes is that we are dealing with a broadly democratic society most of whose members and officials, including legislators, are committed 'to the idea of individual and minority rights' (*PPT* 203).

Given that assumption, Waldron argues as follows. He begins by distinguishing between considerations of 'outcome' and considerations of 'process' (*PPT* 214–5). 'Outcome' is about getting the true or correct result from a decision; 'process' is about having a legitimate procedure independent of the result. These are distinct considerations: it would be possible to get the right answer from an illegitimate procedure and the wrong answer from a legitimate procedure.

It may be tempting, Waldron observes, to align outcome-related considerations with the justification of judicial review and process-related considerations with the case against. That is, it might be supposed that democratic procedure favors legislation while the wisdom and impartiality of the courts is more likely to lead to a correct outcome. In that case, the question of whether judges should be allowed to override legislators would turn into the question of whether outcome should override process.

This way of framing the issue would be a classic instance of the problem of value pluralism. Waldron recognizes outcome and process as not merely distinct but also incommensurable goals when he asks, 'how do we weigh these process-related and outcome-related considerations? We face the familiar problem of trying to maximize the value of two variables, like asking someone to buy the fastest car at the lowest price' (*PPT* 217). Which institutional option is chosen would depend on how we weigh or rank the pertinent considerations. The answer to this question is unclear in the absence of a general system for ranking or commensurating them.

'I think I can cut through this Gordian knot', Waldron writes.

> What I will argue is that the outcome-related reasons are at best inconclusive. They are important, but they do not (as is commonly thought) establish anything like a clear case for judicial review. The process-related reasons, however, are one-sided. They operate mainly to discredit judicial review while leaving legislative decision-making unscathed.
>
> (*PPT* 217)

In effect he cleverly finesses the pluralist choice between norms by canceling one of them out. On the issue of outcome, he declares a draw between judges and legislators, so process becomes decisive. And on process, legislation wins hands-down.

The detailed moves by which Waldron reaches this conclusion need not be rehearsed in their entirety; they can be consolidated into two key lines of argument, corresponding to considerations of outcome and process. First, on the score of outcome it is sometimes said that judicial review is superior because of the impartiality of judges compared with the self- or partisan interest of legislators. Waldron responds that this claim is defeated by his assumption that most legislators are committed to the idea of rights – those of other people are as well as their own and their supporters. To the extent that 'sectarian pressures' nevertheless creep into legislation, these have been known to influence judicial reasoning too (*PPT* 218). For these and other reasons, Waldron sees the rival claims of legislation and judicial review as on a par when it comes to outcome.

When it comes to process, however, Waldron sees legislation as possessing a clear advantage. Legislators are appointed by process of fair election, and the standard procedure of majority decision making within legislatures is neutral among outcomes and reflects a paradigm model of equal treatment. Judges, on the other hand, are appointed by methods at various removes from democratic control. Their decision-making procedures are in no way representative of public opinion. To the argument that they speak for the people through bills of rights, Waldron replies that bills of rights 'bear on' questions of rights without 'settling' them – that is, judges are left with considerable, undemocratic discretion to determine the details of those rights (*PPT* 232). In short, while legislative procedures

> respect the voices and opinions of the persons – in their millions – whose rights are at stake in these disagreements and treat them as equals in the process ... an additional layer of final review by courts adds little to the process except a rather insulting form of disenfranchisement and a legal obfuscation of the moral issues at stake in our disagreement about rights.
> (*PPT* 244)

Waldron's argument against judicial review is debatable at several points, but I focus on his assumption that all members of the society, including legislative representatives, 'take rights seriously' and that their concern for rights 'is not just lip service' (*PPT* 207). Are the public and its legislators really as committed to preserving rights as Waldron supposes?

Unfortunately, there is ample reason to believe that the answer is, in general, no. I concede that in Chapter 7 I argued that the general notion of human rights is widely respected in liberal democracies even though there is limited consensus about which rights should be protected and how they should be prioritized. However, that argument assumed the contribution to the culture of rights made by all the institutions of liberal democracy including, crucially, pillars of liberal constitutionalism such as judicial review. My point in this current chapter is that we cannot rely on legislatures and popular opinion *alone* to respect rights. The 'democratic' elements of liberal democracy need to be supplemented and corrected by liberal constitutionalism, and judicial review is an essential part of the necessary balance.

This is certainly true under current political conditions. Since the events of 9/11 and the start of the subsequent 'war on terror', public attitudes in liberal democracies have shifted away from sympathy with civil liberties and toward greater concern for security at the expense of rights. In the case of the US, for example, studies have shown how readily people give up their commitment to rights, especially the rights of others, in the face of perceived threats to their safety.[12] This change in American public sentiment has translated into legislation in which long-cherished civil liberties have been eroded, the salient example being the USA PATRIOT Act (2001), with its provisions authorizing indefinite detention of non-US citizens, along with expanded powers of search, seizure, and intelligence gathering.[13] Provisions of this kind have been legislated all over the liberal-democratic world.[14]

Another recent anti-rights trend is the rise of 'populism'. Populism is hard to define with precision and in particular difficult to separate from extreme forms of nationalism.[15] But there is widespread agreement that there is a general pattern uniting political phenomena such as the election of Donald Trump, Brexit, and the influence in France of Marine Le Pen. In these and other cases, populists claim to champion the claims of 'ordinary people' against 'elites', including professional politicians and experts, who are alleged to have betrayed the people in favor of economic globalization and the interests of foreigners, asylum seekers, and immigrants. These latter groups are often those whose rights are most severely restricted by populist legislation (Zaslove 2004). But populist legislation is capable of demolishing a much wider range of democratic rights, as demonstrated by Viktor Orbán's Fidesz party in Hungary.[16]

Waldron may reply that the circumstances of the war on terror and of the current wave of populism are exceptional or at any rate contingent. When these phases have passed, his assumption of a majority commitment to individual rights will be satisfied once more. The trouble is that both the war on terror and the rise of populism are sustained by a more deep-seated hostility to minorities that persists in all societies. For example, a recent study has found that the unpopularity of Muslims in the United States has increased little since 9/11, but is maintained by 'a general sense of affect' for non-mainstream groups (Kalkan, Layman, and Uslaner 2009).

Waldron does recognize prejudice against 'discrete and insular minorities' – African Americans in the United States, for example – as a major problem in this connection (*PPT* 241). This is 'the sort of noncore case', he concedes, 'in which the argument for judicial review of legislative decisions has some plausibility. Minorities in this situation may need special care that only nonelective institutions can provide' (*PPT* 241). He insists that not all discrete and insular minorities deserve protection, giving the example of Bolsheviks in the United States, and that not every minority is discrete and insular. However, these observations are not much to the point. Even if American Bolsheviks do not deserve rights-protection (why not?), and even if not all minorities are discrete and insular, it is clear that there are discrete and insular minorities that are subject to persistent prejudice and deserve protection. It is hard to avoid concluding that Waldron has conceded a significant case for judicial review.

Note also that the same phenomena that have reduced the public commitment to rights in liberal democracies can also be seen as objectionable from the perspective of value pluralism. The attitudes and legislation typical of the war on terror make security overriding at the cost of the important values embodied in the rights it displaces. Populism elevates the supposed 'will of the people' to a position of primacy, with the same consequences (Müller 2016). Prejudice against minorities involves a refusal to consider the values implicit in ways of life other than one's own. In short, the denigration of basic rights represents a failure to respect the full range of human values acknowledged by pluralists.

However, to show the limitations of public opinion and elected legislatures when it comes to the protection of rights, and consequently the promotion of plural values, is not necessarily to show that judges will do any better. In terms of Waldron's argument, even if his underlying assumption does not hold and the core argument does not go through, it does not follow automatically that judicial review must be defensible. Could it be that a society's judicial decision making is 'no less corrupt or no less contaminated with prejudice than the society's legislative decision-making' (*PPT* 241)? There is, of course, some truth in this suggestion; judges have often been guilty of adopting biased or limited perspectives.[17] So, it remains for the defenders of judicial review to make a positive case in its favor.

Value-Pluralist Defenses of Judicial Review

I can see three principal lines of argument along which judicial review can be defended on the basis of value pluralism: one appealing to cultural and historical context, another to the judiciary's insulation from public opinion, and a third to the principle of checks and balances.

First, then, one standard way of settling conflicts of incommensurable values is to refer to context, in particular the context of cultural tradition. In this way, a case might be made for judicial review by locating it within just such a tradition. So, for example, judicial review might be defended in the US by invoking American political culture. One obvious weakness of this kind of argument is its limitation to particular cultures, although in the case of judicial review this institution is now endorsed in virtually all liberal-democratic political cultures, even those without written constitutions (e.g., the UK) or Bills of Rights (e.g., Australia). More troublesome is the objection that the mere existence of a cultural tradition is not a guarantee of its desirability.

Second, defenders of judicial review can emphasize that judges are in varying degrees insulated by their institutional position from the kind of populist public opinion that undermines rights. This is also an argument from pluralism given that, as we have seen, the same political tendencies that have threatened rights are also threats to value diversity. Waldron, of course, makes judicial insulation the leading exhibit in his case *against* judicial review: it is this that, in his view, makes judicial review undemocratic. But when public opinion is problematic for reasons such as those already mentioned, judicial insulation begins to look like an advantage. Indeed, it could be argued that, in offering protection to rights under conditions of hostile public opinion, it is the judiciary that is more genuinely 'democratic' in the inclusive as opposed to merely majoritarian sense of the word. This, too, is a pluralist argument, since it is inclusive rather than merely majoritarian democracy that is endorsed by pluralism. Pluralists want voice to be given to all relevant values and interests, not just those backed by the greatest numbers.

I hasten to add that the kind of anti-populist insulation I am commending here is not a matter of demographic elitism. A persistent complaint against the judiciary is that it is unrepresentative of the population at large, its members drawn from a narrow elite that excludes women and minorities (see, e.g., Malleson 1999: 103–5). Few would defend this, least of all pluralists. They would support a more representative judiciary on the same ground on which they would defend democracy: a range of different voices implies respect for a range of different values.

Rather, the insulation I have in mind refers to the judiciary's institutional independence – that is, the courts' independence from other institutions in the political system and consequently their independence from the political pressures channeled by those other institutions. This is not simply a matter of unelected appointment. Most judges in most jurisdictions across the world are appointed by means other than election, but unelected appointment is not essential to judicial independence.

James Gibson (2012) points out that the great majority of American state judges are elected but they are still strongly perceived by the public as impartial decision makers.[18] For Gibson, what makes judges legitimate in the eyes of the public is a combination of several factors, including their procedural rectitude, their expertise in the law, and their capacity to reach decisions that are 'fair and just' (Gibson 2012: 88–9). These are factors that mark the judiciary as independent from other democratic institutions; its role is to make even-handed and fair legal decisions, not to reflect public sentiment. Moreover, that role is endorsed by public opinion itself. Whether judges are elected or not (and even whether they are demographically representative or not), the institution of the judiciary aspires to an independence that equips it to defend rights against populist pressure.

It might be objected that I am unfairly comparing the judiciary at its best with legislatures at their worst. Can judges not be moved by populist concerns that undermine rights, just like legislators? Earlier I conceded that it is possible for judges to be biased or limited in outlook, so where is the superiority of the judiciary in this matter?

The point is about institutions, not individual cases. Even at their best, legislatures can undermine rights because their role is to represent the interests and ideologies of their constituents and supporters. Where these run counter to rights, legislators are only doing their job in opposing the rights in question or at least in arguing for interpretations of those rights that suit their supporters' interests. The courts, on the other hand, aspire to impartiality among competing interests when they interpret and apply the law. Individual judges can fail to meet that aspiration, of course. Moreover, there are also structural obstacles to complete impartiality. Judges inevitably have to decide matters that have a political content, since these involve judgments about the public interest, and to these decisions they cannot help but bring their own political views (Griffith 1985). Judicial independence is sensibly seen less as a fact than 'an ideal or set of normative values about courts' (Peretti 2002: 103). Nevertheless, it is a crucial point of distinction that the judiciary possesses such an ideal while legislatures do not. Judicial independence and impartiality are never complete, but they make the judiciary a more reliable instrument for protecting rights than legislatures.

Third, pluralists might defend judicial review as part of the checks and balances that they regard as essential to a healthy constitution. I argued earlier that pluralists have reason to endorse constitutional checks and balances as a supplement to the separation of powers emphasized by Waldron. Judicial review is an important component of most systems of checks and balances.

An immediate concern may be that judicial review in fact unbalances the system because, by giving the judiciary the last word, it makes the courts dominant. In pluralist terms, are the values promoted by judicial review allowed to override, without justification, those of the other parts of the system? To answer this question is to consider the precise relation implied by judicial review between the judiciary and other branches, especially the legislature. This will vary in different political systems, and within any one system it may be contested.

In the case of the US, for example, the proper relation between the Supreme Court and the Federal and State legislatures whose statutes the Court reviews is a matter of some dispute. Iddo Porat (2009) has identified three different value-pluralist models for that relation proposed in American legal theory.

The first of these is 'contextual balancing'. As Porat explains, the general principle is that, when assessing the constitutionality of legislation,

> judges should not give absolute or categorical preference to any one value at the expense of all the other values. A judge should rather strive to reflect the plurality of values in her decisions, by giving voice to all of the possible values and worldviews in society and balancing between them to the best of her abilities, in accordance with the circumstances of the case. Value pluralism therefore connotes judicial balancing.
>
> (Porat 2009: 919)

This balancing may be regarded as a matter either of 'pragmatic necessity' or of symbolism and expression. In the latter case, 'the judicial decision should express respect to each of the values involved in it by giving voice to each and by making sure that no value or interest is left out of the judicial balance' (Porat 2009: 920). For example, in *University of California v. Bakke*,

> Justice Powell contraposed the value of 'color blindness' with the value of 'affirmative action' and reached a compromise that seems to give voice to both: affirmative action would be allowed, but only through an individualized review of applicants rather than through quotas.
>
> (Porat 2009: 920–1)

However, judicial balancing attracts the familiar democratic objection: these values need to be balanced, but is that not the job of the elected legislature rather than the unelected judiciary? This leads to the second model identified by Porat, that of 'judicial neutrality' or 'judicial deference', in which the court defers to the legislature, since 'the only place to decide between such conflicts would be in the battleground of democratic competition' (Porat 2009: 921).

But can legislatures always be relied upon to balance all the values relevant to the case? Might there not be a danger that important rights of individuals and minorities will sometimes be pushed aside without due acknowledgment or expression? The third model identified by Porat responds to this worry, aiming at a happy medium between the first two approaches. The starting point or default position for balancing plural values in public policy is acknowledged to be the democratic decision making of legislatures. However, 'process theory' recognizes the judiciary as having a role in 'regulating the democratic process and in maintaining that it does indeed reflect the plurality of values in society' (Porat 2009: 923). This is especially so in those cases where 'the rights in view are those that pertain to the democratic process itself or enhance the participation of marginalized groups in that process, such as the rights of free speech and equal protection' (Porat 2009: 923). Again, the argument points to a function for judicial review in response to the kind of problem raised in the previous section, where in a certain climate of public opinion elected legislatures are not reliable guardians of rights.

Armed with this set of alternative models, I am now in a better position to assess whether judicial review tilts the institutional balance too far in favor of the judiciary and against legislatures, at any rate in the American context. In the case of the second model, judicial deference, this is obviously not so; indeed, there may be room for the argument that in this understanding it is the legislature that is too dominant, with corresponding danger to vulnerable rights. Nor is there much cause for complaint in relation to the third model, in which judicial review comes in only to regulate democratic decision making, which is explicitly the norm.

Only the first model invites the question of institutional imbalance, and even in that case the question is not unanswerable. While it is true the first model allows more potential than the others for judicial activism, it is going too far to see the model as enabling the judiciary to dominate the system as a whole. Judicial review on this understanding can shape the law through interpretation, but it cannot initiate or change statutes themselves. Those functions remain the preserve of legislatures; the judiciary can check and balance the legislature, not displace it. Institutional balance is maintained even according to the strongest model of judicial review.

Even in a strong tradition, such as that of the US, and even when this is understood in its strongest interpretation, judicial review is rightly seen as an appropriate institution within a system of checks and balances. Since such a system fits well with a value-pluralist outlook, as argued earlier, judicial review is in tune with pluralism.

Is Pluralism Equivocal About Judicial Review?

As a final issue in relation to judicial review, I consider an objection from Maimon Schwarzschild, who believes that pluralism is an unreliable basis on which to defend any specific legal or institutional line. 'Value pluralism can be invoked, it would seem, on any side, or at least on many sides, of various legal issues' (Schwarzschild 2009: 756). In the case of judicial review, the US Supreme Court, for example, has promoted pluralism through inclusive and tolerant decisions in areas such as equal protection, freedom from censorship, and freedom of religion. On the other hand, 'public policy made by the courts tends to be more uniform than policy made by any other institutions of government' (Schwarzschild 2009: 759). 'More uniform' seems to suggest less pluralistic. The courts are organized in a hierarchy the apex of which (the Supreme Court) decides law for the whole of the United States. 'Constitutional adjudication, in particular, tends to impose a single, almost unchangeable standard across the country' (Schwarzschild 2009: 759). Were it not for judicial review, ultimately at the level of the Supreme Court, there would be a mosaic of different laws in the US, hence a greater pluralist diversity.

The issue here recalls the distinction, familiar from previous chapters, between the plurality and diversity of values on the one hand and the plurality and diversity of whole systems of value on the other.[19] In Chapter 5, for example, I considered Gray's argument that a world containing only liberal political regimes must be less satisfactory from a pluralist perspective than a world in which some political regimes were non-liberal. My reply was that this does not follow, for two reasons. First, value pluralism refers primarily to the plurality and diversity of values and only secondarily to that of cultures and regimes. Second, some regimes and cultures are hostile to value plurality and diversity, so it does not follow that these goals will be promoted merely by multiplying regimes and cultures. Value diversity may be maximized by fewer cultures and regimes if these are more hospitable to value diversity than others.

Parallel points apply to Schwarzschild's argument, although this is subtle and takes some pinning down. At first sight his objection might seem to be that the legal uniformity promoted by judicial review must be opposed to pluralism and that, conversely, pluralism must favor a greater multiplicity of legal jurisdictions. One reason might be that a greater multiplicity of legal systems amounts, in itself, to greater diversity under pluralism. Here my first reply to Gray applies: this is not true because the primary question for pluralists is whether a diversity of *values* is being promoted. A multiplicity of cultures, political regimes, or legal systems is desirable only so far as it tends to maximize the diversity of values.

Alternatively, it may be that Schwarzchild accepts that greater value diversity is the pluralist goal but he supposes that this must be maximized by a greater multiplicity of laws. If so, the same reply can be made as the second urged against Gray. A mosaic of different laws may be a collection of laws that are each strongly monistic in content, amounting in the end to Leslie Green's 'mosaic of tyrannies' (Green 1995: 270). By comparison, value diversity may be increased by a single law that expresses greater toleration and respect for different interests and ways of life. Schwarzschild himself observes that many US constitutional decisions of the twentieth century 'can be seen ... as having greatly promoted pluralism ... enhancing the possibilities for more varied political outcomes, welcoming interest groups hitherto excluded, and hence promoting a climate more tolerant of a plurality of values in American life' (Schwarzschild 2009: 761). Since these are the results of the uniform law created by rulings of the Supreme Court, uniformity cannot be opposed to pluralism of necessity. It is not the uniformity of the law that is crucial but its content.

However, Schwarzchild's objection probably has to be reinterpreted agian to emphasize his theme of equivocation. On this view he allows that a uniform law, if it has the right content, can promote value diversity. But so, too, can a mosaic of different laws, even if each is internally monistic, since a multiplicity of monisms adds up to value diversity overall. So, Schwarzschild argues, on the one hand *Brown v. Board of Education* increased pluralism in the ways mentioned, but on the other hand a legal landscape that still contained Jim Crow laws would be more various and therefore also commended by pluralism (Schwarzschild 2009: 770). In that case, we would be back to Schwarzschild's overall theme of the equivocal nature of value pluralism: favoring judicial review and opposing it in equal degrees.

It is hard to believe that the exchange of Jim Crow segregation for African-American civil rights is not a net gain for value diversity. Pluralists do have to acknowledge that it is not only liberal societies and practices that have value but also non-liberal or illiberal societies and practices. But the loss of Jim Crow is surely outweighed by the gains from *Brown*. On one side, Americans lost the values of a narrow and oppressive culture which suppressed the values, interests, and voices of a substantial minority; on the other, it gained an outlet for those values, interests, and voices, which have opened out into a further diversity of values.

Moreover, it should be remembered that the pluralist criterion here is 'diversity' of values, not mere multiplicity of values. Value diversity contains an element of coherence: as Bernard Williams puts it, 'not all values can be pluralistically combined' (Berlin 2013: xxiii). The legal worlds of *Brown* and Jim Crow cannot simply be added together or happily nested one within the other. In Nagel's terms, they conflict in a 'noncontingent' way, meaning conceptually or necessarily rather than just circumstantially (Nagel 2001: 105–6).[20] Further, they conflict in the strong 'oppositional' sense where one set of values not only excludes but condemns the other. Consequently, there is a choice to be made. Given that *Brown* represents the more pluralist world and Jim Crow the more monist, it is surely *Brown* that should prevail from a pluralist point of view.

Where does that leave us with Schwarzschild's argument that value pluralism is indifferent between judicial review and its absence? It is true that pluralism does not favor judicial review over legislative process in all circumstances – to say otherwise would be to endorse the kind of absolute value ranking that pluralism denies. Democratic legislation is adequate to pluralist concerns when conditions apply that amount to something like Waldron's assumption of a strong and widespread social commitment to individual and minority rights. In that situation, there is no need for judicial back-up, since rights are reliably protected by democratic political negotiation alone.

However, I have argued that those conditions do not always hold. In recent times, the war on terror and the rise of populism have created a climate of opinion in which fundamental rights are under threat. Indeed, there is reason to believe that conditions favorable to rights are to some extent always in doubt because of the persistent possibility of hostility to minorities. To the extent that this is so, a case remains for judicial review to check and balance the legislative process. Of course, the judiciary is itself not always wholly resistant to chilly (or overheated) climates of opinion. Schwarzschild observes that the US Supreme Court has passed through more and less liberal phases in its history, sometimes standing out against conformist attitudes, sometimes reflecting them (Schwarzschild 2009: 761–2). However, it remains the case that, however varied its history may have been, the Court has the capacity to check and balance the anti-rights excesses of legislatures. That is an institution worth retaining, on value-pluralist grounds among others.

Pluralism and Public Policy

We have seen that constitutionalism provides one way in which institutions can help us respond to the problem of value pluralism. Separation of powers, checks and balances, and judicial review are all institutions that fit well with a pluralist outlook, and they all contribute to laying down fundamental rules that legislation and policy making must abide by.

However, we have also noted the limits of constitutionalism in this regard. First, the content of any given constitution will depend on the surrounding political culture, so that we are to some extent returned to the problem of cultural relativism. Second, any constitution provides only a framework within which more specific public policies still have to be formulated. Multiple options for ranking or trading off fundamental values may be consistent with any given constitution. Indeed, conflicts among basic values may break out within the constitution itself in the form of conflicts of rights or other basic constitutional goods.

Might we look for further guidance to the actual practices of public policy makers? In an influential article, 'Managing Value Conflict in Public Policy' (2004), David Thacher and Martin Rein suggest a range of possibilities along these lines. For Thacher and Rein, a rich 'preliminary repertoire' of means by which conflicts among incommensurable values can be managed is revealed by an examination of the familiar practices of public administration (*TR* 463).

They start by noting that much textbook discussion of public policy formation assumes a monistic understanding of values. Such discussions often treat the making of public policy as a matter of 'instrumental rationality' in which the only question is what the best or most efficient means are to a given end that commensurates all the other values involved in the policy (*TR* 457). Typical of this kind of thinking are utilitarianism and cost-benefit analysis, which both apply a single abstract rule in all cases, enabling competing goods to be measured against one another (*TR* 462). In essence, they are both instances of normative monism. Cost-benefit is an especially influential instrument in the world of public policy, conveniently reducing contending values to monetary amounts which can then be weighed against one another in a clear and systematic manner.

Of course, the problem with these administratively convenient procedures is that they assume a commensuration of values that is, in the understated words of Thacher and Rein, 'not particularly plausible' (*TR* 438). Citing Berlin, Weber, Richardson, and others, they accept the basic tenets of value pluralism and the problem that results.

> When only a single overriding goal has primary relevance for policy making, it is clear what kind of argument a policy actor needs to offer to justify her actions: she must show that the choice she made is the best way to achieve that single overriding goal. But when multiple and conflicting values are relevant, it is not clear what kind of argument is needed to vindicate her decision. It will not be enough to show how well the decision serves each value taken in isolation. In addition, she will need to justify her choice to pay more attention to one value at the expense of the others, or offer an alternative reason for her decision.
>
> (*TR* 461)

In spite of the incommensurability of fundamental values, Thacher and Rein still believe that choices among such values can be rational. To some extent, this is a matter of 'situated judgements about what is appropriate in particular times, places, and contexts' (*TR* 458). In this respect, they accept a broadly contextualist approach to the problem.

However, Thacher and Rein also argue that contextual policy judgments can be framed and guided by institutions. Institutions influence decision making by focusing or channeling it. 'Institutions shape the justifications available to policy actors because those justifications rely partly on schemas and resources that institutions provide' (*TR* 461). For example, institutions may enable us to avoid value conflict altogether by setting up 'such a coherent and simplified set of goals that potential conflicts do not arise in the first place', or they may enable conflicts to be readily resolved by establishing 'a fixed decision making structure' (*TR* 461).

If we accept a pluralist outlook, then our institutions should reflect this – the link here is conceptual. Rather than attempting to transcend value conflict, pluralist institutions will aim to manage it. Moreover, that management will not appeal to any intrinsic ranking of fundamental values. Priorities must be established among incommensurable goods while respecting their fundamentally equal status at the same time. For example, 'a policy actor may be able to justify a decision to neglect some values not on the grounds that they are intrinsically unimportant but on the grounds that those values are the responsibility of other institutions' (*TR* 461–2).

In this connection, Thacher and Rein identify three common strategies by which institutions manage conflicts among basic values: cycling, firewalls, and casuistry.[21] In the first of these, institutions deal with commitments to multiple, conflicting values by cycling back and forth between them over time. 'Policy actors may focus on each value sequentially, emphasizing one value until the destructive consequences for others become too severe to ignore' (*TR* 463). Thacher and Rein give the example of pension policy, which usually attempts to balance considerations of need and citizen rights. In the case of Australia, the Age Pension was initially distributed according to need, on the evidence of a means test, but this policy was later (in the 1970s) replaced by a rights-based approach in which most aspects of the means test were replaced by the principle that pensioners were entitled to their benefits as rights after years as taxpayers. Later still (in the 1980s) the policy cycled back to a focus on need, with the means test largely reinstated.

Is such a process not merely unsystematic vacillation? Thacher and Rein concede that this may be so in some cases, but they argue that cycling can be a deliberate policy design that makes sense as a way of tackling complex problems. 'Cycling may facilitate the invention of policies that are better on all dimensions by ... breaking the overall design process into stages and simplifying the designer's task at each stage by focusing attention on a single goal' (*TR* 466). Where trying to advance multiple goals simultaneously may lead to confusion and paralysis, progress can be achieved by concentrating on each goal by turn. Ideally, each phase will lead to gains that will be maintained in the next phase, even if this has a different focus. 'Single-minded pursuit of one value leads to the development of novel tactics that survive into the next phase of the cycle', so that cycling becomes an upward 'spiraling', implying progress (*TR* 467). On the other hand, there is a danger that the opposite effect may be achieved, a 'downward spiraling' in which a phase of focusing on value X results in an institution's being locked into 'a low level of value Y' (*TR* 468).

The second strategy Thacher and Rein consider is that of 'firewalls', in which distinct values are promoted by distinct institutions. 'Policy actors may establish and sustain multiple institutions committed to different values, walling off each institution from the responsibilities of the others' (*TR* 463). Each institution champions a particular value or cluster of values. The separation of powers is an obvious example in the constitutional realm. At the level of public policy, the UK divides the provision of security among three different institutions, each with its own normative brief: the domestic policing agencies are concerned with domestic law and order, MI5 with domestic intelligence, and MI6 with international intelligence.

This is essentially the application to institutions of Walzer's 'art of separation' or segregation already discussed under the heading of compromise in Chapter 7. Some of the strengths and weaknesses of such an approach may be recalled from that earlier discussion. On the positive side, segregation of values allows us to avoid having to confront conflict between them. Similarly, Thacher and Rein note the strength of the idea as residing in the way it enables institutions to simplify the task facing them. 'Each separate institution then faces a simpler task – not to resolve conflicts among values, but only to determine the best way to pursue each value in isolation' (*TR* 472).

On the downside, recall that the objection to Walzerian segregation is that in the real world it is seldom possible to separate the spheres – or maintain the firewalls – as neatly as the model proposes. Separation of powers, for example, is nowhere complete. Moreover, even if segregation is strong initially it can erode over time. Thacher and Rein give the example of Australian retirement policy, which was at one time divided between a public scheme, the Age Pension, concerned mainly with meeting need, and private arrangements that were part of labor contracts governed by the employer's own judgments concerning productivity. This division was blurred by the creation in the 1990s of a compulsory superannuation scheme partly funded by mandated contributions from employers. Considerations of need and productivity now influence both the public and private wings of the policy. Still, Thacher and Rein argue that firewalls may reduce value conflict, or at any rate manage it, for a while. 'An institutionally separated system can temporarily buffer value conflict by focusing different institutions on separate horns of the underlying dilemma' (*TR* 475).

The third approach identified by Thacher and Rein is 'casuistry', in which those deciding public policy compare the case before them with similar past cases. 'Policy actors may eschew general decisions about how conflicting values should be weighed. Instead they encourage and facilitate case-by-case judgement about how decisions should be made, typically using analogical reasoning to do so' (*TR* 464). Over time, policy makers construct 'a moral taxonomy' of cases to which they can refer when a new case arises. When the new case arises, the policy maker looks for guidance to decisions made in similar cases in the past. If the new case is different, she will gauge the extent of the difference with previous experience and the significance of that difference.

There are obvious links between this approach and the 'contextual' approaches discussed in Chapter 3, in particular in the rejection of general rules and attention to concrete circumstances. Casuistry, as described, is also clearly similar to legal reasoning, with its attention to precedent. Another cognate idea, especially influential in the literature of public policy, is the 'incrementalism' of Charles Lindblom (1959, 1979).

An example of casuistry given by Thacher and Rein concerns the use of excessive force by the police in US law. This has proved hard to define and therefore hard to enforce. One proposal is that excessive force should be defined in relation to what would be judged appropriate in the circumstances by 'a highly skilled police officer' (*TR* 478, quoting Klockars). In making this judgment, they would refer to their own experience of cases encountered in the past – their 'moral taxonomy' of hard cases. Out of this experience, officers and departments 'would develop a repertoire of responses to standard police encounters that (ideally) minimize the use of authority while preserving police effectiveness' (*TR* 479).

The main objection to this approach, as with contextualism more generally, is that it is too subjective or relativistic. Its results depend on judgments made in particular cases against criteria that are themselves highly variable – the fruits of personal and cultural experience. Thacher and Rein respond that 'there may be no alternative. Many difficult normative issues, such as those where values are ambiguous or in conflict, can only be worked out case by case' (*TR* 479). More abstract rankings or balances are hard to strike, especially in the face of value incommensurability. Further, 'novel cases often reveal new considerations', so we need a decision procedure that is flexible enough to cope. Such a procedure requires a 'situated judgement' rather than 'a predetermined weighing of values' (*TR* 479).

In addition, the worry about the variable results of casuistry is mitigated by my account of the norms derived from the concept of value pluralism itself (Chapters 5–7). Indeed, these provide reassuring limits to the application of cycling and firewalls too. The policy devices identified by Thacher and Rein will be bounded not only by local culture, history, and other contextual circumstances but also by considerations of diversity (primarily of values, secondarily of cultures), personal autonomy, and inclusive democracy.

Conclusion

Responding to Waldron's thesis, I have conceded that Berlin writes little about institutions in general and about constitutional institutions in particular. However, contrary to Waldron, Berlin is not hostile to constitutionalism. Indeed, his value pluralism can be used as a platform from which to argue for constitutionalism.

Waldron's own democratic constitutionalism can be assessed on the same pluralist grounds. Here I find that pluralism endorses Waldron's support for separation of powers and extends that endorsement to constitutional checks and balances. But Waldron's 'core' rejection of judicial review is another matter. This position depends crucially on Waldron's assumption that most members of liberal democracies are strongly committed to rights, including the rights of others. That assumption is empirically unrealistic. Recent political developments such as the war on terror and the rise of populism show the fragility of public commitment to rights, and this is underlined by the permanence of prejudice against minorities, a point conceded by Waldron himself. The upshot is that democratic legislatures, so strongly influenced by public opinion, cannot be relied upon to protect rights, contrary to a key assumption underpinning Waldron's core argument.

Does a value-pluralist approach suggest that judicial review can do any better? The answer is a qualified yes. The same insulation from public opinion that makes judicial review 'undemocratic' also gives it an advantage in protecting rights when public opinion is monistic and intolerant. Under such conditions, judicial review can play a vital role in a constitutional system of checks and balances that ensures a hearing for all relevant voices and values. When it plays this role, judicial review can be more truly democratic, in the inclusive sense, than a legislature that respects only the wishes of a majority. It is inclusive democracy rather than mere majoritarianism that is endorsed by pluralism. This is not to say that judicial review cannot fail to play such a role; only that it has the capacity to play such a role.

Administrative practices also play an important role in managing conflicts among incommensurable values that arise in the formation of public policy. Although pluralist public policy is broadly contextual, the institutions that frame and guide it must reflect the concept of pluralism itself. Thacher and Rein show this in relation to three familiar policy devices: cycling, firewalls, and casuistry. The chief critical concern about these, their relative open-endedness, is mitigated by the general pluralist norms – diversity, personal autonomy, and inclusive democracy – developed in previous chapters.

Notes

1 Waldron also argues that Berlin neglects and is hostile toward democracy, but I have already defended Berlin on that issue in Chapter 7.
2 See also Crowder 2004.
3 To consider only those influenced by Berlin's value pluralism (rather than his conceptions of negative and positive liberty, etc.), these include authors who have written about matters such as constitutional structure (Bellamy in *LAP*, 2000; Galston in *LP*, 2011; Porat 2009; Schwarzschild 2009); public administration (Wagenaar 1999; Spicer 2001, 2010; de Graaf 2015; Thacher and Rein in *TR*); and transitional justice (Allen 2007).
4 In this respect, 'Two Concepts of Liberty' (in *L*), Berlin's essay on the foundational liberal conception of liberty, is an exception to his more common practice.
5 For various aspects of Berlin's relation to the Enlightenment and Counter-Enlightenment, see Mali and Wokler 2003; Brockliss and Robertson 2016.
6 See, e.g., Berlin 1957; Berlin 2013; Crowder 2004: 54–6, 96–8.
7 This point has already been developed in Chapters 4, 5, and 7.
8 Elsewhere Waldron finds Montesquieu more helpful and chides Berlin for not appreciating this: *PPT* 276–8.
9 Compare the 'segregation' mode of compromise discussed in Chapter 7.

10 See also Waldron 1999. For a range of other views on the merits of judicial review in relation to democracy, see Tushnet 2000; Kramer 2004; Brettschneider 2006; Otter 2009.
11 See Richard Bellamy, who rejects judicial review in favour of democratic negotiation and deliberation: *LAP*, Bellamy 2000.
12 See Davis and Silver 2004; Hetherington and Suhay 2011.
13 See Cole and Dempsey 2002; Whitehead and Aden 2001–2002.
14 See Ramraj, Hor, Roach, and Williams 2012; Davis, McGarrity, and Williams 2014.
15 See Ionescu and Gellner 1969; Taggart 2000; Mudde and Kaltwasser 2013a, b; de la Torre 2015.
16 See Rupnik 2012; Bankuti, Gabor, and Scheppele 2012; Mueller 2014.
17 For an entertaining survey in the UK context, see Pannick 1988: ch. 2.
18 Gibson uses survey evidence to argue that, although some campaign activities are viewed more positively than others, 'the predominant essence of judicial elections is not foul': Gibson 2012: 141.
19 See Chapters 1, 3, 5, and 6.
20 See Chapter 1.
21 Jenny Stewart has argued that, in addition to the three mechanisms for managing conflict among incommensurables discussed by Thacher and Rein, three more can be identified: bias, hybridization, and incrementalism. On inspection, however, these either add little of value or are already included by Thacher and Rein. First, 'bias' involves the more or less arbitrary 'exclusion of alternatives' from policy debate (Stewart 2009: 41–2). This is hardly a legitimate method for dealing with incommensurables since it simply ignores value pluralism rather than addressing it. Second, 'hybridisation' is the coexistence within a single program of 'two policies or practices with different values bases' (Stewart 2009: 39). That does no more than identify a potential site of collision among those values unless some account is provided of how the conflict will be resolved or managed. Third, 'incrementalism' is scarcely distinguishable from the category of 'casuistry' proposed by Thacher and Rein, which itself is cognate with the classic 'incrementalism' of Lindblom (1959, 1979).

References

In-text abbreviations are noted in brackets.

Allen, Jonathan (2007), 'A Liberal-Pluralist Case for Truth Commissions: Lessons from Isaiah Berlin', in George Crowder and Henry Hardy, eds, *The One and the Many: Reading Isaiah Berlin* (Amherst, NY: Prometheus Press).
Bankuti, Miklos, Halmai Gabor, and Kim Lane Scheppele (2012), 'Disabling the Constitution', *Journal of Democracy* 23 (3): 138–46.
Bellamy, Richard (1999), *Liberalism and Pluralism: Towards a Politics of Compromise* (London: Routledge). [*LAP*]
Bellamy, Richard (2000), 'Liberalism and the Challenge of Pluralism', in Richard Bellamy, ed., *Rethinking Liberalism* (London: Pinter).
Berlin, Isaiah (1957), 'Introduction' to Isaiah Berlin, ed., *The Age of Enlightenment: The Eighteenth-Century Philosophers* (New York: George Brazilier, Inc.).
Berlin, Isaiah (2002), *Liberty*, ed. Henry Hardy (Oxford: Oxford University Press). [*L*]
Berlin, Isaiah (2013), *Three Critics of the Enlightenment: Vico, Hamann, Herder*, ed. Henry Hardy, 2nd edn (Princeton: Princeton University Press).
Brettschneider, Corey (2006), 'Popular Constitutionalism and the Case for Judicial Review', *Political Theory*, 34 (4), 516–21.

Brockliss, Laurence and Ritchie Robertson, eds (2016), *Isaiah Berlin and the Enlightenment* (Oxford: Oxford University Press).
Cole, David and James X. Dempsey (2002), *Terrorism and the Constitution: Sacrificing Civil Liberties in the Name of National Security*, 2nd edn (New York: New Press).
Crowder, George (2004), *Isaiah Berlin: Liberty and Pluralism* (Cambridge: Polity).
Davis, Darren W. and Brian D. Silver (2004), 'Civil Liberties vs. Security: Public Opinion in the Context of the Terrorist Attacks on America', *American Journal of Political Science* 48 (1): 28–46.
Davis, Fergal, Nicola McGarrity, and George Williams, eds (2014), *Surveillance, Counter-Terrorism and Comparative Constitutionalism* (London: Routledge).
de Graaf, Gjalt (2015), 'The Bright Future of Value Pluralism in Public Administration', *Administration and Society* 47 (9): 1094–102.
de la Torre, Carlos, ed. (2015), *The Promise and Perils of Populism: Global Perspectives* (Lexington: University of Kentucky Press).
Galston, William (2002), *Liberal Pluralism: The Implications of Value Pluralism for Political Theory and Practice* (Cambridge: Cambridge University Press). [*LP*]
Galston, William (2011), 'Pluralist Constitutionalism', *Social Philosophy and Policy* 28 (1): 228–41.
Gibson, James L. (2012), *Electing Judges: The Surprising Effects of Campaigning on Judicial Legitimacy* (Chicago: Chicago University Press).
Green, Leslie (1995), 'Internal Minorities and Their Rights', in Will Kymlicka, ed., *The Rights of Minority Cultures* (Oxford: Oxford University Press).
Griffith, J. A. G. (1985), *The Politics of the Judiciary*, 3rd edn (London: Fontana).
Hetherington, Marc and Elizabeth Suhay (2011), 'Authoritarianism, Threat, and Americans' Support for the War on Terror', *American Journal of Political Science* 55 (3): 546–60.
Ionescu, Ghita and Ernest Gellner, eds (1969), *Populism: Its Meaning and National Characteristics* (New York: Macmillan).
Jahanbegloo, Ramin (1992), *Conversations with Isaiah Berlin* (London: Peter Halban). [*CIB*]
Kalkan, Kerem Ozan, Geoffrey C. Layman, and Eric M. Uslaner (2009), 'Bands of Others? Attitudes toward Muslims in Contemporary American Society', *Journal of Politics* 71 (3): 847–62.
Kramer, Larry D. (2004), *The People Themselves: Popular Constitutionalism and Judicial Review* (New York: Oxford University Press).
Lilla, Mark (2001), 'Wolves and Lambs', in Ronald Dworkin, Mark Lilla, and Robert B. Silvers, eds, *The Legacy of Isaiah Berlin* (New York: New York Review Books).
Lindblom, Charles (1959), 'The Science of Muddling Through', *Public Administration Review* 19 (2): 79–88.
Lindblom, Charles (1979), 'Still Muddling, Not Yet Through', *Public Administration Review* 39 (6): 517–26.
Mali, Joseph and Robert Wokler, eds (2003), *Isaiah Berlin's Counter-Enlightenment* (Philadelphia, PA: American Philosophical Society).
Malleson, Kate (1999), *The New Judiciary: The Effects of Expansion and Activism* (Aldershot: Ashgate).
Mudde, Cas and C. R. Kaltwasser (2013a), 'Populism', in Michael Feeden et al., eds, *Oxford Handbook of Political Ideologies* (Oxford: Oxford University Press).
Mudde, Cas and C. R. Kaltwasser, eds (2013b), *Populism in Europe and the Americas: Threat or Corrective for Democracy?* (Cambridge: Cambridge University Press).

Mueller, Jan-Werner (2014), 'Eastern Europe Goes South: Disappearing Democracy in the EU's Newest Members', *Foreign Affairs* 93: 14–19.
Müller, Jan-Werner (2016), *What Is Populism?* (Philadelphia: University of Pennsylvania Press).
Nagel, Thomas (2001), 'Pluralism and Coherence', in Ronald Dworkin, Mark Lilla, and Robert Silvers, eds, *The Legacy of Isaiah Berlin* (New York: New York Review Books).
Otter, Ronald C. Den (2009), *Judicial Review in an Age of Moral Pluralism* (Cambridge: Cambridge University Press).
Pannick, David (1988), *Judges* (Oxford: Oxford University Press).
Peretti, Terri Jennings (2002), 'Does Judicial Independence Exist? The Lessons of Social Science Research', in Stephen B. Burbank and Barry Friedman, eds, *Judicial Independence at the Crossroads: An Interdisciplinary Approach* (Thousand Oaks, CA: Sage).
Porat, Iddo (2009), 'The Plural Implications of Value Pluralism: A Comment on Maimon Schwarzschild's *On This Side of the Law and on That Side of the Law*', *San Diego Law Review* 46 (4): 909–24.
Ramraj, Victor V., Michael Hor, Kent Roach, and George Williams, eds (2012), *Global Anti-Terrorism Law and Policy*, 2nd edn (Cambridge: Cambridge University Press).
Rupnik, Jacques (2012), 'How Things Went Wrong', *Journal of Democracy* 23 (3): 132–7.
Schwarzschild, Maimon (2009), 'On This Side of the Law and on That Side of the Law', *San Diego Law Review* 46 (4): 755–72.
Spicer, Michael (2001), 'Value Pluralism and Its Implications for American Public Administration', *Administrative Theory and Praxis* 23 (4): 507–28.
Spicer, Michael (2010), *In Defense of Politics in Public Administration: A Value Pluralist Perspective* (Tuscaloosa: University of Alabama Press).
Stewart, Jenny (2009), *Public Policy Values* (London: Palgrave Macmillan).
Taggart, Paul (2000), *Populism* (Buckingham, UK: Open University Press).
Thacher, David and Martin Rein (2004), 'Managing Value Conflict in Public Policy', *Governance* 17 (4): 457–86. [*TR*]
Tushnet, Mark (2000), *Taking the Constitution Away from the Courts* (Princeton: Princeton University Press).
Wagenaar, Hendrik (1999), 'Value Pluralism in Public Administration', *Administrative Theory and Praxis* 21 (4): 441–9.
Waldron, Jeremy (1999), *Law and Disagreement* (Oxford: Oxford University Press).
Waldron, Jeremy (2016), *Political Political Theory: Essays on Institutions* (Cambridge, MA: Harvard University Press). [*PPT*]
Whitehead, John W. and Steven H. Aden (2001–2002), 'Forfeiting "Enduring Freedom" for "Homeland Security": A Constitutional Analysis of the USA Patriot Act and the Justice Department's Anti-terrorism Initiatives', *American University Law Review* 51: 1081–133.
Zaslove, Andrej (2004), 'Closing the Door? The Ideology and Impact of Radical Right Populism on Immigration Policy in Austria and Italy', *Journal of Political Ideologies* 9 (1): 99–118.

9 Conclusion

I have argued that the problem of value pluralism, as framed by Berlin, should be taken seriously. The idea that fundamental human values are irreducibly plural and incommensurable, and consequently that there is a problem of how to choose among them when they conflict, is compelling. The truth of pluralism cannot be demonstrated beyond doubt, since it is always open to monists to reply that it may be falsified, and an overriding super-value discovered, at some unspecified time in the future. However, this is deeply implausible. The evidence of experience suggests strongly that there is no such super-value and that the picture of human values presented by pluralists is indeed correct.

If pluralism is true, then Berlin's problem of choice or ranking cannot be solved by those approaches to moral and political theory that are most familiar in the contemporary literature. These include monist outlooks, such as utilitarianism and Kantianism, that make one value or principle overriding in all cases. They also include thoroughgoing relativist approaches that make value judgment depend wholly on personal or cultural perspective. These ignore the pluralist commitment to the universality of certain values that contribute to any conception of human well-being: Berlin's 'great goods'. Relativist approaches are also inclined to turn personal preference or cultural tradition into an overriding value and thus a form of monism.

So, how can we respond to the problem of value pluralism? Berlin throws out many suggestions without pursuing any of them systematically. Other writers have taken them up; indeed, all of Berlin's proposals have their defenders. Nevertheless, some of those proposals, I have argued, can be rejected, or at least strongly qualified, fairly quickly.

The tactic of avoidance, for example, where the problem simply does not arise because the conflict of values that produces it has been prevented from arising, is of limited help. A basic insight of pluralism is that conflicts of fundamental values are inevitable and have to be faced at some point.

When they are faced, Berlin's further suggestion that all we can do is 'plump' for one option or another, without regard to reasons, is also of limited application. This may apply to some extreme cases where people are trapped in genuinely irresolvable dilemmas. However, experience shows that this is usually not all we can do. We often decide conflicts of incommensurable values, for good reason, at any rate within context – although not without a vestigial sense of loss. Indeed, Berlin makes this point himself. The point is lost on 'agonistic' pluralists such as Weber, Schmitt, and Mouffe, and it remains unappreciated in the work of many writers, both those attracted to pluralism and those opposed.

Nor is the 'psychological' account of choice under pluralism of much use. According to this, pluralists tend to make certain kinds of choice among conflicting values because, as pluralists, they have a natural or in-built disposition to make those kinds of choice. The psychological argument is often used to link pluralism with liberalism: pluralists are sometimes said to be liberals by disposition. But the personal psychologies of pluralists lead in various ideological directions, not just to liberalism. The truth is that the concept of value pluralism and the psychologies of individual value pluralists are two different things. For those interested in the concept and its implications, the psychologies of its adherents tell us little.

However, this is not to say that Berlin offers us no assistance at all. On the contrary, his proposed approaches to the problem include three main candidates that, together, provide a more persuasive solution. The three principal approaches involve appeals to 'the great goods', to context, and to the concept of value pluralism itself. Each of these is developed in various ways by Berlin's successors.

First, there are the great goods. In Berlin's account the nature of these is left ambiguous and their content looks ad hoc, but Berlin's successors have advanced much more explicit and systematic explanations on both counts. Riley emphasizes the goods necessary to the survival of any society. Hampshire points to the principle of *audi alteram partem*, or hearing the other side, as universal in all systems of justice. Although he presents a philosophical argument in favor of this view, its universality is ultimately an empirical matter. Nussbaum presents a much more extensive and elaborate list of 'central capabilities' said to be essential to human well-being.

The writers in this school make an important point that addresses the problem to a degree. A closer understanding of the great goods enriches pluralism by giving content to the values that are said ultimately to be plural. Nussbaum's theory of the central capabilities constitutes the most elaborate account of this kind. Further, the appeal to the great goods enables us to narrow down the choices that pluralism confronts us with because at least we have reason to accept that the great goods will usually override lesser or more specific values. Nussbaum's central capabilities matter more than more trivial abilities and talents, and it matters more that Riley's survival values be satisfied in some form than that they be satisfied in any particular form. So, attention to the great goods does guide choice to the extent that they have priority in almost any conflict with lesser goods or local forms.

However, theorists of the great goods leave us with two questions. First, the content of these universals remains controversial, since the various accounts tend to be either too thin to have much normative substance or too thick to avoid charges of cultural bias. Second, even supposing that the great goods can be convincingly identified, that leaves the question of what to do when there is conflict among them – the heart of the problem of value pluralism. At this level, the post-Berlinian work has helped to clarify what it is that pluralists say is plural and incommensurable – at bottom it is the great goods. However, the question of how to respond to that plurality remains.

The second major school tackles the problem by appeal to context. The great goods cannot be ranked in the abstract, or according to a rule that applies in every case, but instances of them may perhaps be rankable, for decisive reason, in specific situations. Social justice may come before liberty, or may rightly be allowed to reduce liberty, where that is required to relieve poverty. The trouble is that there are several different kinds or levels of context. Berlin's comments are ambiguous between contexts of personal life, cultural tradition, politics, and history.

At the level of an individual life for example, it may make sense for someone to rank one good ahead of another against the background of her own general values and goals in life. In ethical theory, the model is Aristotle's *phronesis*, and this is advanced as a response to pluralism by Nussbaum and others. The obvious limitation of this approach is that it does not address issues of politics and public policy.

For the purposes of public policy, we need to contextualize at a social level. Here, we might reasonably look to the cultural tradition of the relevant society. Among pluralists, Kekes is a leading exponent of this approach, emphasizing the role of tradition as a criterion for organizing plural concerns, and deriving from this a conservative politics. But in modern societies tradition is routinely disputed, fragmented, multiple, and conflicting. Which tradition should we follow? Perhaps several should be promoted simultaneously, generating a multiculturalist politics. But then we still have the question of what kind of political framework this should have, whether liberal or some alternative.

Talk of a political framework introduces another level of context, 'the political'. But the nature of this is highly contested. Some would still follow Aristotle in upholding the ideal of the good life as the goal of the political, only to be met by the hard fact that in modern societies the nature of the good life is widely and deeply disputed. At the other extreme are those who agree with Hobbes in identifying politics with power and the containment of power by sovereignty, a view in tension with a concern for ethics.

Among pluralists, the 'agonist' school follows broadly Hobbesian lines. For Weber, conflicts of fundamental political values can be resolved only by charismatic leadership. Similarly, on Schmitt's view, political conflicts must be conceived as ultimate antagonisms, resolvable only by the reasonless imposition of the will of the decision-maker – a defense of the authoritarian dictatorship he advocated and then served. In the work of Mouffe, Schmitt's antagonism is moderated into 'agonism', which attempts to constrain power with toleration. The strength of the agonist school is its appreciation of politics as a realm of conflict. Its weakness is its inability to see politics as anything other than conflict, stemming from its one-dimensional view of pluralist choice as necessarily irrational.

A more nuanced view of the political is provided by Bernard Williams, who combines a realist emphasis on the value of social order with a liberal stress on political legitimacy as consent. According to Williams, both of these commitments are internal to the political. But is social order the product *of* politics or an antecedent reason *for* politics? There is as much reason to see it as the latter as the former. Perhaps a demand for legitimacy is inherent in the political, but legitimacy based on consent is a distinctively liberal notion and therefore external to the political as such (and subject to historical contingency). Moreover, even supposing that order and legitimacy are internal to the political, why is justice not also a paramount political concern, as Rawls supposes? The most plausible account of the special place of order and legitimacy in politics is that these are 'preconditions' for other political goods. But this gives order and legitimacy a sequential rather than normative priority, which since it can be accepted by so-called moralists such as Rawls, amounts to the abandonment of a distinctively realist position.

Might we find a way forward by appealing to another dimension of context, the historical? A historical sensibility, Bernard Williams argues, is vital in philosophical argument in general. More specifically, the liberalism that Williams shares with Berlin must be defended not as a timeless abstraction but within historical context. In pluralist terms, this means that distinctively liberal rankings of values must be justified not only politically but also historically. In Williams's account, the key context is 'modernity': liberalism, although not valid eternally, is the only political position valid under modern conditions. Why this should be so receives only the sketchiest treatment in Williams's brief political theory texts. This can be supplemented, however, by the work of Welzel, who explains in detail how modern historical conditions make meaningful the pursuit of the emancipatory values that are characteristic of liberalism.

This historical justification of liberal value rankings is extremely valuable to liberal pluralists because it enables them to show how the defense of liberalism can be contextual rather than absolute or monist. Anti-liberal pluralists, such as Kekes and Gray, typically see liberalism as a monist position that makes its favored values – individual liberty, equality of opportunity, and so on – overriding in all circumstances. Williams and Welzel, by contrast, show that liberal values are not invariably overriding in human experience but claims meriting emphasis within the historical context of modernity.

Thus far, however, there is a significant gap in the pluralist case for liberalism. Welzel argues that the modern phase of human economic development produces conditions under which it makes sense to pursue the emancipatory values of liberalism. The development of the Western liberal democracies does seem to bear this out. But the emergence of the 'East Asia' model appears to present a counter-example. In China and elsewhere, modern economies have developed rapidly but that development has not been accompanied by a move to liberal politics. Welzel asserts that this change will take place eventually, but at this point his prediction remains speculative. There is no immediate sign of political liberalization in China – indeed, at present matters are turning strongly in the opposite direction.

So, we might turn to the third of my highlighted approaches to the problem of ranking fundamental values, one less at the mercy of contingency than the various forms of contextualism. This is a conceptual approach that begins with reflection on the idea of pluralism itself and derives implications from that.

The central feature of value pluralism, in my interpretation, is the thought that there are many distinct goods that constitute human well-being, and these all deserve respectful consideration, so far as they are relevant, when we are deciding on a course of action. Pluralism insists that we should not turn a blind eye to important values; rather, we should promote all such values where possible.

The practical consequence is a broad principle of 'diversity': in public policy we should have appropriate regard to all the fundamental values in play in the matter, promoting, or enabling the promotion of, as many as possible. This is not simply a matter of multiplicity but also of coherence, since not all values fit neatly together in any particular situation. But on the whole we should aim in policy at pursuing or enabling as broad a range of the components of human well-being as is consistent with practicalities.

Diversity is best advanced by a liberal politics. The individual rights and liberties protected and extended by liberalism are more likely than any alternative system to enable people to pursue the diverse range of values indicated as desirable by value pluralism. Pluralism thus provides a grounding for liberalism that does not depend wholly on the contingencies of history. This view reinforces Welzel's expectation of the end of the East Asian model with a normative argument. Not only is that change possible in practice, it is desirable in principle and specifically on pluralist grounds.

Nevertheless, the diversity argument pays its dues to history through its acknowledgment of practicalities. A diversity of values can be promoted only so far as this is possible, and what is possible is determined in part by historical conditions. As Welzel explains, the emancipatory values latent in the human condition are of little use to people until economic development makes them useful. The arming of those values is an achievement of modernity. A case for liberal politics exists in potential before modernity, rooted in the pluralistic character of human well-being. But modern development, in particular economic development, realizes that potential.

At this point the question arises: if pluralism indicates, under modern conditions, a liberal form of politics, what kind of liberalism will this be? I have argued that this will not be a classical or laissez-faire liberalism in which negative liberty is overriding. Rather, it will be an egalitarian or redistributive liberalism in which negative liberty is balanced by other values, including social justice and the effective freedom with which it is associated.

Moreover, in the terms introduced by Galston, I have argued that pluralism will also lead us toward the Enlightenment liberalism of personal autonomy rather than the Reformation liberalism of group toleration. In part this is because the diversity implied by pluralism is primarily a diversity of individual values or goods rather than of whole cultures or ways of life. This must be so because on the pluralist view it is values or goods that are incommensurable, not whole cultures or ways of life. The latter are not incommensurable because they overlap on the great goods they all share. Consequently, pluralists should seek a diversity of cultures or ways of life only so far as these are themselves hospitable to *value* diversity, both internal to the culture and external. Since a diversity of values is linked with liberalism, this means that pluralists should seek a diversity of liberal cultures, not just a multiplicity of cultures with no regard to their content.

From this follows a global concern for individual autonomy in the strong sense that pluralists should want people to have the capacity to reflect critically on how they want to live. In part this conclusion is simply a consequence of a commitment to thoroughgoing diversity, but it is also supported by another pluralist argument. This is that pluralism imposes hard choices on people, especially in the modern world, which can only be navigated, or best be navigated, by those capable of the critical reflection at the heart of strong autonomy. Traditions and other monist instruments will not be adequate to this task.

Note that these are points of principle. It does not follow that liberals must immediately and coercively liberalize illiberal minorities or other illiberal societies. For one thing, considerations of practicality and prudence will be part of any sensible pluralist judgment – to that extent pluralists will agree with realists. For another, pluralists will be democrats.

Pluralism has conceptual links not only with liberalism but also with democracy. The notion of people determining their own government has immediate affinities with the pluralist idea that the best political system is one that respects a diversity of values. Assuming that democracy brings many different voices into politics and that different voices are bearers of different values, democracy fits with pluralism.

This link between democracy and pluralism becomes questionable, however, if it is further assumed that democracy is equivalent to a majoritarianism. What if the majority willfully or ignorantly closes its eyes to significant values that it ought to consider, perhaps those favored by a minority? Democratic majoritarianism, in other words, is not a wholly reliable expression of value pluralism.

One response to this problem is the deliberative turn, where democratic practices are corrected by institutions designed to encourage or require reciprocal reason-giving on the part not just of political leaders but also of ordinary citizens. In its most ambitious form, deliberative democracy displaces liberal democracy altogether. Here there are obvious problems of practicability, given current political realities. Moreover, deliberation itself embodies certain values, and these are distinct from those promoted by other kinds of political practice. Deliberation is a reasonable complement to political action, in pluralist terms, but not a wholesale replacement for it.

Democratic forms naturally suggest the topic of compromise in politics. In Margalit's account, for example, conflicting groups, representing divergent value rankings, might negotiate a settlement involving mutual concessions and mutual recognition. Gray's notion of modus vivendi is an account of compromise emphasizing the goal of peace.

Such an approach is attractive to a degree, but Gray's account in particular reveals its limitations. Will this be a balance of power in which each side pursues its own interests as far as it can, or a settlement based on moral principles dedicated to an overarching goal of peace? Both have their problems. As Rawls points out, the balance of power is inherently unstable because it will change along with alterations in the parties' interests and their power to enforce these. The moral settlement appears to elevate peace to the status of a super-value and thus to become a form of monism.

The greatest problem with compromise, though, is identifying its ethical limits. Margalit points to the phenomenon of the 'rotten' compromise, where the terms are such that they should never have been entered into – the Munich Agreement of 1938 being a prime example. But what makes a compromise rotten? Margalit proposes the Kantian test of respect for persons, but this is looks like a monist, not a pluralist criterion. Gray refers to a universal minimum morality, but the limitations of the great goods approach have already been noted. Universal goods are likely to be so generic in content that they are compatible with most human practices, and it remains open to ask what choices we should make when they conflict – that is, the problem of value pluralism is largely restated.

The conceptual approach also addresses an issue that is often said to be neglected by contemporary political thought, namely that of institutions. On the face of it, the kind of institutions we ought to commend may seem to be simply a reflection of contextual factors. Institutions must answer to the fundamental political need for social order. Once that requirement is satisfied, they are likely to mirror the cultural traditions specific to the relevant society, whatever these may be.

However, given the case for value diversity as a norm required, under modern conditions, by pluralism itself, there is an obvious argument for extending this thought to the shaping of a modern society's institutions. If, within the framework of modernity, the concept of pluralism indicates the superiority of liberal principles, so too does it indicate the superiority of liberal institutions.

What those institutions should be is to some extent uncontroversial. Few liberals dispute the need for constitutional schemes expressing principles such as separation of powers and checks and balances. But disagreement begins to develop over whether the constitution should form a 'higher law' to some extent protected from political debate and revision, and in particular over the role of judicial review. Waldron is one of several recent writers who have questioned whether an unelected judiciary should be the final arbiter of constitutional matters, insisting instead that such a role should fall always to legislators. Here I argue on pluralist principles for a middle ground in which judicial review of legislation on constitutional grounds is maintained subject to constraints. Once again the general strategy is a balancing of considerations in order to serve the overall goal of a maximal diversity of values.

The idea of pluralism also has implications for the way public policy is formed and administered by the bureaucracy. Thacher and Rein show how pluralist considerations are reflected in the familiar administrative devices of cycling, firewalls, and casuistry. The difficulty of identifying a constraining normative framework for these is eased by applying the general principles of value diversity, personal autonomy, and inclusive democracy that are implicit in the pluralist idea.

I shall end by briefly considering the place of the pluralist literature in the wider context of contemporary political philosophy. First, what is the significance of Berlin himself? On one view he is *sui generis*. As Stefan Collini writes,

> it cannot be said that Berlin has commanded an area of 'research' in the way some of the great barons of scholarship have done. There have been many students, but they have not been allotted roles in extending and defending a territory, in the way in which the pupils of Karl Popper or Geoffrey Elton were apparently commanded to do. He has probably had more admirers than any figure in recent British academic life, yet there has not been a widely established style that could lead followers to be labelled as 'Berlinians' in the way in which it was common in post-war university circles to speak of 'Leavisites' or 'Oakeshottians'. Berlin's manner of speech has attracted countless affectionate imitators; one has to wonder whether his manner of writing is likely to die without issue.
>
> (Collini 1997: 3)

There is a good deal of truth in this. Berlin's writing style is all his own. Indeed, his whole approach to intellectual questions, which usually takes the form of imaginative exposition rather than acknowledging a literature and defending a case, is out of place under contemporary academic conventions (Kenny 2000: 1035–6). Moreover, as I have emphasized throughout, Berlin's treatment of value pluralism opens up important questions, only to offer the sketchiest of answers.

Nevertheless, my examination of the post-Berlin literature on pluralism shows that Collini's assessment is not altogether true. Berlin has 'commanded an area of research' in the sense that he has drawn attention to the problem of value pluralism and proposed all of the main lines of response that have been taken up by others. He has not assigned tasks to followers, but his successors have identified and undertaken tasks for themselves. These have not been about defending parts of the Master's territory but rather about exploring the area in their own way. The results have often been at variance with those of Berlin, but they have responded to a problem that he framed and whose implications he pioneered. Whether or not Berlin's successors should properly be called 'Berlinians', they are working within a paradigm he outlined.[1]

Might it be said, however, that the whole paradigm is relatively insignificant? Thus, a recent commentator writes that 'what is safe to say about the twentieth century, though, is that value pluralism played a rather marginal role in Anglo-American political thought', constituting 'a minor strand in what is conventionally understood as Cold War liberalism' (Müller 2012: 85). 'Thus', the same writer continues, 'neither broadly speaking Rawlsian liberalism nor multicultural liberalism adopted value pluralist assumptions'.

Again, there is a degree of truth in these remarks. Anglo-American political theory has for decades been dominated by Rawls rather than Berlin, and by successive waves of theorists – libertarian, communitarian, republican, feminist, and others – responding to Rawls. Berlin's Cold War preoccupation with Soviet totalitarianism has receded in the contemporary consciousness to be replaced by other concerns: distributive justice, the value of community, the claims of culture, the role of gender and other identities, and international and ecological issues.

However, when these contemporary concerns are investigated it does not take long before value-pluralist themes begin to surface. This is hardly surprising given that the problem of value pluralism is the question of how to prioritize fundamental values, a central concern for any area of political philosophy. Consequently, it is unsurprising that the pluralist problem is part of the thinking of Rawls himself. As I argued in Chapters 4 and 7 in particular, Rawls is crucially concerned with justifying value rankings against a background of incommensurablity. This becomes explicit in *Political Liberalism*, where it emerges that his assumed 'burdens of judgement' are in part aspects of value pluralism.

Consequently, it is seriously mistaken to suppose that the themes of value pluralism are confined to 'Cold War liberalism'. Pluralist issues arise in discussions of distributive justice found not only in Rawls but also in Dworkin, Walzer, and Nussbaum. Multicultural theory has taken value pluralism as a starting point in the work of Raz and Parekh. Democracy has been theorized from a pluralist perspective by Bellamy and Galston. Constitutionalism and public administration have received similar treatment from Galston and Thacher and Rein, respectively.

Simply to list these applications of pluralism and the names of those thinkers engaged by these matters is to go some way toward showing that value pluralism and its issues lie much closer to the center of contemporary political philosophy than many people realize. Further, the pluralist outlook has implications for many topics other than those I have been able to cover here. But these must wait for another time.

Note

1 Berlin's legacy may be described as a distinctive kind of 'humanism', of which pluralism is one aspect: Cherniss and Hardy 2018: 23–4, 26.

References

In-text abbreviations are noted in brackets.

Cherniss, Joshua L. and Henry Hardy (2018), 'The Life and Opinions of Isaiah Berlin', in Joshua L. Cherniss and Steven B. Smith, eds, *Cambridge Companion to Isaiah Berlin* (Cambridge: Cambridge University Press).

Collini, Stefan (1997), 'Against Utopia', *Times Literary Supplement*, 22 August.

Kenny, Michael (2000), 'Isaiah Berlin's Contribution to Modern Political Theory', *Political Studies* 48: 1026–39.

Müller, Jan-Werner (2012), 'Value Pluralism in Twentieth-Century Anglo-American Thought', in Mark Bevir, ed., *Modern Pluralism: Anglo-American Debates Since 1880* (Cambridge: Cambridge University Press).

Index

Note: Entries followed by "n" refer to endnotes.

Agonism 4, 34–6, 38n23, 66–77, 91, 169, 220
Appiah, Kwame Anthony 150–1
analytical vs holistic pluralism *see* incommensurability of values vs cultures
Antigone 31, 136
Aristotle 4, 21, 64n18, 66, 78–80, 87n11, 95–6, 119–20, 134, 186, 220
audi alteram partem see hearing the other side
Australia 119, 197, 211–12
authoritarianism 2, 15, 69, 71, 73, 92, 109–11, 116, 121–2
autonomy, individual 3, 6, 8, 36, 54–6, 63n10, 97, 109–11, 113n14, 142–162n9, 165–6, 176, 186–8, 192, 213–14, 222–5

Bellamy, Richard 2, 6, 36, 38n24, 63n9, 70, 165, 167, 215n11
Berlin, Isaiah viii, ix, Ch. 1, 2, 11–36n1, 44, 104, 193; and conceptual approach viii, 3–5, 7, 32, 187, 222, 224; and contextual approach 31–2, 35, 78, 81, 84, 87n10, 91, 170, 212; intellectual development of 15; on compromise 36, 166, 174; on constitutionalism viii, ix, 7, 71, 74, 123–4, 139n8, 192–9, 201, 209, 213, 226; on cultural diversity 3, 86, 132–3, 143–5, 152–5, 165, 187, 192; on democracy viii, 3, 6, 13, 16, 35–6, 54, 60, 74–7, 94, 109–11, 116, 139n16, 165–73, 178, 187–8, 192–3, 198–9, 201, 204, 213–215n10, 223–6; on great goods viii, 3–4, 6–7, 12, 28–9, 34, 36, 43–5, 51, 62, 81, 85–6, 116, 132, 153, 155, 157, 159, 165, 173, 185, 218–20, 223–4; on historical context viii, 3, 5, 7, 31–2, 34, 116; on negative and positive liberty 214n3; on monism 1–2, 11, 15–16, 19, 21, 23, 29, 87n11, 92–3, 99, 125, 128, 146, 160, 181–3, 196, 208–10, 218, 224; on plumping (agonism) 67–8, 87n7; on pluralism viii, 44–5, 49–50, 57, 60, 62–72, 75, 77–8, 81–6, 91–5, 98, 103–5, 109, 112, 116–18, 120–1, 125–132, 135–139n16, 142–3, 146–7, 151–7, 160–3, 166, 168, 171–3, 175–6, 178–81, 184–5, 187–189n25, 192, 196, 199, 203, 205–227n1, Ch. 1, 1–8, 11–29, 31–37n3; on pluralism and liberalism 6, 33–4, 125, 135, 138, 165; on psychological approach 33, 38n28; on relativism vs pluralism ix, xv, 12, 18, 21, 24–8, 32, 36–37n16, 56–7, 62, 85, 88n21, 93–4, 112–14, 132, 138, 153, 156, 161; 'Pursuit of the Ideal' 12, 15, 29; 'Two Concepts of Liberty' 5, 12, 162n2, 214n4
Brown v. Board of Education 208

Callan, Eamonn 149
Churchill, Winston 184
Collini, Stefan 225
compromise viii, 3–4, 6–7, 18, 24, 28, 30, 32–3, 36, 50, 52, 63n8, 123–4, 188n5–189n18, 192, 206, 212, 214n9, 224; Ch. 7, 165–7, 169–70, 172–80, 183–8; definition of 7, 18, 174; limits of 166, 183–5, 187–8; rotten 7, 166, 173, 185–6, 224; types of 166, 169–70, 172, 174–7, 188

Index

conceptual responses to pluralism 220; *see also* autonomy; compromise; democracy; value diversity
Condorcet, Marie Jean Antoine Nicolas Caritat, marquis de 196
conservatism 33, 82, 85, 93, 180–1
Constant, Benjamin 13, 47
constitutionalism viii, 7, 71, 74, 123–4, 139n8, 226, Ch. 8, 192–9, 201, 209, 213
contextual responses to pluralism 4–8n2, 11–12, 31–2, 34–6, 63n1, 77–8, 81, 220–2, 224, Ch. 4, 91, 93, 95, 98–9, 105, 118, 128, 135–8; *see also* cultural context; historical context; personal context; political context; tradition
cost–benefit analysis 210
cultural context 38n35, 94, 105; *see also* tradition
cultural relativism 21, 25, 56–7, 85–6, 88n21, 93, 132, 138n3, 153, 156, 209

Democracy viii, ix, 3, 6, 8, 13, 16, 35–6, 54, 60, 74–7, 94, 109–10, 116, 139, 192–3, 198–9, 201, 204, 213–215n10,223,225–6;Ch. 7,165–71, 173, 178, 187–8; deliberative 6, 20, 36, 54, 146, 167–72, 187–189n20, 223; inclusive 3, 8, 79, 165, 167, 173, 187–8, 192–3, 204, 207, 213–14, 225; liberal ix, x, 2–3, 5–7, 11–13, 16, 21, 23, 25, 27–9, 34–6, 38n31, 44, 46–51, 53–6, 59–60, 63–64n18, 66, 68–77, 81, 83–6, 88n17, 91, 93–6, 98, 101–2, 105–113n14, 116–17, 121–5, 130–139n8, 142–54, 157–8, 160–1, 163n12, 165, 167–71, 175–6, 180–1, 183–188n3, 192, 194–7, 199, 201–3, 207–9, 213–214n4, 219–24
De–Shalit, Avner 58
diversity *see* value diversity
Dworkin, Ronald 2, 21, 34, 55, 124

Freeden, Michael 96, 100–1, 113n7
freedom *see* liberty

Galston, William 2, 6, 20, 36, Ch. 6, 143–4, 149, 196
Geuss, Raymond 98
Gibson, James 204
Gill, Emily 154
Gray, John 2, 3, 6, 36n1–38n21, 109–10, 113n14, 123, 130–1, 180–2, 189n14; *vs* liberalism viii, ix, x, 2–3, 5–7, 13, 21, 25, 28, 33–6, 38n31, 44, 46, 50, 56, 58, 62, 66–7, 69–72, 75–6, 84–6, 88n17, 91, 93–8, 101, 104–6, 108–12, 116–17, 121–5, 130–1, 133–139n7, 142–4, 146–7, 150–3, 155, 161, 165–6, 168–9, 171, 176, 180, 187, 192, 195, 219, 221–3, 226; on modus vivendi 6, 185
great goods vii, 3–4, 6–7, 12, 28–9, 34, 36, 185, 218–20, 223–4, Ch. 2, 43–4, 51, 62, 81, 85–6, 116, 132, 153, 157, 159, 165, 173, 185
Green, Leslie 208
Green, Thomas Hill 125
Griffin, James 129

Hamann, Johann Georg 195
Hayek, Friedrich 102, 175, 188n11
Habermas, Jürgen 75, 94, 109
Hall, Edward 100
Hampshire, Stuart 2, 44, 50; on hearing the other side 44, 50, 53–6, 59, 62–3, 169, 219
Hart, H. L. A. 45, 63n7, 189n15
Hegel, Georg Wilhelm Friedrich 15–16, 33, 107
Herder, Johann Gottfried 11, 16, 18, 25–6, 28, 31, 35, 37n2, 195
Hirst, Paul 72–4
historical context viii, 3, 5, 7, 31–4, 36, 84, 91, 94–5, 97, 101, 105–6, 110–12, 116, 121, 135–6, 138, 157, 192, 203, 221
Hitler, Adolf 69, 73, 182, 186–7
Helvétius, Claude Adrien 196
Hirschmann, Albert 151
Hobbes, Thomas 96, 220
Holbach, Paul Heinrich Dietrich, baron d' 196
Horton, John 54, 182–4, 189n23
Hume's law 6, 33–4, 70, 126–7, 138

Incommensurability: concept of 12, 17, 32, 35, 71, 116–17, 128, 135–7, 143, 145, 157, 162n9, 185, 224; of values *vs* cultures (analytical vs holistic pluralism) 16, 22–3, 80–1, 125, 145–6, 198, 212

Jinping, Xi 111
Johnston, David 149–51
Jubb, Robert 102, 104, 112n6
judicial review 7, 87n9, 192–3, 205–9, 213–215n10, 224

justice viii, 1, 5, 13, 15, 18, 20, 23, 31, 34, 51–8, 63n6, 78, 80, 91, 93, 96–7, 99, 100–5, 112–113n8, 121, 123, 125, 137, 149–50, 154–5, 157, 162n10, 174–8, 183, 187, 189n19, 193, 198, 206, 214n3, 219–22, 226

Kant, Immanuel 59, 93, 144, 186
Kekes, John 2–3, 5, 28, 35, 37n6, 81, 83, 88n16, 139n15, 146; argument for conservativism 2, 4, 32, 62, 78, 149, 210; on practical reasoning 34, 38n24, 52–3, 77–8, 81, 83, 87n12, 156, 158, 160, 162n10, 174; vs liberalism viii, ix, 2–3, 5–7, 13, 21, 25, 28, 33–6, 38n31, 44, 46, 50, 56, 58, 62, 66–7, 69–72, 75–6, 84, 86, 88n17, 91, 93–8, 101, 104–6, 108–12, 116–17, 121–5, 130–1, 133–139n7, 142–4, 146–7, 150–3, 155, 161, 165–6, 168–9, 171, 176, 180, 187, 192, 195, 219, 221–3, 226
Kukathas, Chandran 148, 160–162n4
Kymlicka, Will 86, 147, 151, 160–1

Larmore, Charles 72, 78, 87n13, 100, 113n7
Le Pen, Marine 202
liberalism viii, ix, 2–3, 5–7, 13, 21, 25, 28, 33–6, 38n31, 44, 46, 50, 56, 58, 62, 66–7, 69–72, 75–6, 84, 86, 88n17, 91, 93–8, 101, 104–6, 108–12, 116–17, 121–5, 130–1, 133–139n7, 142–4, 146–7, 150–3, 155, 161, 165–6, 168–9, 171, 176, 180, 187, 192, 195, 219, 221–3, 226; and historical context viii, 3, 5, 7, 31–2, 34, 36, 84, 91, 94–5, 97, 101, 105–6, 110–12, 116, 121, 135–6, 138, 157, 192, 203, 221; and value pluralism viii, ix, 1–8n1, 11–12, 14, 16–21, 24, 27–9, 32–4, 36–37n3, 43–5, 49, 56–7, 60, 62–63n10, 66–72, 75, 77–8, 82, 84–6, 88n13, 91–3, 98, 103–5, 112, 116–18, 120, 125–6, 128, 131–3, 135–7, 139n17, 142–3, 146–7, 151–3, 155–62, 162n9, 165–8, 173, 175, 180–1, 184–5, 187–188n12, 192–3, 196–200, 203, 205, 207–10, 213–215n21, 218–20, 222–6, Ch. 5; classical vs egalitarian 139n7; Enlightenment vs Reformation 6, 36, Ch. 6, 143–4; of fear 14, 20, 36, 87n9, 95, 97–8
liberty viii, 1–2, 4–6, 11–15, 18–23, 25, 27, 30, 34–5, 43–50, 57, 59, 75–6, 84, 92–3, 95–6, 98–9, 103–4, 107, 111, 122–5, 129–31, 134–5, 137–138n7, 144–8, 151–2, 154–5, 157–8, 162, 166, 173–4, 181–2, 188n2, 189n15, 195–6, 198, 214n3, 220–2; effective 77, 96, 104, 125, 143, 149, 154, 158, 160–1, 183–4, 213, 222; expressive 6, Ch. 6, 145–8, 151, 155, 158, 162; negative 12–15, 22–3, 25, 34–5, 44, 46–7, 50, 57, 84, 95, 98, 124–5, 128, 144–5, 148, 152, 154, 158, 162n1, 166, 214n3, 222; positive 12–15, 34, 51, 54, 69, 83, 85, 125, 128, 144, 149, 161–162n1, 171, 192–3, 203, 212, 214n3
Lindblom, Charles 213, 215n21
Locke, John 85, 95, 123

Machiavelli, Niccolò 11, 16, 18–19, 25, 28, 30, 37n2, 53, 96
MacIntyre, Alasdair 63n6, 84
Madison, James 124, 194
Maistre Joseph Marie, comte de 195
Margalit, Avishai 2–3, 7, 37n1, 166, 173–4, 182, 184–189n26, 224
Marx, Karl 15–16, 33, 59, 107
Mill, John Stuart 13, 22, 47, 55, 64n18, 77, 95, 122, 134, 144–5, 149–50, 160, 167, 201
modus vivendi 6–7, 36, 165, 180–8, 189n23, 224
Montesquieu, Charles Louis de Secondat, baron de 124, 178, 194, 198
Mouffe, Chantal 2–4, 35, 38n34, 66, 74–7, 86–87n1, 123, 170, 180n3, 219–20
multiculturalism 38n27, 66–7, 85–6, 88n23, 121, 125, 131–2, 138n3, 153, 187, 192
Munich Agreement 181–7, 224

Nagel, Thomas 19, 61, 138n2, 208
Nazi Germany 27, 46, 48–9, 53, 108, 111, 185
Neal, Patrick 128–30, 133–5
Nietzsche, Friedrich 150
Nozick, Robert 124
Nussbaum, Martha 2–4, 31, 35, 38n24, 44, 56–64n18, 66, 78–81, 87, 92, 117, 125–7, 131, 138n2–139n10, 146, 185, 219–20, 226; on capabilities 35, 44, 56–63, 64n18–65, 92, 117, 125, 127, 131, 138n2, 162n10, 185, 219; on practical reasoning 34, 38n24, 52–3, 77–8, 81–3, 87n12, 156, 158, 160, 162n10, 174

Index

Okin, Susan Moller 148–9, 151
Orbán, Viktor 202

Parekh, Bhikhu 28, 36, 38n21, 55, 86, 226
Parfit, Derek 129
personal context 4, 87, 197
Plato 1, 15–17, 19, 33, 78–80, 127, 154, 189n19
pluralism *see* value pluralism
political context 5, 12, 98–9
Porat, Iddo 205–6, 214n3
populism 193, 202–3, 209, 214
problem of value pluralism viii, 2–5, 7, 21, 28–9, 33, 36, 43–4, 56–7, 60, 62–3, 66–9, 71–2, 77–8, 82, 91, 105, 116–17, 137, 142, 167, 173, 175, 185, 200, 209, 218, 220, 224–6
public policy viii, 5, 7, 57–8, 61, 66–7, 81, 91, 125, 142, 150, 160, 193, 197, 199, 206–7, 210, 212–14, 220, 222, 225

Rawls, John 5, 34, 38n31, 56, 58, 60, 62–64n18, 72–3, 75–6, 84, 95–6, 99, 102–5, 109, 113n8, 119–20, 125, 131, 137, 173, 176–7, 181, 183, 193, 221, 224, 226
Raz, Joseph 37n11–38n27, 86, 113n14, 162n9, 226
realism, political viii, 3, 5, 91, 95–6, 98, 103, 108, 113n7, 183–4
Rein, Martin 7, 193, 210–14, 214n3–215n21, 225–6
relativism *see* cultural relativism
Richardson, Henry S. 38n24, 88n13, 210
rights: individual 50, 110–111, 123, 169, 183, 193, 199, 202, 222; group Ch. 6
Riley, Jonathan 2–4, 37n11, 44–50, 62–63n1, 59, 73, 78, 83, 113n15, 138n1, 219
Roosevelt, Franklin Delano 184
Rousseau, Jean–Jacques 16, 87n4

Sandel, Michael 37n14, 106, 154
Schmitt, Carl 2–4, 35, 38n34, 66, 71–7, 86–87n5, 96, 138n4, 170, 188n3, 219–20
Schumpeter, Joseph 32, 106
Schwarzschild, Maimon 207–9, 214n3
Sen, Amartya 57, 61, 63n13
Shklar, Judith 87n4, 95
social democracy 13

Sophocles 31, 136
Stalin, Josef 184

Talisse, Robert 38n33, 126, 128, 139n12
Thacher, David 7, 193, 210–215n21, 225–6
Thornton, John 111
Tolstoy, Leo 15
tradition viii, 2–3, 5–6, 31, 38n27, 55–7, 59–60, 66–9, 78, 81–88n17, 91, 93–4, 98, 109, 113n14, 119, 125, 134, Ch. 6, 142, 145, 148, 150, 152, 155–6, 159, 161, 178, 180–1, 183, 197, 199, 203, 207, 218, 220, 224; *see also* cultural context
Truman, Harry 187
Trump, Donald 202
Turnbull, Colin 120

United Kingdom 69, 197, 203, 212, 215n17
United States 69–70, 142, 170, 199, 202, 207
universal values *see* great goods
utilitarianism 1, 29, 57, 92, 128, 146, 156, 210, 218

Value diversity 3, 6–7, 86, Ch. 5, 121–2, 125–6, 131–6, 153, 155–7, 159–60, 165–6, 173, 187–8, 203; vs cultural diversity 3, 86, 132–3, 143–5, 152–3, 155, 186–7, 192–3
value pluralism: and constitutionalism 7, 71, 74, 123, 187–90; and democracy 165–88; Berlin on Ch. 1, 166, 188n1, 195; Williams on 86–8; definition of 1–2, 47, 49; interpretations of 3, 27; truth of 21, 160, 176; vs realism 3, 5, 91–12; vs relativism 4, 12, 18, 21–8, 32, 36, 56–7, 62, 85–6, 93–4, 112, 132, 153, 156; *see also* analytical vs holistic pluralism; conceptual responses to pluralism; contextual responses to pluralism; incommensurability; liberalism and pluralism; problem of value pluralism
values 2–7, 11–13, 15–18, 33–37n5, 43–7, 49–51, 54, 56, 58–64, 66–87, 91–9, 102–3, 108, 110–12, 116–139n10, 142–4, 146–57, 159–62, 165–88, 192–7, 199, 203–215n21, 218–23, 225–6
Vico, Giambattista 11, 16, 18, 25–6, 28, 31, 37n2, 195

Voltaire (François Marie Arouet) 194, 196

Waldron, Jeremy ix, 2, 7, 123–4, 139n8, 166, 188n1, Ch. 8, 192–5, 197–203, 205, 209, 213–215n10, 224
Walzer, Michael 28, 36–37n20, 102, 125, 172, 177–9, 212, 226
Weber, Max 2–4, 11, 35, 38n34, 66–71, 74–7, 86–87n5, 94, 96, 109, 135, 138n4, 188n3, 210, 219–20

Welzel, Christian 3, 5, 110–12, 147, 221–2
Wendt, Fabian 173–4, 186, 188n7
Williams, Bernard ix, x, 2–3, 5, 20, 23, 31, 36, 38n24, 56, 84, 87n10–88n13, Ch. 4, 91–5, 97–110, 112n7–13, 117–18, 121, 126, 135–6, 138, 146–7, 160, 208, 215n14, 221
Wolff, Jonathan 58

Young, Iris Marion 172

Made in United States
North Haven, CT
05 May 2022